Youth Empowerment and Volunteerism

Youth Empowerment and Volunteerism

Principles, Policies and Practices

Edited by
Elaine S. C. LIU
Michael J. HOLOSKO
T. Wing LO

City University of Hong Kong Press

©2009 City University of Hong Kong

First published 2009

ISBN: 978-962-937-137-1

Published by
       City University of Hong Kong Press
       Tat Chee Avenue
       Kowloon, Hong Kong
       Website: www.cityu.edu.hk/upress
       E-mail: upress@cityu.edu.hk

Printed in Hong Kong

Contents

Foreword

The Youth Studies Net (YSNet) at City University of Hong Kong was founded in 2000 by a group of scholars and professionals who are interested in promoting the wellbeing of young people and conducting research in different areas of youth studies. Being an inter-institutional and inter-disciplinary research network, YSNet serves to consolidate the interests and potentials of youth studies scholars and professionals who come from various disciplines, including psychology, sociology, criminology, social work, education and media studies. Maximising the use of limited academic resources through coordinated and collaborated efforts, YSNet aims to foster a profound understanding of the psychological, social, cultural, technological and political issues confronting young people in the cyber era by conducting comparative youth research and organising periodic conferences, seminars and workshops on youth-related issues. To facilitate youth development in this region, YSNet also provides comprehensive information, professional advice and consultancy on youth policy and youth services to local and overseas governments and organisations.

In 2005, YSNet collaborated with City University of Hong Kong Press to launch the Caring for Youth Series, with the objective to share its scholarly research output with the professional and academic community. Since then, five books have been published by academics or professionals in youth research and youth work. The first book, co-authored by T Wing Lo, Alfred Choi and Songxing Su, is a comparative study of juvenile delinquency and youth services in Hong Kong, Singapore and Shanghai. Xiaodong Yue authored the second and fourth books of this Series. The first one is a psycho-social and cultural analysis of idol worship by young people, whereas the second one is about the promotion of positive psychology among young people. Based on the result of her PhD thesis, Jessica Li authored the third book in which she analyzed the decision-making process of juvenile thieves and recommended related crime prevention strategies. The fifth book was written by a group of social workers who documented their intervention experiences with police cautioned youth, midnight drifters and at-risk youth in relation to violence, gang and triad involvement, drug abuse, runaway from home, school dropout, love and sex.

The continued publication in this Series signifies the advancement of applied youth research in Hong Kong. It also provides a platform for experts, academics, government officials, politicians, social workers, teachers, parents, young people and other interested individuals to share their concerns and examine issues that affect youth development, and explore means to meet the needs of young people. This book provides another fruitful opportunity for such valuable exchange. Being the first edited volume of this Series, it is a collection of quality academic papers presented in two international conferences on youth empowerment and volunteerism held in City University of Hong Kong over the last four years. Apart from the analysis and synthesis of theoretical concepts related to the subject by distinguished scholars, practice experiences from Canada, United States, England, France, Singapore and China are shared by experts of the countries. Their enthusiasm, ideas and international endeavours will add immeasurably to our understanding of the challenges faced by young people around the world and how they are empowered through volunteerism.

Series Editor
Professor T. Wing Lo

Preface

Youth studies have always been an important part of the curriculum design and academic research of Department of Applied Social Studies of City University of Hong Kong. Over the years, the Department has successfully involved teachers and students to launch a series of international and national cross-cultural learning and social service programmes. With the teachers of the department as the core, these networks of youthful activities finally rolled and grew to a bigger idea of Youth Empowerment and it paved the road for the two international conferences to be held in City University of Hong Kong for academics, practitioners as well as young people to further gather together for sharing and conferencing. The two youth conferences are "International Conference on Youth Empowerment: A Cross-cultural Exchange" held in 2004 and "2nd International Conference on Youth Empowerment: Empowering Youth through Volunteerism" held in 2006. The two conferences received overwhelming support as attended by over 800 delegates from 14 countries. Today, the Department of Applied Social Studies continues to encourage students and teachers to stay in touch with the contacts they developed over the years and is still running a volunteer training and servicing project for students in City University of Hong Kong—The City-youth Empowerment Project.

Subsequent to the two international conferences, we have collected eleven full text papers presented in the plenary sessions from the two conferences. All of these have been refereed and edited for this book. The submissions are about the various theories, concepts, ideas, programmes, examples, projects, and issues about youth, volunteerism, and youth empowerment. This edited book serves as a testimony and memory for all who had participated in this series of youth focused projects. In the collection, one clearly sees how youth potential is unlimited all over the world. Given the chance to serve their communities, youth can indeed become responsible citizens of tomorrow.

The chapters and numerous examples herein, clearly demonstrate the synergistic, energising, and dynamic relationship between those who hold social resources for youth, those who initiate and coordinate youth programmes, and the youth themselves who participate in such projects. Youth empowerment is thus, a "Win-Win" scenario for both youth and the communities in which they live.

This book is organised into three parts: Youth Empowerment and Volunteerism: Concepts, Models and Theories, Selected Examples in Countries around the World and Conclusions. Part One presents the various theories, models, paradigms, and concepts related to youth empowerment and volunteerism. All of these are both "field tested" and practical approaches which set the context for a better understanding of the numerous examples which follow in Part Two.

Although the chapters in this first part are written by authors from the United States, China, and Canada, they all convey that: a) empowerment is a dynamic process, b) youth volunteerism is an actualising and empowering process, and c) such a process holds the potential for positive outcomes not only of an immediate nature, but for healthy life long fulfilment.

Chapters 1, 2, and 3 can be viewed as a set of cornerstones concerned with empowerment model-building through volunteerism. In Chapter 1, Snyder and Omoto use empirical studies mainly from their own extensive body of research and present a three stage Volunteer Process Model (VPM), comprised of antecedents of volunteerism, experiences of volunteerism, and consequences of volunteerism. They clearly address the underpinning psychology of volunteerism and empirically answer the important question—who gets involved in volunteerism and why? In Chapter 2, Omoto and Snyder extend their model to illustrate and justify the role of community context, linkages, and connections to their volunteer model. Using their earlier VPM (in Chapter 1), they clearly argue the case that any model purporting to understand volunteering that is devoid of community context, is seriously remiss. In Chapter 3, Risler and Holosko present the core elements, distilled from the literature, of a youth empowerment model. Their model is presented as a blueprint for implementation. It includes a series of examples and open-ended process questions for others to address, in planning for and applying this approach. In Chapter 4, Yue concludes by using the underlying concepts of hardiness and resilience nested in dispositional empowerment, to demonstrate how these important aspects of empowerment are interrelated. He discusses how they impact positively on intrinsic factors such as well-being, optimism, cognitive re-appraisal of self and coping effectiveness. Finally, in Chapter 5, Kam draws on examples from Hong Kong to describe factors and processes that not only empower youth but others that may disempower them. He concludes the chapter and this part with an eight-step model to direct a successful empowerment approach. Interestingly, when one reads these eight steps and looks at them as essentials for successful empowerment through volunteerism, they form a set of assumptions that underline all of the examples in the remaining chapters that follow.

Part Two includes six chapters showcasing selected examples from different countries of the world including England, Canada, Singapore, United States, China, and France. They clearly show how different cultures infuse their own history, language, mores, laws, policies, demographics, and socio-political infrastructures in facilitating youth empowerment and volunteerism.

In Chapter 6, Payne describes the development of youth work in England, illustrating not only how it has evolved but how it has evolved toward empowering youth in society. Using case examples from numerous youth empowering projects, he concludes that youth empowerment is "alive and well" in England—and there are many important lessons to be learned about it. In Chapter 7, Ungar, Langlois and Hum showcase the Phoenix Programmes in Eastern Canada. They demonstrate how a variety of innovative programmes can address unique needs in the community. These programmes have developed with "an eye to the community", in an effort to be responsive and provide timely initiatives to local citizens.

Tan, in Chapter 8, presents data on how Singapore has valued the importance of youth in developing the future of Singapore. He highlights numerous examples of "The Singapore Model" which focuses on education, youth aspirations and community development. In Chapter 9, Cheung describes a unique youth volunteer "Asset Development" programme being implemented in a Teen Health Clinic in Houston, Texas with African American women. "Project Passport" helps those young women assess their assets/strengths in order to develop and enhance resiliency in the areas of support and empowerment; boundaries and expectations; positive values; social abilities; and positive identity.

In Chapter 10, Lo, Su and Jiang show how a paradigm shift, supporting youth empowerment, has occurred in China since the post-cultural revolution period. Using numerous case examples from Shanghai, they show how volunteerism associations promote youth empowerment through projects such as caring for disadvantageous groups, to providing professional services, and to supporting large scale community activities.

Finally, in the last of these main example chapters of Part Two, Ferrand-Bechmann (in Chapter 11) examines how young adults in non-governmental and non-profit organisations in France help youth become active members of society, as well as help them to operate "junior associations" or Reseau National de Jeunes Associations. She presents a range of numerous examples of these empowering associations and shows how they benefit French communities in general, and French youth, in particular.

Last but not least, in Part Three, Liu and Holosko in Chapter 12 look retrospectively across the spectrum of the collections in this edited reading set, offer a simple way to understand the relationship between youth volunteerism and empowerment. They are convinced, and the hope is that so will be the readers, that indeed, we live in a rather small "global village", and youth hold the future keys to how countries all over the world will develop. The real trick is—in getting those countries to truly believe in their youth's true power and potential.

Elaine S. C. LIU
Michael J. HOLOSKO
T. Wing LO

Acknowledgements

A book that is an international undertaking of this nature involved a cast of many to bring it to fruition. We would like to first acknowledge those individuals in Hong Kong and Athens, Georgia of the U.S.A. who made this project possible. In Hong Kong, we would like to thank the Department of Applied Social Studies, the College of Humanities and Social Sciences and the Office of the Dean of Student Learning of the City University of Hong Kong for giving the much needed support to launch this series of youth themed programmes, expediting the Cross-Cultural Learning Programme, the International Conference on Youth Empowerment and the City-Youth Empowerment Project. The City-Youth Empowerment Project is still operational for groups of City University students to further their social commitments in the Hong Kong community and for a group of international scholars to be able to cluster together and continue pursuing academic exchanges on the concepts of youth empowerment and volunteerism. Thanks to those many colleagues and students at City University of Hong Kong who participated in these projects. Without their effort and initiative, all dreams and ideas such as these, are just empty words. The students truly brought them to life. This project also would not have been achieved without the dedication and commitment of Sally Hung, the Project Assistant to these projects who networked both with the Georgia team and liaised with all of the authors in all of the countries for their contributions. Her ability to facilitate this overall process was much appreciated.

At the University of Georgia a special thanks goes out to the Berger family for providing the resources to allow Professor Holosko to take a lead role in this editing process. In addition, two tireless workers who served as assistants to this project need special acknowledgement. Many thanks go out to Katherine Spencer and Irina Ciurea for their dedication, commitment and perseverance in following this project through to completion, often working on compressed time constraints and deadlines.

We would also like to thank all of the contributors to this book, for their input, ideas, and knowledge, and for allowing us to share these with you in an East meets West global exchange about academic and practical experiences concerning the concepts of youth, volunteerism and youth empowerment. The range of the materials that we share with you was based on these insightful and interesting submissions that to our knowledge have not been presented in published form anywhere else.

The individuals noted above were the real "story behind the book". However, they are not alone as formal sponsorship from a variety of individuals, departments, agencies and organisations believed in this endeavour and supported the two International Conferences on Youth Empowerment (ICOYE) held in 2004 and 2006 at City University of Hong Kong and from where most of the articles in this book were firstly presented.

Elaine S. C. LIU
Michael J. HOLOSKO
T. Wing LO

About the Editors

ELAINE SUK CHING LIU, Ph.D., M.S.W., is Associate Professor of Department of Applied Social Studies, City University of Hong Kong. She had ten years experience serving as a School Social Worker and a Youth Counsellor before joining the Department of Applied Social Studies, City University of Hong Kong as a faculty member. For the last 17 years as a faculty member in City University of Hong Kong, she has taught courses in social work theories, social casework, counselling and children, youth and family work. She also has supervised social work practicum to more than 50 social work students in the areas of youth and family. She has published in the areas of school social work, help-seeking behaviour, parent-child relationship and young adolescents running away from home. As a consultant, she assisted with various projects and trainings in the areas of youth development and youth policy in Hong Kong, Macau and Singapore. Recently, she has been advocating and promoting youth development and empowerment, youth volunteerism and youth cross-cultural learning both locally and internationally. She had convened the International Conference on Youth Empowerment: A Cross Cultural Exchange in May 2004, and the 2nd International Conference on Youth Empowerment: Empowering Youth through Volunteerism in 2006. She is one of the founding members of the Youth Studies Net of City University of Hong Kong and was its Director from 2004–2006. She is a member of the Commission on Youth of Hong Kong Government since 2004. She was awarded the Faculty of Humanities and Social Science Contribution to Learning Award in 2001.

MICHAEL J. HOLOSKO, Ph.D., M.S.W., is the Pauline M. Berger Professor of Family and Child Welfare at The University of Georgia, School of Social Work, and adjunct instructor at Norfolk State University. He has taught in schools of: social work (primarily), nursing, public administration, and applied social science in Canada, the United States, Hong Kong, Australia, and the U.S. Virgin Islands. He has published extensively in the areas of evaluation, health care, gerontology, social policy, research, music intervention, and spirituality. For the past 28 years, he has been a consultant to a variety of large and small health and human service organisations in the areas of: program evaluation, outcomes, accreditation, organisational development, communication, leadership, visioning, organisational alignment, and stress management. He has published numerous monographs, chapters, articles, and texts in the areas of evaluation, health care, gerontology, social policy, research, music intervention, and spirituality. He serves on the editorial boards of: *Research on Social Work Practice; Journal of Health and Social Policy; Stress, Trauma and Crisis; Journal of Human Behavior and Social Environment; the Hong Kong Journal of Social Work; Journal of Social Service Research* and the *Journal of Evidence-based Social Work Practice.* He has had both radio and television shows advocating for social justice in North America.

T. WING LO, Ph.D., M. Phil., is a Professor at City University of Hong Kong, teaching counselling, social work and criminology. He received his education in social work and criminology in Hull and Cambridge, England and had been a frontline youth worker for 17 years before joining the academia. Being the founding director of City University's Youth Studies Net, he has led over twenty research projects in the past ten years. Many of these were large-scale consultancy projects, and/or blueprint studies on youth services commissioned by the Hong Kong and Macau governments. He has published numerous journal articles, research monographs, books and book chapters in the areas of youth service, juvenile justice, group counselling and community service. He has been active in community service and served as a member on the board of directors or committees of a number of government departments and NGOs. He has recently founded the "Caring for Youth Series" with the City University of Hong Kong Press, and is an editorial board member of *Crime, Media and Culture*, and the *Asian Journal of Criminology*. He is the holder of the Teaching Excellence Award by City University of Hong Kong in 2007.

List of Contributors

Monit CHEUNG
Graduate College of Social Work
The University of Houston
Houston, TX, USA
mcheung@uh.edu

Dan FERRAND-BECHMANN
Centre d'études des solidarités sociales
Université de Paris
Paris, France
bechmann.cesol@wanadoo.fr

Michael J. HOLOSKO
School of Social Work
University of Georgia
Athens, GA, USA
mholosko@uga.edu

Melissa HUM
Phoenix Youth Program
Halifax, Canada
mhum@phoenixyouth.ca

Guoping JIANG
Department of Applied Social Studies
City University of Hong Kong
Kowloon Tong, Hong Kong
ssjiang@cityu.edu.hk

Ping Kwong KAM
Department of Applied Social Studies
City University of Hong Kong
Kowloon Tong, Hong Kong
sspkk@cityu.edu.hk

Marc LANGLOIS
Heartwood Institute
Bridgewater, Nova Scotia, Canada
hw-youth@istar.ca

Elaine S. C. LIU
Department of Applied Social Studies
City University of Hong Kong
Kowloon Tong, Hong Kong
elaine.au@cityu.edu.hk

T. Wing LO
Department of Applied Social Studies
City University of Hong Kong
Kowloon Tong, Hong Kong
sstwl@cityu.edu.hk

Allen M. OMOTO
School of Behavioral & Organisational Sciences
Claremont Graduate University
Claremont, CA, USA
Allen.Omoto@cgu.edu

Malcolm PAYNE
Youth Affairs Unit
De Montfort University
Leicester, United Kingdom
mpayne@dmu.ac.uk

Edwin RISLER
School of Social Work
University of Georgia
Athens, GA, USA
erisler@uga.edu

Mark SNYDER
Department of Psychology
University of Minnesota
Minneapolis, Minnesota, USA
msnyder@umn.edu

Songxing SU
Insititue of Youth and Juveniles Population
Shanghai Population and Development Research Centre
Shanghai, China
susongxing47@sina.com

Ngoh Tiong TAN
Department of Social Work
Augsburg College
2211 Riverside Avenue
Minneapolis, Minnesota, USA
tan@augsburg.edu

Michael UNGAR
School of Social Work
Dalhousie University
Halifax, Nova Scotia, Canada
Michael.Ungar@dal.ca

Xiaodong YUE
Department of Applied Social Studies
City University of Hong Kong
Kowloon Tong, Hong Kong
ssxdyue@cityu.edu.hk

Future contacts please direct to:
Elaine S. C. LIU
Department of Applied Social Studies
City University of Hong Kong
Kowloon Tong, Hong Kong
elaine.au@cityu.edu.hk

List of Illustrations

Youth Empowerment
and Volunteerism

Principles, Policies and Practices

part one

Youth Empowerment and Volunteerism
Concepts, Models and Theories

This set of five chapters is written by authors from Hong Kong and the United States. Together they serve as the building blocks for the remaining chapters in parts two and three. It is important that the relationship between theory and practice is always maintained, as one without the other is contextually remiss. Indeed, sound concepts, models, and theories form the very scaffolding and frameworks that empirically tested ideas stand on. Each chapter in this part presents unique concepts, models, or theories; some are derived from extensive and critical appraisals of the literature; some are derived from qualitative anecdotal evidence, and others are derived from quantitative data collected on various populations of individuals. To build a good house, one needs a solid foundation, and we offer this set of chapters to you as the foundation for the remainder of the text.

WHO GETS INVOLVED AND WHY? THE PSYCHOLOGY OF VOLUNTEERISM

Mark SNYDER and Allen M. OMOTO

Acknowledgements

The research described in this chapter was supported by grants from the National Institute of Mental Health to Mark Snyder and to Allen M. Omoto.

Introduction

Every year, millions of people all over the world volunteer and devote substantial amounts of their time and energy to helping others, e.g. providing companionship to the elderly, tutoring to the illiterate, counselling to the troubled, or providing health care to the sick. In fact, in the United States, in the year 2000 alone, 83.9 million American adults, or 44% of the adult population, engaged in some form of volunteerism each year, doing so for an average of 3.6 hours per week, contributing a total of 15.6 billion hours of volunteer services with a monetary value in excess of 239.2 billion dollars (Independent Sector, 2001). These legions of adult volunteers are joined by substantial numbers of young volunteers (in fact, high school volunteering in the United States recently reached its highest levels in the past 50 years; Independent Sector, 2001) and elderly volunteers. Whereas the United States has long been marked by relatively high rates of volunteerism, voluntary action can be found in countries throughout the world (Curtis, Grabb, & Baer, 1992).

Volunteerism is one of the many and varied ways in which people try to do good for others, their communities, and society at large. There are important ways in which volunteerism stands apart from these other forms of doing good works. Volunteerism can be distinguished from charitable giving and philanthropy, in that participants in volunteer efforts provide valuable time, resources, and energy to causes and recipients of service rather than necessarily donating money or goods. Whereas philanthropic efforts are crucial to the success of many organisations and service programmes, our research focus is on volunteer behaviour itself.

It is also important here to distinguish between "forced" and freely chosen volunteer efforts. That is, many schools, businesses, and other institutions provide volunteer opportunities that are mandatory for students or employees or are perceived as all but required (e.g. service learning programmes, some corporate-community partnerships). And, although some of the outcomes of these programmes may be similar (cf., Clary, Snyder, & Stukas,

1998; Stukas, Snyder, & Clary, 1999), our interests have been focused on the instances and organisations in which individuals provide assistance to other people and causes, without receiving compensation or having been obviously coerced. In short, for us, volunteerism is a form of pro-social action in which people actively and freely seek out opportunities to provide non-monetary assistance to others in need.

Volunteerism benefits the recipients of service and the broader community as well; as such, volunteer service is one way that people can help others and, simultaneously, help alleviate some of the society's problems. Volunteer service also intrinsically rewards volunteers by promoting community spirit, offering evidence of people's kindness and commitment to others, by increasing feelings of helpfulness and self-worth, by providing opportunities to develop and exercise one's skills, and by actually improving physical health (Andrews, 1990). Volunteer service, to put it simply, provides opportunities to, at one and the same time, do good for other people, for society, and for oneself.

In addition to these practical considerations of volunteerism and leading volunteer organisations, studying volunteerism provides a distinct perspective on the nature of helping and pro-social action. In psychology, helping has long been studied in terms of brief, low cost, generally spontaneous assistance provided by strangers (i.e. bystander intervention) or, more recently, in terms of care provided to chronically sick or severely debilitated members of one's own family (Piliavin & Charng, 1990; Schroeder, Penner, Dovidio, & Piliavin, 1995; Wilson, 2000). However, a careful consideration of features of volunteerism makes it clear that it is a distinctive form of pro-social action that, as a hybrid, incorporates aspects of both of these forms of helping that have received research attention (Omoto & Snyder, 1995; Snyder, Clary, & Stukas, 2000). Specifically, volunteerism typically involves people choosing to help others in need. Moreover, their acts of helping are often ones that have been actively sought out by the volunteers themselves and that may be sustained over extended periods of time and considerable efforts.

And, since volunteers typically help people with whom they have no prior association, it is a form of helping that occurs without any bonds of prior obligation or commitment to the recipients of volunteer services.

Because of its defining and characteristic features, volunteerism is something of a curious phenomenon. For a variety of reasons, it simply should not occur. Unlike the helping that occurs in response to emergencies, there is no press of circumstances. Unlike the helping that occurs in families and in existing relationships, there are no bonds of obligations. Volunteerism is effortful, time consuming, and presents opportunity costs to volunteers. For example, people may forego other activities and social relations to make time for their volunteer activities, which in turn, may introduce additional social costs and possible rejection. Yet, people do seek out opportunities to volunteer, and they do sustain their volunteer efforts over extended periods of time. The question then, is "Why?" Why do some people get involved in helping others as volunteers? What is it that moves people to seek out opportunities to help, that guides them toward some helping opportunities and away from others, and that sustains their efforts over time and through adversity? In our research, we seek to answer such questions.

Overview of the Processes of Volunteerism

Our research on volunteerism is guided by a conceptual model of the volunteer process that takes account of the defining and characteristic features of volunteerism as a form of sustained helping without obligation. The model conceptualises volunteerism as a process that unfolds over time (Omoto & Snyder, 1995, 2002; Snyder & Omoto, 2007). Specifically, it specifies interrelated psychological and behavioural features associated with each of three sequential and interactive stages. At the antecedents stage, it identifies personality, motivational, and circumstantial characteristics of people that predict who becomes involved as volunteers and, if they do, who will be most effective and satisfied in their volunteer service. At the experiences stage, the model explores psychological and behavioural aspects of the interpersonal relationships that develop between volunteers and recipients of their services, paying particular attention to the behavioural patterns and relationship dynamics that facilitate the continued service of volunteers and positive benefits to the recipients of their services. Finally, at the consequences stage, the Volunteer Process Model (VPM) focuses on the impact of volunteer service on the attitudes, knowledge, and behaviour of volunteers, the recipients of their services, and the members of their social networks. Taken together, then, the stages of the VPM speak to the initiation and to the maintenance of volunteer service and its effectiveness.

Moreover, the VPM seeks to characterise volunteerism as a phenomenon that is situated at, and builds bridges between, many levels of analysis, and that unfolds over time. At the level of the individual, the model calls attention to the activities and psychological processes of individual volunteers and recipients of volunteer services. For example, volunteers make decisions to get involved as volunteers, seek out service opportunities, engage in volunteer work for some period of time, and eventually cease their efforts. At the interpersonal level, the model expands this focus further and incorporates the dynamics of the helping relationships between volunteers and recipients of service. At an organisational or agency level, the model focuses on the goals associated with recruiting, managing, and retaining an unpaid work force as well as associated concerns about work performance, compensation, and evaluation. That is, many volunteer efforts take place through or in cooperation with community-based organisations or other institutions. Accordingly, we have incorporated aspects of organisational structure, roles, and operations into the VPM. Finally, at a broader societal level, the model considers the linkages between individuals and the social structures of their societies as well as collective and cultural dynamics.

Thus, the VPM conceptualises volunteerism as a process that unfolds over time and that involves multiple levels of analyses. (For further discussion on the VPM, see Omoto, Snyder, & Berghuis,

1993; Omoto & Snyder, 1990, 1995, 2002; Snyder & Omoto, 1992a, b). Although we believe that our conceptual model and the issues of interest are applicable to many, if not most forms of volunteerism, much of our empirical research on the volunteer process has focused on volunteer service programmes that have emerged in the United States in response to the epidemic of HIV and AIDS. HIV disease, including AIDS, has had and continues to have major medical, economic, social, and societal impact throughout the world. A critical component of the societal response to the HIV epidemic in the United States has been community-based organisations of volunteers involved in caring for people living with HIV or AIDS (Person with AIDS [PWAs]) and in educating the public about HIV and PWAs. Some volunteers provide emotional and social support as "buddies" to PWAs, others help PWAs with tangible household chores or transportation, and still others staff information and referral hotlines, make educational presentations, or engage in advocacy. Although the importance and prevalence of some of the specific roles that volunteers play have shifted over the course of the epidemic and with changes in medical treatments and government support, volunteer efforts continue to be important in shaping HIV services and education. They remain at the heart of community-based responses to HIV and other societal problems.

Like volunteers for other causes, AIDS volunteers seek out opportunities to help, make substantial commitments to their work, and provide assistance to people who initially are strangers to them. As well, many AIDS volunteers provide care and assistance in potentially trying and stressful situations (i.e. spending time with seriously ill PWAs) and at some personal and emotional cost. For these reasons, we see AIDS volunteerism as paradigmatic of volunteerism, more generally. In our research, we have examined the processes of volunteerism as they occur in the real world, focusing on "real" individuals involved in "real" acts of volunteerism in "real" world settings. In so doing, we have entered into a naturally occurring laboratory in order to investigate a phenomenon of significance for individual and collective action. Moreover, we have supplemented our field studies with focused laboratory experiments that have permitted us to more carefully identify causal mechanisms and processes of volunteerism. And finally, our research has employed both longitudinal and cross-sectional designs and has drawn data from diverse populations of volunteers and non-volunteers.

The Three Stages of the Volunteer Process Model

Antecedents of Volunteerism

Among the questions at the antecedents stage of the volunteer process that we have sought to answer in our empirical work is: What motivates some people to become AIDS volunteers? We attempted to identify personality, motivational, and circumstantial characteristics of AIDS volunteers that predict who becomes an effective and satisfied volunteer, and ultimately to build on this knowledge to develop effective strategies for recruiting and retaining volunteers.

The special concerns in research at this stage have been the motivations of AIDS volunteers. In this regard, our work has been informed by a functional approach to personality, motivation, and social behaviour, one in which the purposive and agentic nature of human action is emphasised (Snyder & Cantor, 1998). Consistent with functional theorising (Clary & Snyder, 1991; Smith, Bruner, & White, 1956; Snyder & Omoto, 2000, 2001; Snyder et al., 2000), we have found that different people volunteer in the service of different goals, functions, or motivations. Specifically, we utilised exploratory and confirmatory factor analytic techniques in multiple samples to identify five primary motivations for AIDS volunteerism (Omoto & Snyder, 1995; for related measures of volunteer motivations, see Clary et al., 1998; Omoto, Snyder, & Martino, 2000; Ouellette, Cassel, Maslanka, & Wong, 1995; Schondel, Shields, & Orel, 1992; Simon, Stürmer, & Steffens, 2000).

Investigations of the motivations behind volunteerism indicated that some people volunteer to express their personal values or to satisfy felt humanitarian obligations to help others, whereas another relatively other-focused motivation expressed by volunteers is that of community concern. In terms of AIDS volunteerism (in the United States), this has meant volunteering out of concern for people affected by HIV disease and the communities most affected by it. The remaining motivations are more self-focused: some people volunteer in search of greater understanding of AIDS and how people live with HIV disease; some for reasons related to personal development such as to challenge themselves or enlarge their social networks, and some to fulfil esteem enhancement needs (e.g. to feel better about themselves or escape from other pressures).

Of the motivations that we have identified, values motivation tends to be endorsed most and esteem enhancement least among the AIDS volunteers that we have studied, with the other three motivations falling in between (Omoto & Snyder, 1993, 1995), a pattern that is typical of volunteers in many other domains (Clary, Snyder, & Stukas, 1996). Moreover, volunteers typically score higher on these motivations than non-volunteers (Clary et al., 1996). In addition, volunteers can be motivated by more than one motive. In fact, in one study of AIDS volunteers, we observed that fully 62.9% had multiple motives for volunteering; however, multiple motivations can constitute "too much of a good thing" as volunteers with many important motives also reported greater stress and less satisfaction with their volunteer service than volunteers with only a clear and single motive for volunteering (Kiviniemi, Snyder, & Omoto, 2002).

In short however, it is clear that the same acts of volunteerism can be motivated by quite different considerations and that volunteers often have many motives for volunteering. Moreover, the functional theoretical perspective guiding our research on volunteer motivations, and the motivations that we have identified in our research, serve as reminders that volunteers act both on behalf of others (e.g. volunteering to alleviate the problems of homelessness, poverty, etc.) and on behalf of themselves (e.g. volunteering in order to make friends, to acquire new skills, to boost one's self-esteem, and/or to affirm personal values). That is, many of the motivations for volunteer service are ones that bring together a mutual concern for benefiting others and a concern for benefiting oneself. At the same time, as volunteers are motivated to do good for others, they may also be motivated to volunteer as a way of doing good for themselves.

An appreciation of the strength and variety of different motivations that lead people to volunteer as well as the interweaving of motivations to do good for others and to do good for oneself, have implications for designing effective methods of attracting people to involve themselves in volunteer activities and associations. Indeed, research on persuasive messages for recruiting volunteers has focused on appeals to prospective volunteers' motivations for volunteering. A recurring theme in these investigations is the importance of the matching of messages to motivation. That is, building on research indicating a diversity of potential motivations for volunteering (Clary et al., 1998; Omoto & Snyder, 1995), these studies have demonstrated that the persuasive impact of a message is greater when it directly addresses the recipient's primary motivations than when it does not (Clary, Snyder, Ridge, Miene, & Haugen, 1994; Clary et al., 1998; Smith, Omoto, & Snyder, 2001; Snyder, Omoto, & Smith, in press).

For example, to examine the use of motivation matching in a field setting, Smith et al., (2001) created three newspaper-type advertisements encouraging AIDS volunteerism. One ad contained a self-focused motivational appeal (e.g. "volunteer to feel better about yourself"); one contained an other-focused motivational appeal (e.g. "volunteer to help people in need"), and one ad contained no appeal to any specific motivation. When volunteers at an AIDS service organisation evaluated these ads, the results revealed a clear matching pattern. First, the ads that emphasised a motivation or reason for volunteering were generally preferred to the control ad. Further, preference for the other-focused ad over the control ad was strongly predicted by volunteers' reported other-focused motivation for their own current volunteer work, but not by their reported self-focused motivation. When preference for the self-focused motivation ad over the control ad was examined, the converse pattern was obtained: volunteer self-focused motivation predicted this preference, but their other-focused motivation did not.

We extended this research by next placing these ads in university newspapers to see how effective they would be in recruiting young people to volunteer. The different ads ran in campus newspapers at two large U.S. universities. We were able to track which ads people responded to by listing a telephone number to call but by changing the name of the contact person mentioned in the different ads. The results of this study revealed that more people responded to the motivational ads than to the control ad, with the other-focused ad attracting the most respondents. In addition, the other-focused motivational ad was more successful than the control ad in attracting callers who followed through with their intent to pursue the advertised volunteer opportunity. Callers later completed questionnaire measures that assessed their motivations for volunteering and, of particular relevance to the matching effect, we found that participants who responded to the other-focused ad were higher in other-focused motivation than participants who responded to the other two ads, although a strong matching pattern was not observed for the self-focused ad. These findings provide evidence supporting the use of specific motivationally based appeals to recruit volunteers, with these appeals also especially likely to attract motivationally matched prospective volunteers.

Experiences of Volunteerism

The second stage of the volunteer process concerns the experiences of volunteers over the course of their service. At this stage, we explored the interpersonal relationships that develop between volunteers and recipients of their services (especially PWAs in buddy programmes), the extent to which volunteers feel their service has met their expectations and fulfilled their needs, and volunteers' perceptions of their work, their service organisation, and their perceptions of other people's reactions to their work.

Illustrating with findings at this stage, we found that volunteers have relatively high expectations for the quality of the relationships they will develop with client PWAs and those actual volunteer-PWA relationships generally fall short of these expectations (Omoto, Gunn, & Crain, 1998). Volunteer satisfaction also falls short of expectations and volunteers report some stress from these relationships, with this stress related to relationship closeness and client health. Specifically, volunteer stress increases with relationship closeness early on, and working with a relatively healthy client is related to less stress.

Moreover, the extent to which volunteers' experiences match the motivations that drew them into volunteer service and the expectations that they formed early on about volunteering, they are likely to be satisfied with their service as volunteers. As part of a longitudinal study of the volunteer process, Crain, Omoto, and Snyder (1998) examined the role that the matching between volunteers' motivations, expectations, and experiences played in determining volunteers' satisfaction and their burnout. In this study, AIDS volunteers completed four questionnaires at different points in time in which they reported the importance of each set of functional motivations for volunteering: Time 1, prior to their training to serve as volunteers, the extent to which they expected that volunteering would fulfil their motivations; Time 2, immediately following training, the extent that their experiences met these expectations; Time 3, after volunteering for three months, and their feelings of satisfaction and burnout; Time 4, after having volunteered for six months. Overall matching between motivations, expectations, and experiences was predictive of greater satisfaction and less burnout, suggesting that a stronger match is associated with more positive consequences of volunteerism. Similar evidence of the importance of matching volunteers' experiences to their motivations in predicting satisfaction is provided by Clary et al., (1998) and Davis, Hall, and Meyer (2003).

Moreover, the matching of volunteers' experiences to their motivations may have implications for their commitment to their volunteer service and their intentions to continue in service as volunteers. For example, in a longitudinal field study of AIDS volunteers, commitment to sustained service was greater among volunteers whose experiences were congruent with, or matched, their motivations for volunteering as espoused 6-months earlier (O'Brien, Crain, Omoto, & Snyder, 2000; Crain et al., 1998). Moreover, in a pair of laboratory experiments in which college students were induced to participate in activities conceptually related to volunteer service, attitudes and intentions facilitative of continuing service were increased by interventions designed to encourage them to frame their volunteer service in ways that were congruent with their own motivations (O'Brien et al., 2000; Williamson, Snyder, & Omoto, 2000).

It is important to recognise that volunteers' experiences may include both positive and negative feelings. On the positive side, volunteers experience empathy, and/or liking for their clients, with empathy being particularly important in predicting helping behaviour and intentions to continue helping when the volunteer and client share a common identity of membership in a social group (i.e. "the in-group"), and liking being particularly important when the client is a member of a different social group (i.e. "the out-group"; Stuermer, Snyder, & Omoto, 2005; Stuermer, Snyder, Kropp, & Siem, 2006). The volunteer experience may also include some negative downsides. In research on AIDS volunteerism, findings show that some volunteers reported feelings of stigmatisation and discomfort resulting from their work as AIDS volunteers. In fact, many reported that the reactions of members of their own social networks have caused them to feel embarrassed, uncomfortable, and stigmatised because of their volunteerism (Snyder, Omoto, & Crain, 1999).

Consequences of Volunteerism

Our research questions at the consequences stage of the VPM focused on changes in attitudes, knowledge, and behaviour among volunteers as a result of their service, as well as their ultimate longevity of service and their perceived and judged effectiveness as volunteers. In longitudinal research with repeated measurements over time, we found that volunteers are indeed changed by their experiences, for example, increases in knowledge about safer sex practices, less stereotyped beliefs about PWAs, and significantly greater comfort with AIDS and AIDS-related issues (Omoto, Snyder, Chang, & Lee, 2001). In their self-reports, moreover, volunteers revealed that their experiences have powerfully affected and changed them directly (Omoto & Snyder, 1995).

In exploring longevity of service, we also found that the duration of service of one group of AIDS volunteers was related to their satisfaction with their work, the amount of support they perceived from their social support network, and the motivations they reported for becoming AIDS volunteers (Omoto & Snyder, 1995). Specifically, volunteers served longer to the extent that they were more satisfied with their work, had less social support, and reported stronger, and particularly self-focused, motivations for volunteering. The fact that greater social support was actually related to shorter length of service time is consistent with previously discussed findings about the stigmatisation of AIDS volunteers. To the extent that being a volunteer disrupts harmonious relations with members of one's social network, and to the extent that these social network members responded negatively to this disruption and to the AIDS volunteerism that has occasioned this disruption, volunteers may be likely to quit sooner than if their work is supported by others.

The findings with respect to volunteers' motivations, although initially surprising, are understandable, in retrospect. Engaging in volunteerism for self-focused reasons such as to gain understanding, personal development, or esteem enhancement all predicted longer durations of service, whereas ratings of other-focused motivations such as values and community concern were unrelated to longevity of service. Thus, volunteers who can and did get something back from their work were likely to stay involved longer. Volunteering for relatively more other-focused reasons however, may not sustain people in the face of the stress and stigmatisation they are likely to encounter as volunteers. Said another way, volunteering for personal reasons, and not just out of relatively selfless desire to serve others, not only is common, but is likely to lead to longer service as a volunteer.

As well, research on the consequences of volunteerism has examined the impact of volunteers on the clients who are served. Such research addresses the key question — Do volunteers make a difference? In a study of the helping relationships between AIDS volunteers and their clients, clients with volunteers (relative to those without) had higher psychological functioning, with this effect seeming to be linked to greater active coping, which was in turn, promoted by the quality of the relationship between the volunteer and client (Crain, Snyder, & Omoto, 2000). And further, what makes for a high quality, effective and productive volunteer-client helping relationship? A critical ingredient seems to be a psychological sense of community — to the extent that volunteers are connected with their communities, they are effective as volunteers and, to the extent that clients feel a psychological connection to their communities, they benefit most from the services provided to them by volunteers (Omoto & Snyder, 2002). In short, both volunteers and clients benefit from heightened community connections.

Moreover, research on volunteerism has yielded recurring indications that connections to community can draw people into volunteerism and sustain their involvement over time. In reciprocal fashion, moreover, involvement in volunteerism seems to strengthen and build connections to community. Specifically, community concern and the influences of other community members figure prominently in the motivations of new volunteers (Omoto & Snyder, 1995; Stuermer & Kampmeier, 2003). Moreover, over the course of their service, volunteers become increasingly connected with their surrounding communities, including the communities defined by the volunteers, staff, and clients associated with their volunteer service organisations (Omoto & Snyder, 2002). In this way, volunteering also appears to build and foster a sense of community. For example, in research in which changes in the social networks of volunteers over the course of their service was investigated, we found that volunteers were increasingly surrounded by a community of people who are somehow connected to their volunteer service, including people they had recruited to be volunteers (Omoto & Snyder, 2002). Moreover, as connections to a community of shared concerns increase, participation in the community, including in forms of social action other than volunteerism (such as giving to charitable causes, attending fund-raising events, and engaging in social activism), also increases (Omoto & Malsch, 2005; Omoto & Snyder, 2002).

The Psychology of Volunteerism in Context

The dynamics of volunteerism that we have observed in our studies of AIDS volunteers have also been observed in related studies of other populations of volunteers. For example, it has been possible to develop measures of volunteer motivations for use in diverse samples of actual volunteers and prospective volunteers (e.g. Clary et al., 1998), to demonstrate that persuasive messages, whether in videotape or brochure form, designed to motivate people to volunteer are persuasive to the extent that they target the motivations of individual prospective volunteers (Clary et al., 1994; Clary et al., 1998), to demonstrate that the satisfaction experienced by diverse groups of volunteers is predicted by the match between their motivations and the benefits that they derive from volunteering (Clary et al., 1998; Crain et al., 1998), and that volunteers' intentions to continue volunteering both in the immediate and longer terms is predicted by the match between their motivations and the benefits that they perceive to accrue as volunteers (Clary et al., 1998).

Further, research on volunteerism has revealed important differences in the ways in which this form of helping manifests itself across the life course. Rates of volunteerism in the United States tend to increase as individuals move from adolescence to young adulthood to middle age, and then decline as people move toward old age. For those under 25, less than 50% reported having volunteered in the previous year; for those aged 25–34, it's 53%; for those 35–44, it's 61%; for those 45–54, it's 56%; and, for those over 55, it drops below 50% (Clary et al., 1996). Some motivations for volunteering are accorded equal importance across age groups. For example, values are always highly rated, in fact as highly rated for 18–24 year olds, as for those over the age of 65. However, some motivations are quite different by age; for example, motivations revolving around career development and acquiring new skills and knowledge through volunteering seem to be more important to younger than to older people (Clary et al., 1996).

Moreover, volunteering in adults appears to have its roots in youth volunteerism, according to survey research conducted by Independent Sector (2001). Key findings from this research are that, among adults who volunteer, two-thirds began volunteering when they were young. Moreover, adults who began volunteering as youth are twice as likely to volunteer as those who did not volunteer when they were younger. And, in every income and age group, those who volunteered as youth, gave and volunteered more than those who did not. Finally, those who volunteered as youth and whose parents volunteered became the most generous adults in giving their time as volunteers.

Where, then, does this important pattern of youth volunteering come from? In studies of volunteering during high school years, it appears that certain critical events in the early years of high school foreshadow volunteering that occurs in the later high school years. Thus, in one study of high school students in Minnesota, those with higher educational plans and higher intrinsic motivation toward school work (as measured in their first year in high school), were also more likely to become involved in volunteer activities.

In turn, their volunteering strengthened their work values and the importance they attached to involvement in their communities (Eccles & Barber, 1999; Johnson, Beebe, Mortimer, & Snyder, 1998; Lo & Au, 2004; Youniss, McLellan, & Yates, 1997).

In later stages of the life course, volunteering is prevalent among the elderly. However, the motivations for volunteering do show important shifts in emphasis over the life course. Whereas, among younger and middle aged adults, motivations revolving around relationship concerns are particularly pronounced, among elderly volunteers, motivations related to concerns with service to society and community obligation seem to be particularly prominent (Omoto et al., 2000). Moreover, among the elderly, volunteerism and other forms of social participation seem to be associated with higher psychological functioning, better physical health, and increased longevity (House, 2001; House, Robbins, & Metzner, 1982).

Just as volunteerism may vary across stages of life, so too does there seem to be meaningful variation across cultures and countries in the meanings and manifestations of volunteerism and other forms of citizen participation and civic engagement (Curtis et al., 1992; Levine, Norenzayan, & Philbrick, 2001). Much of this variation tracks the disparity in individualism and collectivism across cultures and regions of the world, with cultural orientations influencing whether getting involved in solving societal problems is seen as a matter of personal choice and individual responsibility (i.e. an individualistic orientation) or whether it is construed as one of normative obligation and collective concern (i.e. a collectivistic orientation). For example, Miller (1994) proposed that the moral foundations of caring and helping may vary across cultures, especially with respect to the extent that caring and helping reflect personal and individual considerations (which might be especially pronounced in individualistic cultures), versus the extent to which these pro-social actions reflect interpersonal and social obligations (an orientation that might be particularly characteristic of collectivistic cultures). In addition, there appear to be associations between individualism/collectivism and various indicators of civic engagement and citizen participation. Thus, in the United States, the states with the greatest amounts of charitable giving and volunteerism also tend to be the most individualistic (Kemmelmeier, Jambor, & Letner, 2006). Similarly, there is a positive association between individualism and social capital across different countries (Allik & Realo, 2004). These associations may suggest that the apparent liberation from social bonds that may come with individualistic cultural views may also make people dependent on being or staying involved with society (as suggested over a century ago by Durkheim, 1893/1984).

Conclusion

Clearly, the emergence of volunteer service organisations in the United States in response to the challenges of the HIV/AIDS epidemic has provided us with considerable opportunities to explore the unique dynamics of volunteerism as a form of pro-social action and as a case example of people mobilising themselves to respond to a pressing social problem. Moreover, the lessons learned from our studies of AIDS volunteers have been generally corroborated by studies of volunteers working for other causes and engaging in other forms of social action (Snyder & Omoto, 2007). Taken together, such research has been informative about the nature of helping and pro-social action, especially those forms of helping and pro-social action that are planned, sustained, and that occur in the absence of bonds of obligation.

In addition to the theoretical benefits of the study of volunteerism for understanding the nature of pro-social action, we believe that an understanding of the psychology of volunteerism offers practical messages as well. Among the practical implications of our research are the lessons that suggest the practice of volunteerism itself, specifically about the ways that the recruitment, placement, and retention of volunteers can be enhanced. Systematic attention to the experiences and motivations of individual volunteers may go a long way in making more effective the efforts of grass roots and volunteer organisations. Specifically, to the extent that organisations dependent on the services of volunteers can identify the motivations of prospective volunteers, including motivations that vary reliably with one's stage of life, they can systematically tailor their recruitment efforts to the actual motivations of potential volunteers. And, to the extent that these organisations can and do attend to the motivations of their actual volunteers, they may be able to channel them toward volunteer assignments that provide opportunities to best serve their particular motivations, and thereby enhance their effectiveness, satisfaction, and longevity of service.

From the perspective of the concerns of society, studying volunteerism is likely to yield valuable information of societal significance, including how to understand and expand the roles of volunteers and volunteer organisations in confronting and surmounting many of the problems that challenge societies. Quite conceivably, a focus on the motivations of volunteers could be an important foundation for large-scale campaigns to promote awareness of and interest in volunteerism and other forms of civic involvement. If successful, these campaigns would increase the involvement of individuals in the affairs of their societies, and thereby contribute to an active citizenry and a fully engaged civil society. The implications of this work for youth who choose or do not choose to volunteer to benefit themselves and society, as a whole are profound all over the world.

References

Allik, J., & Realo, A. (2004). Individualism-collectivism and social capital. *Journal of Cross-Cultural Psychology, 35*, 29–49.

Andrews, H. F. (1990). Helping and health: The relationship between volunteer activity and health-related outcomes. *Advances, 7*, 25–34.

Clary, E. G., & Snyder, M. (1991). A functional analysis of altruism and prosocial behaviour: The case of volunteerism. *Review of Personality and Social Psychology, 12*, 119–148.

Clary, E. G., & Snyder, M. (1993). Persuasive communications strategies for recruiting volunteers. In D. R. Young, R. M. Hollister & V. A. Hodgkinson (Eds.), *Governing, leading, and managing nonprofit organisations: New insights from research and practice* (pp. 121–137). San Francisco, CA: Jossey-Bass.

Clary, E. G., Snyder, M., & Stukas, A. A. (1996). Volunteers motivations: Findings from a national survey. *Nonprofit and Voluntary Sector Quarterly, 25*, 485–505.

Clary, E. G., Snyder, M., & Stukas, A. A. (1998). Service-learning and psychology: Lessons from the psychology of volunteers' motivations. In R. G. Bringle & D. K. Duffy (Eds.), *With service in mind: Concepts and models for service-learning in psychology* (pp. 35–50). Washington, DC: American Association of Higher Education.

Clary, E. G., Snyder, M., Ridge, R. D., Copeland, J. T., Stukas, A. A., Haugen, J. A., et al. (1998). Understanding and assessing the motivations of volunteers: A functional approach. *Journal of Personality and Social Psychology, 74*, 1516–1530.

Clary, E. G., Snyder, M., Ridge, R. D., Miene, P., & Haugen, J. (1994). Matching messages to motives in persuasion: A functional approach to promoting volunteerism. *Journal of Applied Social Psychology, 24*, 1129–1149.

Crain, A. L., Omoto, A. M., & Snyder, M. (1998, April). *What if you can't always get what you want? Testing a functional approach to volunteerism.* Paper presented at the annual meetings of the Midwestern Psychological Association, Chicago, IL.

Crain, A. L., Snyder, M., & Omoto, A. M. (2000, May). *Volunteers make a difference: Relationship quality, active coping, and functioning among PWAs with volunteer buddies.* Paper presented at the annual meetings of the Midwestern Psychological Association, Chicago, IL.

Curtis, J. E., Grabb, E., & Baer, D. (1992). Voluntary association membership in fifteen countries: A comparative analysis. *American Sociological Review, 57*, 139–152.

Davis, M. H., Hall, J. A., & Meyer, M. (2003). The first year: Influences on the satisfaction, involvement, and persistence of new community volunteers. *Personality and Social Psychology Bulletin, 29*, 248–260.

Durkheim, E. (1984). *The division of labour in society.* London: Macmillan (Original work published 1893).

Eccles, J. S., & Barber, B. L. (1999). Student council, volunteering, basketball, or marching band: What kind of extracurricular involvement matters? *Journal of Adolescent Research, 14*, 10–43.

House, J. (2001). Social isolation kills, but how and why? *Psychosomatic Medicine, 63*, 273–274

House, J. S., Robbins, C., & Metzner, H. L. (1982). The association of social relationships and activities with mortality: Prospective evidence from the Tecumseh Community Health Study. *The American Journal of Epidemiology, 116*, 123–140.

Independent Sector (2001). *Giving and volunteering in the United States: Findings from a national survey.* Washington, DC: Author.

Johnson, M. K., Beebe, T., Mortimer, J. T., & Snyder, M. (1998). Volunteerism in adolescence: A process perspective. *Journal of Research on Adolescence, 8*, 309–332.

Kemmelmeier, M., Jambor, E. E., & Letner, J. (2006). Individualism and good works: Cultural variation in giving and volunteering across the United States. *Journal of Cross Cultural Psychology, 37*, 327–344.

Kiviniemi, M. T., Snyder, M., & Omoto, A. M. (2002). Too many of a good thing? The effects of multiple motivations on stress, cost, fulfilment, and satisfaction. *Personality and Social Psychology Bulletin, 28*, 732–743.

Levine, R. V., Norenzayan, A., & Philbrick, K. (2001). Cross-cultural differences in helping strangers. *Journal of Cross-Cultural Psychology, 32*, 543–560.

Lo, T. W. & Au, E. (2004). *Youth empowerment: International experiences.* Hong Kong: City University of Hong Kong.

Miller, J. G. (1994). Cultural diversity in the morality of caring: Individually oriented versus duty-based interpersonal moral codes. *Cross-Cultural Research, 28*, 3–39.

O'Brien, L. T., Crain, A. L., Omoto, A. M., & Snyder, M. (2000, May). *Matching motivations to outcomes: Implications for persistence in service.* Paper presented at the annual meetings of the Midwestern Psychological Association, Chicago, IL.

Omoto, A. M., Gunn, D. O., & Crain, A. L. (1998). Helping in hard times: Relationship closeness and the AIDS volunteer experience. In V. J. Derlega & A. P. Barbee (Eds.), *HIV and social interaction* (pp. 106–128). Thousand Oaks, CA: Sage.

Omoto, A. M., & Malsch, A. M. (2005). Psychological sense of community: Conceptual issues and connections to volunteerism-related activism. In A. M. Omoto (Ed.), *Processes of community change and social action* (pp. 83–103). Mahwah, NJ: Lawrence Erlbaum Associates.

Omoto, A. M., & Snyder, M. (1990). Basic research in action: Volunteerism and society's response to AIDS. *Personality and Social Psychology Bulletin, 16,* 152–165.

Omoto, A. M., & Snyder, M. (1993). AIDS volunteers and their motivations: Theoretical issues and practical concerns. *Nonprofit Management and Leadership, 4,* 157–176.

Omoto, A. M., & Snyder, M. (1995). Sustained helping without obligation: Motivation, longevity of service, and perceived attitude change among AIDS volunteers. *Journal of Personality and Social Psychology, 68,* 671–686.

Omoto, A. M., & Snyder, M. (2002). Considerations of community: The context and process of volunteerism. *American Behavioral Scientist, 45,* 846–867.

Omoto, A. M., Snyder, M., & Berghuis, J. P. (1993). The psychology of volunteerism: A conceptual analysis and a programme of action research. In J. B. Pryor & G. D. Reeder (Eds.), *The social psychology of HIV infection* (pp. 333–356). Hillsdale, NJ: Erlbaum.

Omoto, A. M., Snyder, M., Chang, W., & Lee, D. H. (2001, August). *Knowledge and attitude change among volunteers and their associates.* Paper presented at the annual meeting of the American Psychological Association, San Francisco, CA.

Omoto, A. M., Snyder, M., & Martino, S. C.(2000). Volunteerism and the life course: Investigating age-related agendas for action. *Basic and Applied Social Psychology, 22,* 181–198.

Ouellette, S. C., Cassel, J. B., Maslanka, H., & Wong, L. M. (1995). GMHC volunteers and hopes for the second decade of AIDS.

AIDS Education and Prevention, Supplement, 64–79.

Piliavin, J. A., & Charng, H. (1990). Altruism: A review of recent theory and research. *Annual Review of Sociology, 16*, 27–65.

Schondel, C., Shields, G., & Orel, N. (1992). Development of an instrument to measure volunteers' motivation in working with people with AIDS. *Social Work in Health Care, 17*, 53–71.

Schroeder, D. A., Penner, L. A., Dovidio, J. F., & Piliavin, J. A. (1995). *The psychology of helping and altruism: Problems and puzzles.* New York: McGraw-Hill.

Simon, B., Stürmer, S., & Steffens, K. (2000). Helping individuals or group members? The role of individual and collective identification in AIDS volunteerism. *Personality and Social Psychology Bulletin, 26*, 497–506.

Smith, D. M., Omoto, A. M., & Snyder, M. (2001, June). *Motivation matching and recruitment of volunteers: A field study.* Presented at the annual meetings of the American Psychological Society, Toronto, Canada.

Smith, M. B., Bruner, J., & White, R. (1956). *Opinions and personality.* New York: Wiley.

Snyder, M., & Cantor, N. (1998). Understanding personality and social behaviour: A functionalist strategy. In D. Gilbert, S. Fiske, & G. Lindzey (Eds.), *The Handbook of Social Psychology: Vol.1* (4th ed., pp. 635–679). Boston: McGraw-Hill.

Snyder, M., Clary, E. G., & Stukas, A. A. (2000). The functional approach to volunteerism. In G. R. Maio & J. M. Olson (Eds.), *Why we evaluate: Functions of attitudes* (pp. 365–393). Mahwah, NJ: Erlbaum.

Snyder, M., & Omoto, A. M. (1992a). Volunteerism and society's response to the HIV epidemic. *Current Directions in Psychological Science, 1*, 113–116.

Snyder, M., & Omoto, A. M. (1992b). Who helps and why? The psychology of AIDS volunteerism. In S. Spacapan & S. Oskamp (Eds.), *Helping and being helped: Naturalistic studies* (pp. 213–239). Newbury Park CA: Sage.

Snyder, M., & Omoto, A. M. (2000). Doing good for self and society: Volunteerism and the psychology of citizen participation. In M. Van Vugt, M. Snyder, T. Tyler & A. Biel (Eds.), *Collective helping in modern society: Dilemmas and solutions* (pp. 127–141). London, UK: Routledge.

Snyder, M., & Omoto, A. M. (2001). Basic research and practical problems: Volunteerism and the psychology of individual and collective action. In W. Wosinska, R. Cialdini & D. Barrett (Eds.), *The practice of social influence in multiple cultures* (pp. 287–307). Mahwah, NJ: Erlbaum.

Snyder, M., & Omoto, A. M. (2007). Social action. In A. W. Kruglanski & E. T. Higgins (Eds.), *Social psychology: A handbook of basic principles* (2nd ed., pp. 940–961). New York: Guilford.

Snyder, M., Omoto, A. M., & Crain, A. L. (1999). Punished for their good deeds: Stigmatization of AIDS volunteers. *American Behavioral Scientist, 42,* 1175–1192.

Snyder, M., Omoto, A. M., & Smith, D. M. (in press). The role of persuasion strategies in motivating individual and collective action. In E. Borgida, J. L. Sullivan & C. Federico (Eds.), *The political psychology of democratic citizenship.* New York: Oxford University Press.

Stuermer, A., Snyder, M., Kropp, A., & Siem, B. (2006). Empathy-motivated helping: The moderating role of group membership. *Personality and Social Psychology Bulletin, 32*(7), 943–956.

Stuermer, S., & Kampmeier, C. (2003). Active citizenship: The role of community identification in community volunteerism and local participation. *Psychologica Belgica, 43,* 103–122.

Stuermer, S., Snyder, M., & Omoto, A. M. (2005). Prosocial emotions and helping: The moderating role of group membership. *Journal of Personality and Social Psychology, 88,* 532–546.

Stukas, A. A., Snyder, M., & Clary, E. G. (1999). Service learning: Who benefits and why. *Social Policy Report, 13,* 1–19.

Williamson, I., Snyder, M., & Omoto, A. M. (2000, May). *How motivations and re-enlistment frames interact to predict volunteer attitudes and intentions: A test of the functional matching effect.* Paper presented at the annual meetings of the Midwestern Psychological Association, Chicago, IL.

Wilson, J. (2000). Volunteering. *Annual Review of Sociology, 26,* 215–240.

Youniss, J., McLellan, J. A., & Yates, M. (1997). What we know about generating civic identity. *American Behavioral Scientist, 40,* 620–631.

THE ROLE OF COMMUNITY CONNECTIONS IN VOLUNTEERISM AND SOCIAL ACTION

Allen M. OMOTO and Mark SNYDER

2

Acknowledgements

The research described in this chapter was supported by grants from the National Institute of Mental Health to Allen M. Omoto and to Mark Snyder, and funding from the Fetzer Institute and Institute for Research on Unlimited Love to Allen M. Omoto.

Introduction

In many ways, working alone and working together, people take action that benefits society. Not all of these efforts are necessarily motivated by an explicit desire to benefit society, certainly, but the combined effects of individual action can have profound effects on society, overall. Consider several examples from North America. People may practise the habits of recycling and conserving energy, as well as use mass transit, in order to preserve and conserve natural resources or even to save a few dollars or to avoid the stress of driving at rush hour. They may serve as volunteers and provide services to other people who have difficulty in caring for themselves. They may participate in programmes in schools and in the workplace that provide opportunities for community service. Or, in an effort to spend more time with their children and have positive influence in their lives, parents may coach little league sports teams or serve as the leader or chaperone of youth groups. People join neighbourhood groups and organisations and, where none exist to meet the needs of their communities, take the initiative to find them and assume leadership roles in them. They may vote or work on political campaigns, and even run for office themselves, in order to elect political leaders who will work on behalf of causes that they personally value. They may engage in lobbying and advocacy efforts to arouse the passions and efforts of other people or to work for the passage of legislation of concern to them. They may join and be active in social movements dedicated to causes of concern to them, such as improving the living conditions of disadvantaged groups in society, protecting and expanding human rights, and working for peace at home and abroad. Similar activities and commitments can be found throughout the world (e.g. Allik & Realo, 2004; Curtis, Grabb, & Baer, 1992; Lo & Au, 2004; Van Vugt, Snyder, Tyler, & Biel, 2000).

These activities are all instances of individuals seeking to address problems of society by engaging in what is often referred to as civic engagement, citizenship behaviours, or more generically, social action (Boyte & Kari, 1996; see also Snyder & Omoto, 2007).

Promoting various forms of social action may be one way of solving many of the society's most pressing problems (Oskamp, 2000; Omoto, 2005; Omoto & Snyder, 2002; Snyder & Omoto, 2000, 2001; Van Vugt & Snyder, 2002), and a way to generate "social capital," or bonds of trust among citizens (Coleman, 1990; Portes, 1998; Putnam, 1993, 1995, 2000). In fact, there is a substantial body of research that examines such citizenship behaviours and the ways in which coordinated activities of individuals serve the common good (Kymlicka & Norman, 1994; Putnam, 1993, 1995; Verba, Schlozman, & Brady, 1995; Van Vugt et al., 2000).

Involvement in, or service to, a community is generally deemed pro-social behaviour or action that is intended to help others, or to have beneficial social impact. Most often, this involvement is in local and geographically defined communities, like a city, but it can also take place in relational or interest-based communities in which members are geographically dispersed and may or may not know one another personally (e.g. work on environmental protection or on behalf of people living in poverty in other locations; see Omoto & Malsch, 2005).

A specific form of social action is volunteerism, when individuals willingly give time or work for the good or welfare of others without expectations of compensation or reward. Volunteering can be informal, as when neighbours help one another, or it can be formally institutionalised in organisations and agency-based programmes. Every year, millions of people around the world devote substantial amounts of their time and energy to volunteering. In the United States, in fact, it is estimated that 65.4 million people, or nearly 30% of the U.S. population, volunteered through or for an organisation at least once during 2004–2005 (Bureau of Labour Statistics, 2005). Meanwhile, another recent survey estimates that nearly 45% of the U.S. adult population engages in regular volunteer work, doing so for an average of 3.6 hours each week (Independent Sector, 2001). In our research, we have focused most extensively on volunteerism conducted in the context of formal organisations, especially AIDS service organisations.

The Volunteer Process Model

As indicated in the previous chapter, our research has been ongoing for close to twenty years and is guided by a conceptual model, the Volunteer Process Model (VPM), that conceptualises volunteerism as a process that unfolds over time; individuals decide to get involved, seek out volunteer opportunities, engage in volunteer activities, and eventually cease their efforts (see Omoto & Snyder, 1990, 1995, 2002; Omoto, Snyder, & Berghuis, 1993; Snyder & Omoto, 2000, 2007). This model, summarised in Figure 2.1, specifies psychological and behavioural features associated with each of the three sequential and interactive stages (i.e. antecedents, experiences, and consequences) and speaks to activity at multiple levels of analyses (i.e. the individual, the interpersonal, the organisational, and the social system). Guided by this model, we have conducted coordinated field and laboratory studies employing longitudinal and cross-sectional methodologies and sampling from diverse populations.

Figure 2.1   The Volunteer Process Model embedded in community context

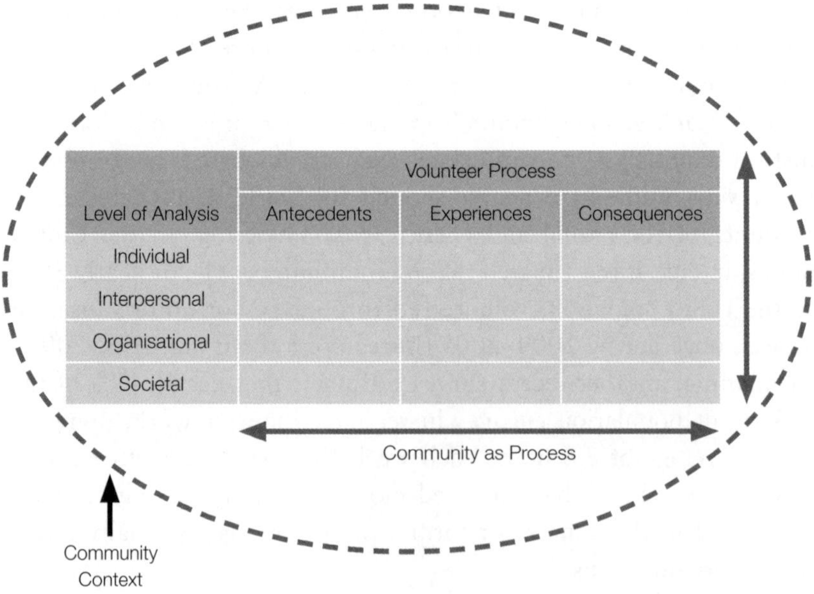

Level of Analysis	Volunteer Process		
	Antecedents	Experiences	Consequences
Individual			
Interpersonal			
Organisational			
Societal			

Community as Process

Community Context

At the antecedents stage, we have identified both theoretically and empirically, personality and motivational factors, as well as characteristics of people's life circumstances that predict who becomes a volunteer and who is most effective and satisfied as a volunteer (Omoto & Snyder, 1990, 1993, 1995; Omoto, Snyder, & Martino, 2000; Snyder & Omoto, 1992a, b; Snyder, Omoto, & Smith, in press). At the experiences stage, we have explored the interpersonal relationships that develop between volunteers and recipients of their services and the ways that these relationships lead to the continued service of volunteers and positive benefits to the recipients of their services (Crain, Snyder, & Omoto, 2000; Lindsay, Snyder, & Omoto, 2003; Omoto, Gunn, & Crain, 1998). We have also examined correlates of satisfaction for volunteers and recipients of service, as well as factors that may make for more pleasant and rewarding experiences (such as organisational integration) and those that detract from enjoyment (such as stigmatisation by others) (Kiviniemi, Snyder, & Omoto, 2002; Snyder, Omoto, & Crain, 1999). Finally, at the consequences stage, we have studied the impact of volunteer service on the attitudes and behaviours of volunteers, the recipients of their services, and members of their social networks, including such "bottom line" behaviours as continuing involvement and willingness to recruit others to the volunteer service organisation (O'Brien, Crain, Omoto, & Snyder, 2000; Omoto & Snyder, 1995; Omoto, Snyder, Chang, & Lee, 2001; Snyder et al., 1999).

At the level of the individual, the VPM calls attention to the activities and psychological processes of individual volunteers and recipients of volunteer services. For example, volunteers make decisions to get involved, seek out service opportunities, engage in volunteer work for a period of time, and eventually cease their efforts. At the interpersonal level, the model expands this focus further and incorporates the dynamics of the helping relationships between volunteers and recipients of service. At the organisational level, the model focuses on the goals associated with recruiting, managing, and retaining an unpaid work force as well as associated concerns about work performance, compensation, and evaluation. That is, many volunteer efforts take place through, or in cooperation with community based organisations or other institutions. Thus, we have incorporated aspects of organisational structure, roles, and operations into the VPM. Finally, at a broader societal level, the VPM considers the linkages between individuals and the social structures of their societies as well as collective and cultural dynamics. (See Chapter 1 by Snyder and Omoto for a more detailed discussion of the VPM.)

Conceptualising Community: Context and Process

Although a good deal of our research has focused on the unfolding process of volunteerism at the individual level (see Figure 2.1), we have recently begun to attend more systematically to the other levels of analysis in the VPM, or the embeddedness of volunteerism in broader levels of analyses such as communities. In conceptualising community, we consider it both as context and process for volunteer efforts (Omoto & Snyder, 2002).

To begin, we seek to place volunteerism and social action in the broader context of the communities in which, and on behalf of which, they occur. That is, many volunteer service organisations are situated in a community domain—they have community origins, roots, and connections that are acknowledged in their histories, mission statements, and public relations efforts. Moreover, the standards, norms, resources, and institutions of the community provide backdrop for volunteer efforts. As such, the community provides a context for volunteer efforts and social action. And, in reciprocal fashion, a community is often directly and indirectly changed by the activities of volunteers and the time and energy that they invest in responding to community needs. For example, in response to demands and unmet needs, new programmes and even agencies are developed (e.g. after school programmes, homeless shelters) and new patterns of behaviour are promoted and take hold (e.g. recycling and energy conservation). In fact, many organisations are conceived, developed, and continue to exist for purposes of community change (Hughey, Speer, & Peterson, 1999). Simply put, the community provides a backdrop for individuals and organisations to undertake volunteer activities aimed at promoting social change, and that may contribute to societal cooperation and civic participation. Occasionally, the community provides only backdrop for the actions of individuals and groups, but sometimes the target of social action is to change the community itself.

In fact, traditional definitions of community and related research refer to a specific place (Dunham, 1986) and are generally illustrative of a locational, territorial, geographical, or structural community. Hence in such definitions, the focus is on a college dormitory, a village, a small town, or simply a network of individuals living in close proximity to people they know. In fact, most of the theorising and research on sense of community has been focused on feelings about specific places or geographic entities (Hill, 1996), or on "community" as a descriptor or characteristic of a locality (Sonn & Fisher, 1998). In our analysis, this emphasis is most similar to community as context.

Our second interest in community, community as process has a decidedly more psychological flavour, and emphasises how concerns about, and connections to, community can motivate and sustain the actions of individuals. In addition, we consider some of the potential effects of belonging to communities on individuals in terms of feelings of empowerment, efficacy, responsibility, support, and ultimately their behaviours. As such, we seek to extend the concept beyond a geographically bounded area and focus on communities that are formed out of shared interests, characteristics, experiences, or opinions, and that are not restricted to individuals in proximity to each other. To identify with or belong to psychological communities, an individual does not need to have direct knowledge or the acquaintanceship of other community members or even disclose community-defining characteristics or status to others. Psychological communities are potentially quite diffuse and are also changeable.

We believe that the meanings, attachments, and consequences of psychological communities and especially their implications for motivating social action are important to explore.

In our work, we propose that a psychological sense of community (see also McMillan, 1996; McMillan & Chavis, 1986; Sarason, 1974) may be importantly implicated in the volunteer process, overall. Consider for example, the case of community-based organisations that emerged in the United States in response to the HIV/AIDS epidemic—organisations of volunteers involved in caring for persons living with HIV and AIDS, in educating the public about HIV disease, and in raising awareness of HIV and AIDS and pushing for supportive legislation and funding mechanisms.

In the specific case of AIDS volunteerism, we suggest a conceptualisation of community as the broad and diverse community of people concerned with HIV. In this sense, community includes not only those individuals with HIV and at risk for it, but also extends to the members of their social networks, as well as the volunteers and staff of organisations that provide services relevant to HIV. This broader conceptualisation of community and the feelings of connection, attachment, and esteem that the individual derives from it, are what we mean by a psychological sense of community for the community affected by HIV/AIDS.

The Importance of Psychological Sense of Community

What, then, are the connections between psychological sense of community and the volunteer process? Theoretically, psychological connections to a broader and more diverse community of concern may promote feelings of efficacy and support. That is, they should lead to increases in feelings of responsibility and obligation to help others, and in the confidence that one's service as a volunteer can and will make a difference and, in so doing, motivate individuals not only to become volunteers but also to persist longer in their service and to strive to be as effective as they can possibly be in their work. Psychological sense of community should also increase an individual's confidence that support is available to those with problems and that he or she is surrounded by a community of caring and compassionate others. This knowledge should empower individuals and make it easier for them to seek out assistance when they need it. Thus, they should also be receptive to the services offered by volunteers and community-based organisations, and ultimately to derive greater benefits from working with volunteers and volunteer agencies.

In short, considerations of psychological sense of community focus attention on the processes by which community can positively affect individuals involved in volunteer efforts, including the volunteers and clients in the AIDS service organisations that we have studied in our research. For example, for clients living with HIV, a bolstered sense of community may help to ease the sense of isolation and indifference that many feel. Similarly, as evidenced in our previous research, some volunteers experience stigmatisation that could be eased through a sense of community.

Heightening and broadening a sense of community may also be likely to have beneficial effects on feelings of personal efficacy and support for persons living with HIV or AIDS (PWAs) and volunteers. That is, increases in sense of community should lead to increases in feelings of responsibility and comfort—in seeking assistance, in helping others, and in helping oneself by way of health maintenance behaviours. The increased confidence that comes with greater sense of community should make individuals more optimistic about facing their problems, whether related to physical health, care giving, stigmatisation, or social isolation. The community as an entity also possesses more and different resources to draw on, for both PWAs and volunteers. Not only is there an expanded network of people from whom to get and offer social support, but there are greater and potentially more specialised collective material and psychological resources available through numerous community connections.

Self-esteem is likely to increase with increased community connections for several reasons. First, community is likely to provide a source of collective self-esteem (Crocker & Luhtanen, 1990) and valued social identity (Tajfel & Turner, 1986; Turner, Hogg, Oakes, Reicher, & Wetherell, 1987) for individuals as they connect and identify with it. The sense of belonging that comes with community also enhances and reaffirms an individual's worth as an individual and as a member of a valued social group. And, possessing a community identity that is valued and shared by others may offer additional positive regard due to social consensus and validation. To the extent that the community is successful (particularly those organised for purposes of action; Hughey et al., 1999), community members should enjoy increased feelings of efficacy and accomplishment. Individuals also can bask in the accomplishments of successful community members (Cialdini et al., 1976; Tesser, 1988). In addition, members may experience pride in a community's ability to provide services and support for its members.

Furthermore, successful community members may become models for upward social comparison (Gibbons & Gerrard, 1989; Suls & Wills, 1990) and motivate or trigger others to strive for success and greater community contribution. Thus, social comparison processes may encourage PWAs to seek out and persist with their medical care and regular social activities, and may lead volunteers to serve longer and recruit others to AIDS volunteerism. Community connections and identity are also likely to provide members with consensus and support for solving problems and overcoming barriers to effective action that they may face. Thus, sense of community should contribute simultaneously to individual and collective action (Simon, 1998; Simon et al., 1998).

Finally, a broader conceptualisation and sense of community should facilitate other civic participation, including helping and being helped. Members of a community are thus likely to feel obligated to work on behalf of the community and to be good team players. They should work to improve their own conditions and those of the community. In addition, feelings of reciprocity for past help received (and possibly for future needs) should be heightened by community connections. The increased resources, confidence, and esteem provided by sense of community should also breed feelings of psychological empowerment (Chamberlin, 1997; Corrigan, Faber, Rashid, & Leary, 1999; Rogers, Chamberlin, Elison, & Crean, 1997; Zimmerman & Rappaport, 1988; Zimmerman, Israel, Schultz, & Checkoway, 1992). As a consequence, attempts at effective action are likely to be enacted, whether in the sphere of volunteerism or other forms of community involvement and civic participation. In this way, then, psychological sense of community may lead individuals to act to change or participate in their surroundings and communities through volunteerism and other forms of civic participation.

Community and the Volunteer Process Model

Based on our analyses, psychological sense of community is not only relevant to, but is predicted to benefit, volunteers and clients in community-based organisations. As an initial test of our theoretical notions, we examined data from several studies of AIDS volunteers and the people living with HIV disease with whom they were paired to work (i.e. PWA clients). Specifically, we examined data from several multi-site, longitudinal field studies that we had conducted for empirical evidence relevant to the role of community in the volunteer process. Our goal here was to articulate and better understand psychological sense of community in the VPM as illustrated in Figure 2.1.

Antecedents

When it came to individuals' decisions to become volunteers, our data revealed that motivations reflecting concern for community figure prominently in such decisions. That is, people have different reasons for getting involved as volunteers and indeed, we have successfully identified a diverse set of motivations for volunteer work. We know from several investigations (Omoto & Crain, 1995; Omoto & Snyder, 1993; 1995; Omoto et al., 2000) that one main impetus for volunteering revolves around motivations reflecting concern for community. For example, when new volunteers rate their reasons for volunteering, community concern or connection typically receive high ratings. Some items that reflect these concerns are: "Because of my concern and worry about communities affected by AIDS," "Because of my obligation to communities affected by AIDS," and "To get to know people in communities affected by AIDS".

In addition to volunteering out of community concern motivations, participants seem to have been drawn to volunteerism by the influences of other members in their communities. In fact, the majority of new volunteers in one longitudinal study (Omoto & Snyder, 1999) claimed community-based routes to volunteering; that is, they began their volunteer work because they were asked to volunteer by someone they knew, they already knew people who were volunteers, or because they participated in other community events (e.g. an AIDS fundraising walk). In addition, over two-thirds of these new volunteers claimed that their parents had modelled some volunteer activities, and over three-quarters of them said that they knew at least one other person doing non-AIDS volunteer work.

These findings are not unique to our AIDS research context. According to data from the 2005 Current Population Survey conducted by the U.S. Department of Labour, when asked how they became involved with their volunteer organisation, a large percentage of respondents (42.8%) claimed that they were asked by someone, with the majority of these respondents having been asked by someone in the organisation itself. As these data suggest, people's sense of community and their social networks may be important at the antecedents stage of the volunteer process—in people's decisions to become volunteers.

Experiences

Moreover, over the course of their service, volunteers become increasingly connected to other members of their communities, including communities defined by the volunteers, staff, and clients associated with their volunteer service organisations. Many AIDS service organisations have so called "buddy programmes," in which volunteers are assigned to work one-on-one with a PWA for purposes of providing daily living assistance, emotional support, and a general social outlet. When we looked at the extent to which volunteers introduced their clients to other members of their existing social networks and the extent to which they were introduced to members of their clients' social networks, we found that, over time, both volunteers and clients became increasingly likely to be integrated into each other's social networks. That is, they did not keep their relationship with each other separate from other aspects of their lives, but instead, they worked to create a broader and more inclusive community, or at least an expanded and integrated social network. After 6 months of working together, a total of 76% of volunteers had been introduced to PWA social network members and 52% of volunteers had introduced their client to members of their own social networks.

Furthermore, these community connections were related to positive benefits for the recipients of volunteer services. For example, the more volunteers were motivated by community concern and the more that they integrated their PWA clients into their (previously separate) personal communities, the better their clients' health. And, for PWAs, the more that they connected to broader communities and had larger social networks, the more they engaged in health maintenance behaviours, the less severe their functioning problems, and the better their mental health. Of particular interest for the community affected by HIV/AIDS, the more close friends at their AIDS service organisation that PWAs reported, the better their own personal ratings of health, the higher their life satisfaction and feelings about themselves, and the less they reported problems of daily living, loneliness, and general depression and listlessness. Taken together, these findings speak to the potential importance of community in understanding the experiences of volunteers as well as other levels of the volunteer process. That is, data supporting the importance of community emerged in the reports of volunteers as well as in the experiences reported by PWAs.

Consequences

Taking things a step further, it appears that volunteering also builds community. For instance, our longitudinal data revealed that, as a consequence of their work, volunteers were increasingly surrounded by people connected to their volunteer service and agency, including people they had recruited to be volunteers. For instance, after only three months of service, over 80% of the volunteers claimed to have at least one friend at their AIDS service organisation, and after six months of service, 28% reported having recruited at least one new volunteer to the organisation. Over the same six-month period, the proportion of each volunteer's social network that was made up of other volunteers also increased by over 1.5 times. In short, as a consequence of their volunteer work, the social networks of volunteers were changed so as to have greater focus on HIV/AIDS and to have a larger community of people working on behalf of HIV/AIDS.

Our data also suggest that, as connections to a community of shared concerns increase, so too does broader civic participation, including participation in forms of social action other than volunteerism (e.g. giving to charitable causes, attended fund-raising events, and engaging in social activism). Tracking the behaviours of AIDS volunteers over their first six months of service in a longitudinal study, we found that the frequency with which these individuals made donations to AIDS groups, attended AIDS fundraisers, and involved themselves further in AIDS activism increased significantly. That is, they tended to act on behalf of the community affected by HIV/AIDS in more and diverse ways.

In summary, research on the VPM has yielded recurring indications that connections to community can draw people into volunteerism and sustain their involvement over time. In reciprocal fashion, moreover, involvement in volunteerism seems to strengthen and build community connections. Specifically, community concern and the influences of other community members figure prominently in the motivations of new volunteers (Omoto & Snyder, 1995;

Stuermer & Kampmeier, 2003). As well, over the course of their service, volunteers become increasingly connected with their surrounding communities, including the communities defined by the volunteers, staff, and clients associated with their volunteer service organisations (Omoto & Snyder, 2002). And, their effectiveness as volunteers is enhanced by a sense of connection to a relevant community (Omoto & Snyder, 2002).

Reversing the causal order, volunteering also appears to build and foster a sense of community. For example, as a consequence of their work, volunteers are increasingly surrounded by a community of people who are somehow connected to their volunteer service, including people they have recruited to be volunteers (Omoto & Snyder, 2002). In addition, volunteering apparently contributes to the creation of bonds of social capital (Stukas, Daly, & Cowling, 2005), and even has been considered a central indicator or measure of social capital itself (Putnam, 2000). Research also suggests that as connections to a community of shared concerns increase, participation in the community, including in forms of social action other than volunteerism, also increases (Malsch, 2005; Omoto & Malsch, 2005; Omoto & Snyder, 2002).

Psychological Sense of Community

Does Psychological Sense of Community Differ from Other Constructs?

So far we have described why we believe that the construct of psychological sense of community is important for theoretical and practical reasons, as well as reviewed some suggestive results from our programme of research supporting this contention. The findings reviewed all utilised indirect or proxy measures of psychological sense of community. In the remaining sections of this chapter, we turn our attention to research and measures that directly tap psychological sense of community and its purported effects.

For example, we sought to distinguish psychological sense of community from two related constructs, namely social identity and social support (Omoto & Malsch, 2005; Lindsay, Snyder, & Omoto, 2006). Briefly, social identity perspectives (Tajfel & Turner, 1986; Turner et al., 1987) stress the distinctiveness and esteem benefits that accrue from categorisation processes. That is, individuals are hypothesised to automatically categorise other individuals as similar, and hence members of their in-group, or as dissimilar and thus, as out-group members. Following categorisation, there is a tendency to positively evaluate in-group members and their characteristics and to derogate out-group members and their attributes. Similar to psychological sense of community, then, social identity emphasises social group membership, shared connections, and common group symbols and norms. However, social identity also stresses the distinctiveness between groups, especially the perceived or created status differences between in-groups and out-groups. This concern is largely absent in psychological sense of community that focuses on inclusiveness rather than distinctiveness.

Similarly, conceptualisations of social support partially overlap with psychological sense of community. The literature on social support tends to emphasise the behaviours or social network members that are or are not deemed to be helpful and comforting by individuals. Social support involves networks of individuals embedded in larger social systems, and the focus is generally on supportive relationships with specific individuals within these networks (Felton & Shinn, 1992). For psychological sense of community, as made clear earlier, individuals need not be personally acquainted with community members, or even have face-to-face contact with them, in order to feel supported and/or affirmed. Their feelings of membership, connection, and attachment may persist even with changes in the membership of their social support networks. Psychological sense of community, therefore, is less rooted in actual behaviours and specific individuals than the usual ways of understanding social support.

To investigate whether these conceptual distinctions would hold up under empirical scrutiny, we conducted a study using data from AIDS volunteers in which we created proxy measures of psychological sense of community, social identity, and social support. We examined the differential ability of these three constructs to predict intentions to engage in AIDS-related activism that were assessed six months later. Our results revealed that the psychological sense of community measure was a unique and independent predictor of later AIDS-related activism and civic participation. That is, although the three constructs shared conceptual overlap, and in fact were empirically related to each other, both the measures of social support and sense of community were significant individual predictors of subsequent AIDS-related activism and civic participation. However, the measure of social identity was unrelated to later reported activism (see also Lindsay et al., 2006).

As anticipated from our theoretical analyses, AIDS volunteers who reported getting involved to enhance community connections and to help meet current community needs and who also knew more people affected by HIV disease (i.e. those who scored higher on our measure of psychological sense of community) engaged in more AIDS-related activities six months later. That is, greater psychological sense of community predicted more efforts to work on behalf of the community. Moreover, these effects of community concern and connection predicted civic participation and social action better than the related constructs of social identity and social support. We have replicated this general pattern of effects—that psychological sense of community is a significant predictor of later social action—in a different data set and using different measures of psychological sense of community, social support, and social identity (Lindsay et al., 2006). Together, these results speak to the potential importance and influence of psychological sense of community in understanding volunteerism and broader forms of social action.

Can Psychological Sense of Community be Created?

In our most recent, and ongoing, field-based work, we are beginning to disentangle some of the bi-directional processes that link sense of community, volunteerism, and broad social action by using more stringent experimental research designs. Specifically, we have examined ways of creating and enhancing psychological sense of community and attempted to harness some of its impact in promoting volunteerism and other forms of social action.

Specifically, we have worked to develop a more fully articulated theoretical analysis of the construct of psychological sense of community, one anchored in the literature on sense of community and also informed by our past research. In this conceptualisation, psychological sense of community is posited to include six key facets or dimensions, some of which reflect relatively cognitive processes, some affective in emphasis, and others relatively behaviourally based. The first facet is knowledge; individuals must know that there is a broad community, who its members are, and that community resources are potentially available to all members. Second, as an adjunct to this knowledge, individuals may re-define their personal conceptualisation of a community. Often, this re-definition involves broadening a narrow conceptualisation of community so that it is more inclusive and encompassing, and so that a wide variety of community resources can be easily identified.

The next facet we named identity, and it refers to individuals focusing on commonalities across community members (rather than differences) and coming to feel a sense of shared identity or community membership. The strengths and rewards of connection to a community represent the next facet. Here individuals develop and feel an affective bond or attachment to the community. They become invested in their community membership, and it is a source of pride and esteem.

The fifth facet is community success. This facet involves the ability of communities to accomplish more when working together than individuals who work alone. As community members work together and succeed, they should begin to take greater responsibility for one another and come to feel greater and lasting efficaciousness, empowerment, and mutual concern. Personal actions are also then undertaken not only out of self interest but on behalf of the community.

Finally, all of the aforementioned actions and attachments lead to an enduring sense of legacy for the community. Community members care not only about themselves and current community members, but strive to create and preserve a shared history and future for the community. The community itself is viewed as an entity and resource worth sustaining, nurturing, and growing together. We expect that in its fullest form, with all six facets, psychological sense of community should lead to increases in helping, sharing, reciprocity, and trust among community members.

Armed with this conceptualisation, we subsequently attempted to create a recipe for creating psychological sense of community, taking care to include each key facet in the mix. That is, rather than simply attempting to measure or approximate psychological sense of community, we sought to intentionally foster it among individuals who were previously unacquainted with each other. Specifically, we developed interventions designed to engender psychological sense of community based on these six facets, interventions that we implemented in our research by way of a series of workshop sessions conducted in small groups. As well, we developed a psychometrically sound, 18-item inventory to measure psychological sense of community which included items designed to tap each of the six facets of community.

We incorporated both the interventions and our measure in a field-based experiment conducted with over 600 participants recruited through AIDS service organisations in two different states. In this investigation, participants were randomly assigned to one of the three conditions. In one condition, the community-building condition, participants took part in the key workshop sessions with group exercises designed to teach and foster our six facets for the community affected by HIV/AIDS. In a comparison condition, workshop sessions were of similar size and length but did not include community-building activities. Instead, participants took part in educational activities designed to increase their knowledge, skills, and confidence in negotiating the AIDS service system. Finally, participants in a control condition did not take part in any workshops.

By way of these experimental conditions, then, we can assess whether our carefully planned workshops increased psychological sense of community relative to other workshops and conditions, and also track different effects of research involvement among participants. Specifically, all participants completed an extensive battery at baseline (enrollment in the study), again soon after they completed their workshops, and several months later in a delayed follow-up. Included in this battery were measures of psychological sense of community, organisational involvement, motives for participation, health, attitudes, and civic participation.

Preliminary results indicate that the community-building intervention did indeed enhance psychological sense of community. We detected significant increases in overall scores on our measure of psychological sense of community, as well as for five of its six facets. In addition, our interventions increased feelings of empowerment, as reflected in increases in reports of efficacy, feelings of responsibility, and confidence in participants' knowledge about the community and its resources. Finally, and as assessed after the workshops, the increased psychological sense of community engendered by the intervention results in increased intentions to become involved in the community through diverse forms of social action (e.g. giving money and goods to charity, joining community groups and organisations, participating in social activism), and increased intentions to help and educate others in the community. This pattern of results was exactly as we predicted. It suggests to us that not only can psychological sense of community be created, but that doing so can influence individuals to take action that can benefit themselves, others, and the broader social system or community in which they act.

Community and Social Action

Looking beyond our specific focus on volunteerism and activism, there are indications of positive associations between community connections and other forms of social action. For example, individuals who report stronger psychological sense of community, as gauged by a variety of different measures, are more likely to be registered voters and active in their neighbourhoods (Brodsky, O'Campo, & Aronson, 1999), to engage in neighbouring behaviours such as lending their neighbours food or tools (Kingston, Mitchell, Forin, & Stevenson, 1999), and to participate in community organisations (Chavis & Wandersman, 1990; Perkins & Long, 2002; Wandersman, 1980; Wandersman, Florin, Friedmann, & Mier, 1987) and political activities (Davidson & Cotter, 1989). Moreover, bonds of connection within communities and the social capital associated with them have been implicated in the provision of public goods (Anderson, Mellor & Milyo, 2004), the reduction of crime within specific localities (Saegert, Winkel, & Swartz, 2002), and the promotion of the health of community members (Kawachi, Kennedy, Lochner, & Prothrow-Stith, 1997). Finally, residential stability has been implicated in identification with one's community which in turn, manifests itself in diverse forms of helping behaviours, pro-community involvement, collective efficacy, and social action (Kang & Kwak, 2003; Kasarda & Janowitz, 1974; Oishi et al., 2007; Sampson, Raudenbush, & Earls, 1997).

It appears likely that there is a dynamic, cyclical process at work here, one in which connections to community lead individuals to engage in social action which in turn, further builds community connections and social capital. As a result of this self-perpetuating and accretionary process, social action becomes more likely and sense of community is increased. More generally, it may be that social action begets social action via sense of community such that one of the more significant consequences of social action is the creation and perpetuation of a culture of service, participation, and involvement.

Conclusion

Taken together, it appears that community concern, community connection, and psychological sense of community are clearly, consistently, and powerfully implicated in the many and varied ways in which individuals involve and invest themselves in society and work for the common good of its members. These findings and observations are important; we believe, for what they say scientifically about the nature of community and its linkages to diverse forms of social action, and what they say practically about creating and promoting an actively engaged society, one in which citizens individually and collectively work to address and solve the problems that confront and challenge society.

Our research findings lend credence to a purely psychological conceptualisation of community, not necessarily with reference to an identifiable area or institution, measured at an individual level. It seems reasonable, therefore, to devote future theorising and research to understanding communities based on shared experiences and interests (e.g. the community affected by HIV/AIDS) and communities with inclusive membership that extend beyond traditional boundaries of region, ethnicity, and nationality. Indeed, with communication and technological advances (e.g. the Internet), psychologically meaningful communities that literally cut across the global village are being formed and sustained everyday.

Quality of life and the well-being of both communities and individuals may depend importantly on psychological sense of community and the connections that people share. Whereas some scholars and commentators have decried the breakdown of social capital in contemporary society, along with decreases in its psychological concomitants, we feel optimistic that this apparent trend can be reversed. Specifically, based on our results, we suggest that one way to build social capital would be by intervening to increase people's sense of community. This suggestion derives from the reciprocal relationship between sense of community and behaviours indicative of social capital (Putnam, 2000), as well as our findings that psychological sense of community generally predicts subsequent volunteerism and social action.

A strong tradition already exists in many cultures, including among North American countries, whereby people should give back to society and engage in pro-social actions (cf. Curtis et al., 1992). The question does not seem to be "do people believe in the value of doing social good?" but rather, "why do they not act on their beliefs?" (Snyder et al., in press) One strategy for motivating action might be to bolster people's psychological sense of community and to call attention to the responsibility of community members to mobilise and work on behalf of the community. As our findings suggest, to the extent that individuals experience psychological sense of community, they are likely to engage in more frequent activism and social action in the future. In short, community involvement and volunteerism seems to lead individuals to feel more positively about and more strongly connected to the people around them and their communities. In reciprocal and synergistic fashion, these feelings are linked to greater willingness to engage in community affairs and to work for the reduction of social problems. Thus, communities can be transformed and societies changed through the service work of their citizens (Omoto, 2005).

In the end, knowledge gained from research on psychological sense of community, and especially interventions designed to create it, can be put to use in making more effective social programmes geared toward enhancing quality of life, ameliorating social problems, and increasing general civic participation for people around the globe and at all stages of the life cycle. The world, we believe, would be a better place for these efforts, and we are optimistic that youth will play an important role in helping to create and shape it.

References

Allik, J., & Realo, A. (2004). Individualism-collectivism and social capital. *Journal of Cross-Cultural Psychology, 35*, 29–49.

Anderson, L. R., Mellor, J. M., & Milyo, J. (2004). *Social capital and contributions in a public goods experiment.* Unpublished manuscript, College of William and Mary, Williamsburg, VA.

Boyte, H. C., & Kari, N. N. (1996). *Building America: The democratic promise of public work.* Philadelphia, PA: Temple University Press.

Brodsky, A. E. (1996). Resilient single mothers in risky neighbourhoods: Negative psychological sense of community. *Journal of Community Psychology, 24*, 347–363.

Brodsky, A. E., O'Campo, P. J., & Aronson, R. E. (1999). PSOC in community context: Multi-level correlates of a measure of psychological sense of community in low-come, urban neighbourhoods. *Journal of Community Psychology, 27*(6), 659–679.

Bureau of Labour Statistics (2005, December 9). *Volunteering in the United States, 2005.* Washington, DC: United States Department of Labour.

Chamberlin, J. (1997). A working definition of empowerment. *Psychiatric Rehabilitation Journal, 20*, 43–46.

Chavis, D. M., & Wandersman, A. (1990). Sense of community in the urban environment: A catalyst for participation and community development. *American Journal of Community Psychology, 18*, 55–81.

Cialdini, R. B., Borden, R. J., Thorne, A., Walker, M. R., Freeman, S., & Sloan, L. R. (1976). Basking in reflected glory, Three (football) field studies. *Journal of Personality and Social Psychology, 34*, 366–375.

Coleman, J. S. (1990). *Foundations of social theory.* Cambridge, MA: Harvard University Press.

Corrigan, P. W., Faber, D., Rashid, F., & Leary, M. (1999). The construct validity of empowerment among consumers of mental health services. *Schizophrenia Research, 38*, 77–84.

Crain, A. L., Snyder, M., & Omoto, A. M. (2000, May). *Volunteers make a difference: Relationship quality, active coping, and functioning among PWAs with volunteer buddies.* Paper presented at the annual meetings of the Midwestern Psychological Association, Chicago, IL.

Crocker, J., & Luhtanen, R. (1990). Collective self-esteem and ingroup bias. *Journal of Personality and Social Psychology, 58*(1), 60–67.

Curtis, J. E., Grabb, E., & Baer, D. (1992). Voluntary association membership in fifteen countries: A comparative analysis. *American Sociological Review, 57,* 139–152.

Davidson, W. B., & Cotter, P. R. (1989). Sense of community and political participation. *Journal of Community Psychology, 17,* 119–125.

Davidson, W. B., & Cotter, P. R. (1991). The relationship between sense of community and subjective well-being: A first look. *Journal of Community Psychology, 19,* 246–253.

Dunham, H. W. (1986). The community today: Place or process? *Journal of Community Psychology, 14,* 399–404.

Felton, B., & Shinn, M. (1992). Social integration and social support: Moving "social support" beyond the individual level. *Journal of Community Psychology, 20,* 103–115.

Gibbons, F. X., & Gerrard, M. (1989). Effects of upward and downward social comparison on mood states. *Journal of Social and Clinical Psychology, 8,* 14–31.

Hill, J. L. (1996). Psychological sense of community: Suggestions for future research. *Journal of Community Psychology, 24,* 431–438.

Hughey, J., Speer, P. W., & Peterson, N. A. (1999). Sense of community in community organisations: Structure and evidence in validity. *Journal of Community Psychology, 27,* 97–113.

Independent Sector (2001). *Giving and volunteering in the United States: Findings from a national survey.* Washington, DC: Author.

Kang, N., & Kwak, N. (2003). A multilevel approach to civic participation: Individual length of residence, neighbourhood residential stability, and their interactive effects with media use. *Communication Research, 30,* 80–106.

Kasarda, J., & Janowitz, M. (1974). Community attachment in mass society. *American Sociological Review, 39,* 328–339.

Kawachi, I., Kennedy, B. P., Lochner, K., & Prothrow-Stith, D. (1997). Social capital, income inequality, and mortality. *American Journal of Public Health, 87,* 1491–1498.

Kingston, S., Mitchell, R., Forin, P., & Stevenson, J. (1999). Sense of community in neighbourhoods as a multi-level construct. *Journal of Community Psychology, 27*, 384–394.

Kiviniemi, M. T., Snyder, M., & Omoto, A. M. (2002). Too many of a good thing? The effects of multiple motivations on task fulfilment, satisfaction, and cost. *Personality and Social Psychology Bulletin, 28*, 732–743.

Kymlicka, W., & Norman, W. (1994). Return of the citizen: A survey of recent work on citizen theory. *Ethics, 104*, 352–381.

Lindsay, J. J., Snyder, M., & Omoto, A. M. (2003, May-June). *Volunteers' impact on psychological and physical functioning of persons living with HIV.* Paper presented at the annual meeting of the American Psychological Society, Atlanta, GA.

Lindsay, J. J., Snyder, M., & Omoto, A. M. (2006, May). *Antecedents and consequences of psychological sense of community.* Paper presented at the annual meeting of the Midwestern Psychological Association, Chicago, IL.

Lo, T. W. & Au, E. (2004). *Youth empowerment: International experiences.* Hong Kong: City University of Hong Kong.

Malsch, A. M. (2005). *Prosocial behaviour beyond borders: Understanding a psychological sense of global community.* Unpublished doctoral dissertation, Claremont Graduate University, Claremont, CA.

McMillan, D. W. (1996). Sense of community. *Journal of Community Psychology, 24*, 315–325.

McMillan, D. W., & Chavis, D. M. (1986). Sense of community: A definition of theory. *Journal of Community Psychology, 14*, 6–23.

O'Brien, L. T., Crain, A. L., Omoto, A. M., & Snyder, M. (2000, May). *Matching motivations to outcomes: Implications for persistence in service.* Paper presented at the annual meetings of the Midwestern Psychological Association, Chicago, IL.

Oishi, S., Rothman, A. J., Snyder, M., Su, J., Zehm, K., Hertel, A., Gonzales, M. H., & Sherman, G. D. (2007). The socioecological model of procommunity action: The benefits of residential stability. *Journal of Personality and Social Psychology, 93*, 831–844.

Omoto, A. M. (Ed.) (2005). *Processes of community change and social action.* Mahwah, NJ: Lawrence Erlbaum Associates.

Omoto, A. M., & Crain, A. L. (1995). AIDS volunteerism: Lesbian and gay community-based responses to HIV. In G. M. Herek & B. Greene (Eds.), *Contemporary perspectives on lesbian and gay issues (Vol. 2): AIDS, identity, and community* (pp. 187–209). Thousand Oaks, CA: Sage Publications.

Omoto, A. M., Gunn, D. G., & Crain, A. L. (1998). Helping in hard times: Relationship closeness and the AIDS volunteer experience. In V. J. Derlega & A. P. Barbee (Eds.), *HIV infection and social interaction* (pp. 106–128). Thousand Oaks, CA: Sage Publications.

Omoto, A. M., & Malsch, A. (2005). Psychological sense of community: Conceptual issues and connections to volunteerism-related activism. In A. M. Omoto (Ed.), *Processes of community change and social action* (pp. 83–102). Mahwah, NJ: Lawrence Erlbaum Associates.

Omoto, A. M., & Snyder, M. (1990). Basic research in action: Volunteerism and society's response to AIDS. *Personality and Social Psychology Bulletin, 16*, 152–165.

Omoto, A. M., & Snyder, M. (1993). AIDS volunteers and their motivations: Theoretical issues and practical concerns. *Nonprofit Management and Leadership, 4*, 157–176.

Omoto, A. M., & Snyder, M. (1995). Sustained helping without obligation: Motivation, longevity of service, and perceived attitude change among AIDS volunteers. *Journal of Personality and Social Psychology, 68*, 671–686.

Omoto, A. M., & Snyder, M. (2002). Considerations of community: The context and process of volunteerism. *American Behavioural Scientist, 45*(5), 846–867.

Omoto, A. M., Snyder, M., & Berghuis, J. P. (1993). The psychology of volunteerism: A conceptual analysis and a programme of action research. In J. B. Pryor & G. D. Reeder (Eds.), *The social psychology of HIV infection* (pp. 333–356). Hillsdale, NJ: Erlbaum.

Omoto, A. M., Snyder, M., Chang, W., & Lee, D. H. (2001, August). *Knowledge and attitude change among volunteers and their associates.* Paper presented at the annual meetings of the American Psychological Association, San Francisco, CA. August, 2001.

Omoto, A. M., Snyder, M., & Martino, S. C. (2000). Volunteerism and the life course: Investigating age-related agendas for action. *Basic and Applied Social Psychology, 22*, 181–198.

Oskamp, S. (2000). A sustainable future for humanity? How can psychology help? *American Psychologist, 55*, 496–508.

Perkins, D. D., & Long, D. A. (2002). Neighbourhood sense of community and social capital: A multi-level analysis. In A. Fisher, C. Sonn, & B. Bishop (Eds.), *Psychological sense of community: Research, application, and implications* (pp. 291–318). New York: Kluwer.

Piliavin, J. A., & Charng, H. (1990). Altruism: A review of recent theory and research. *Annual Review of Sociology, 16*, 27–65.

Portes, A. (1998). Social capital: Its origins and applications in modern sociology. *Annual Review of Sociology, 24*, 1–24.

Putnam, R. D. (1993). *Making democracy work: Civic traditions in modern Italy.* Princeton: Princeton University Press.

Putnam, R. D. (1995). Bowling alone: America's declining social capital. *Journal of Democracy, 6*, 65–78.

Putnam, R. D. (2000). *Bowling alone: The collapse and revival of American community.* New York: Simon & Schuster.

Rogers, E. S., Chamberlin, J., Ellison, M. L., & Crean, T. (1997). A consumer-constructed scale to measure empowerment among users of mental health services. *Psychiatric Services, 48*, 1042–1047.

Saegert, S., Winkel, G., & Swartz, C. (2002). Social capital and crime in New York City's low-income housing. *Housing Policy Debate, 13*, 189–226.

Sampson, R. J., Raudenbush, S. W., & Earls, F. (1997). Neighbourhoods and violent crime: A multilevel study of collective efficacy. *Science, 277*, 918–927.

Sarason, S. B. (1974). *The psychological sense of community: Prospects for a community psychology.* San Francisco: Jossey-Bass.

Simon, B. (1998). Individuals, groups, and social change: On the relationship between individual and collective self-interpretations and collective action. In C. Sedikides, J. Schopler, & C. Insko (Eds.), *Intergroup cognition and intergroup behaviour* (pp. 257–282). Mahwah, NJ: Lawrence Erlbaum Associates.

Simon, B., Loewy, M., Stürmer, S., Weber, U., Freytag, P., Habig, C., et al. (1998). Collective identification and social movement participation. *Journal of Personality and Social Psychology, 74*, 646–658.

Simon, B., Stürmer, S., & Steffens, K. (2000). Helping individuals or group members? The role of individual and collective identification in AIDS volunteerism. *Personality and Social Psychology Bulletin, 26*, 497–506.

Snyder, M., & Omoto, A. M. (1992a). Volunteerism and society's response to the HIV epidemic. *Current Directions in Psychological Science, 1*, 113–116.

Snyder, M., & Omoto, A. M. (1992b). Who helps and why? The psychology of AIDS volunteerism. In S. Spacapan & S. Oskamp (Eds.), *Helping and being helped: Naturalistic studies* (pp. 213–239). Newbury Park CA: Sage.

Snyder, M., & Omoto, A. M. (2000). Doing good for self and society: Volunteerism and the psychology of citizen participation. In M. Van Vugt, M. Snyder, T. Tyler, & A. Biel (Eds.), *Collective helping in modern society: Dilemmas and solutions*. London, UK: Routledge.

Snyder, M., & Omoto, A. M. (2001). Basic research and practical problems: Volunteerism and the psychology of individual and collective action. In W. Wosinska, R. Cialdini & D. Barrett (Eds.), *The practice of social influence in multiple cultures*. Mahwah, NJ: Erlbaum.

Snyder, M., & Omoto, A. M. (2007). Social action. In A. W. Kruglanski & E. T. Higgins (Eds.), *Social psychology: A handbook of basic principles* (2nd ed., pp. 940–961). New York: Guilford.

Snyder, M., Omoto, A. M., & Crain, A. L. (1999). Punished for their good deeds: Stigmatisation of AIDS volunteers. *American Behavioural Scientist, 42*, 1175–1192.

Snyder, M., Omoto, A. M., & Smith, D. M. (in press). The role of persuasion strategies in motivating individual and collective action. In E. Borgida, J. Sullivan & C. Federico (Eds.), *The political psychology of democratic citizenship*. New York: Oxford University Press.

Sonn, C. C., & Fischer, A. T. (1998). Sense of community: Community resilient responses to oppression and change. *Journal of Community Psychology, 26*, 457–472.

Stuermer, S., & Kampmeier, C. (2003). Active citizenship: The role of community identification in community volunteerism and local participation. *Psychologica Belgica, 43*, 103–122.

Stukas, A. A., Daly, M., & Cowling, M. J. (2005). Volunteerism and the creation of social capital: A functional approach. *Australian Journal of Volunteering, 10*, 35–44

Suls, J., & Wills, T. A. (Eds.). (1990). *Social comparison: Contemporary theory and research.* Hillsdale, NJ: Erlbaum.

Tajfel, H., & Turner, J. C. (1986). The social identity theory of intergroup behaviour. In S. Worchel & W. G. Austin (Eds.), *Psychology of intergroup relations* (pp. 7–24). Chicago: Nelson-Hall.

Tesser, A. (1988). Toward a self-evaluation maintenance model of social behaviour. In L. Berkowitz (Ed.), *Advances in experimental social psychology* (Vol. 21, pp. 181–227). San Diego, CA: Academic Press.

Turner, J. C., Hogg, M. A., Oakes, P. J., Reicher, S. D., & Wetherell, M. S. (1987). *Rediscovering the social group: A self-categorisation theory.* Oxford, UK: Basil Blackwell.

Van Vugt, M., & Snyder, M. (2002). Cooperation in society: Fostering community action and civic participation. *American Behavioural Scientist, 45*, 765–768.

Van Vugt, M., Snyder, M., Tyler, T., & Biel, A. (Eds.) (2000). *Cooperation in modern society: Promoting the welfare of communities, states, and organisations.* London, UK: Routledge.

Verba, S., Schlozman, K. L., & Brady, H. E. (1995). *Voice and equality: Civic voluntarism in American politics.* Cambridge, MA: Harvard University Press.

Wandersman, A. (1980). Community and individual difference characteristics as influences on initial participation. *American Journal of Community Psychology, 8*, 217–228.

Wandersman, A., Florin, P., Friedmann, R. R., & Meier, R. B. (1987). Who participates and who does not, and why? An analysis of voluntary neighbourhood organisations in the United States and Israel. *Sociological Forum, 2*, 534–555.

Zimmerman, M. A., Israel, B. A., Schulz, A. J., & Checkoway, B. (1992). Further explorations in empowerment theory: An empirical analysis of psychological empowerment. *American Journal of Community Psychology, 20*, 707–727.

Zimmerman, M. A., & Rappaport, J. (1988). Citizen participation, perceived control and psychological empowerment. *American Journal of Community Psychology, 16*, 725–750.

BLUEPRINT FOR A YOUTH EMPOWERMENT MODEL (YEM) THROUGH VOLUNTEERISM

3

Edwin A. RISLER and Michael J. HOLOSKO

Introduction

All societies and cultures have processes that educate and enable young people to socially integrate into their adult lives. While such methods are often constructed and facilitated through formal social structures, they are often embedded in long-standing cultural mores, beliefs, traditions and rituals. Overall, their fundamental assumption is that they provide functional activities and opportunities to enable youth to become responsible adults. An important activity designed to increase youth understanding of what it means to be a participatory and contributing member of a larger community is volunteerism.

When viewed together conceptually, youth empowerment and volunteerism present a distinct reciprocal and developmental relationship. Moreover, this conjoint relationship serves as an inherent cornerstone in the social and psychological growth for youth. As youth become empowered and mature, they embrace and act upon the ideal of community participation through volunteerism. Correspondingly, the experience of volunteerism enhances and legitimises a youth's sense of empowerment. Empowerment is reinforced through volunteerism, which in turn, enhances empowerment and leads to an increase in volunteerism. This chapter examines the salient factors between empowerment and volunteerism as expressed in a dynamic relationship, and establishes the blueprint and core elements for the development of a model for youth empowerment.

Youth Empowerment

Empowerment is typically viewed broadly depending on the way in which it is conceptualised. It has been characterised as a theory, a framework, a goal, an ideology and a process (Gutierrez, 1995; Lo & Au, 2004; McWhirter, 1991; Rose, 2000; Yip, 2004). For example, one can observe social work models of empowerment in an individual or a community context. Empowerment may also be conceptualised at various micro/mezzo/macro levels including personal, interpersonal, political, professional, societal, and organisational (Wallerstein, 2002; Wehmeyer & Gragoudas, 2004; Yip, 2004). Regardless of how it is conceptualised, attributes of empowerment generally refer to the belief in the ability of an individual, group, community, or social structure, to exercise a degree of autonomy, self-determination, and control over events for the mutual benefit of all (Gutierrez, 1995). However, when viewed developmentally, empowerment serves a unique and important purpose for youth. The principal assumptions and factors contributing to the understanding of youth empowerment have been well documented in the social work literature (Gutierrez, 1995; Hyde-Hills, 1998; Moody, Childs, & Sepples, 2003; Rose, 2000; Yip, 2004).

The concept of empowerment is deemed, both psychologically and socially, as the actualisation of significant and dynamic knowledge, values, or skills that contribute to youths' development of a sense of maturity which ultimately, making them contributing members of a society (Cleary & Zimmerman, 2004; Wehmeyer & Gragoudas, 2004; Risler, Sutphen, & Shields, 2000). Empowerment not only serves to enhance a young person's sense of personal identity, autonomy, and emotional security, but also serves as a catalyst for the cultivation of one's confidence in the development of complex decision-making competencies necessary for adult life. Ideally, empowerment moves a youth from an internal and autonomous locus of control, to one that is more external and socially conscious (Bandura, 1997; Nowicki & Strickland, 1973).

Theoretically, an individual's adolescence has been historically viewed as a psychological period of significant change and development through specific stages in their early life (Erikson, 1950; Kohlberg, 1984; Piaget, 1957). Each stage is thought to present specific tasks to be accomplished developmentally, that contribute to a youth's creation of an identity and exercising mastery over their life. In this way, a youth becomes self-actualised through such a process when s/he becomes aware and the belief is cultivated in a way that they are able to express power and effect changes in their life (Pipher, 1994).

Gutierrez (1995) suggested that youth empowerment is inherently founded on a young person first developing a socially critical consciousness. This involves three developmental psychological processes (Freire, 1973). First is related to group identification and the development of feelings of shared fate, where group membership becomes a central component of an individual's self-concept. Here, youth identify and develop attachments to groups that share common values or emotional needs.

Raising group consciousness is the second process in this development. This relates to a youth's development of the understanding of the relationship between personal problems and social problems impacting a group, in which the youth is affiliated. This involves the increasing awareness of the differential status and power relationships among groups and the identification of shared feelings of the members. Self and collective efficacy is the final stage in this sequence. This involves youth's recognition that they are group participants in a dynamic social interaction capable of effecting change in their life (Gutierrez, 1995).

The congruency between the concept of power and the formulation of youth's critical consciousness is noteworthy in understanding the elements of empowerment. McWhirter (1991) discussed four specific requirements, which highlighted this progression and contributed to the development of full (or actualised) empowerment. Contextually, these prerequisites emerge and are accomplished by any youth, group, or organisation, perceived initially, as powerless.

The first is related to a youth's awareness of the power dynamics at work in their life context. The second pertains to one's ability to develop the necessary skills and capacity for establishing reasonable control over their life. While the first and second requirements seem basic and easily understood; the third and fourth of these conditions significantly influence the development of a youth's overall critical consciousness (Gutierrez, 1995). Cumulatively, the latter requirements pertain to the ability of a youth to exercise power and control in his/her life without infringing upon the rights of others, and an enhanced ability to advocate and support the empowerment of others in their group or community. For the actualisation and development of empowerment in youth (in this developmental progression), these represent an expression of integrity through the incorporation of identifiable community values and beliefs.

In order to fully comprehend the implications for youth empowerment as a means to effective and personal efficacy, it is important to recognise the contextual framework, or environment, in which it is nested. The contextual framework or environment essentially facilitates the actualisation of empowerment, i.e. it enables it to happen. As such, a number of characteristics have been identified as being associated with empowering environments including: group settings, a shared belief system, skill and knowledge development, community development, and leadership (Gutierrez, 1995).

As noted, there are a number of conceptual and dynamic factors associated with the development of empowerment in youth that often serve as the theoretical basis for various social work treatment models and interventions (Coble, Risler, & Nackerud, 1999). Methodologically, each incorporates the previously mentioned processes and environmental conditions that promote youth empowerment. The following descriptions illustrate two such programmes, one is a clinical intervention, and the other, a community-based initiative.

There are a variety of outdoor experiential programmes for troubled and delinquent youth in North America. Typically, youth assigned to these programmes have experienced significant failures in life. They are mistrustful, have authority/defiance issues, and/or have limited coping skills. Therapeutically, these programmes aim to foster the development of a youth's critical consciousness, an essential component of empowerment. Surviving in any wilderness setting as a participating member of a group, youth may develop interpersonal skills to exercise control and make responsible decisions, not only for themselves but also for the mutual benefit of the group (Loughmiller, 1965). As such, they are coerced by the challenges of wilderness survival to become aware and understand the power of group dynamics which, in theory, promote the acceptance and commitment to the group's belief system.

There are also a wide range of community-based social work interventions and programmes designed to foster skills and enhance capacities for self-efficacy that may also contribute to the development of youth empowerment. The following programme description of Youth Empowerment Systems (YES), a local community-based initiative in Athens, Georgia, provides an illustration of a collaborative system of community partners who supported a mechanism to involve youth in community affairs.

This collaborative was comprised of numerous sub-committees which focused on specific problem areas in the local community, e.g. while all the sub-committees involved youth to some degree, one sub-committee consisted entirely of youth who, as a group themselves, were empowered to develop and coordinate service initiatives for the community. The Chair of the YES also served, along with the other committee heads, as a member of the Executive Committee of YES.

One service initiative implemented by this youth-only sub-committee involved developing strategies to address the problems associated with youth dropping out of high school. Organisationally, this committee conducted a problem assessment, designed and coordinated an integrated programme to improve the high school completion rate for the community. Noteworthy was the fact that some youth from the community who had dropped out of high school participated as members of this sub-committee. Other committees within the community collaborative that involved youth included, among others, health, the environment, and family and child well being.

As could be inferred from the previous examples, various social work programme models and interventions for the development of empowerment may be seen as falling on a continuum. Some, by design, are tailored for specific youth with the intervention targeted at a particular need, while others are community-initiated programmes with a broader focus designed to promote empowerment in youth, collectively. Regardless of the proposed model or intervention, each shares and incorporates similar strategies, opportunities and activities to engage youth and facilitate their development as responsible and contributing members of a community. A key activity, which seemingly triggers and promotes the cognitive development of empowerment among youth and the achievement of programme goals, is volunteerism.

Volunteerism

If empowerment is seen as a belief in an individual's self-determination, then conjointly volunteerism may be viewed as a true altruistic expression of that value. Each year, millions of individuals, both young and old, throughout the world commit significant amounts of personal time and energy to assist others through volunteerism (Curtis, Grabb & Baer, 1992). Approximately 45% of the adults and an equal percentage of youth in the United States regularly volunteer in some capacity, and the dollar amount for their services is estimated to exceed $239 billion (Independent Sector, 2006). Through volunteerism, people are involved in a variety of service activities including counselling, advocacy, companionship, and other assistance to people in need. Not only is the idea that an individual would willingly make significant personal sacrifices to others who are often unknown to them intriguing, but also the context and motivation in which the assistance is offered is equally compelling (Clary et al., 1998; Omoto & Snyder, 1995).

While the phenomenon of assisting others occurs in a variety of circumstances and contexts, expressions of volunteerism appear to emerge from two perspectives above all others. The first is referred to as spontaneous helping, where an individual is faced with a decision to act upon an opportunity to assist someone in need. Usually, this spontaneous expression of aid is unexpected and limited to one brief act. An example would be an individual who assisted an elderly person who appeared in distress or someone who responded to a sudden request for financial assistance from a charitable organisation (Clary et al., 1998).

A more prototypic expression of volunteerism is commonly referred to as planned helping. Purposeful in nature, the expression of planned helping incorporates several deliberate factors including an individual's knowledge and interest, personal commitment, and motivational processes. While this could serve different functions and mean different things (for different people), typically in expressions of planned helping, individuals thoughtfully seek out opportunities to address specific issues and commit themselves for longer periods of time to a particular service organisation (Clary et al., 1998). The assumptions that support this expression are attributed to: an individual's satisfaction and commitment to the organisation, positive regard about their role as a volunteer, and the congruency between one's personal identity and the outcome of the activity.

These individual attributes are further highlighted when examining the characteristics and motivational factors associated with youth engaged in volunteer activities (Johnson, Beebe, Mortimer, & Snyder, 1998; Oesterle, Johnson, & Mortimer, 2004). Although the evidence is limited and mixed, some studies suggest that equal numbers of males and females who have a personal connection to a community are more likely to participate in volunteer activities (Johnson et al., 1998; Raskoff & Sundeen, 1994).

While not related to social status or one's background, volunteering has also been found to be more associated with youth who were academically successful and had high educational aspirations (Johnson et al., 1998). Some studies have also suggested that youth whose parents had volunteered were more likely to engage in similar acts of volunteerism (Keith, Nelson, Schlabach, & Thompson, 1990). Finally, research suggests two concurrent issues when attempting to identify the common intangible factors that motivate youth to participate in volunteer activities. One pertains to the idea that participation in volunteer activities is driven by some particular incentive. For example, volunteering could improve the possibility of a youth's future employment or acceptance into a particular college. The parallel view holds that volunteerism emerges out of the intrinsic social and psychological benefits a youth gains from the altruistic nature of the activity (Holosko, Leslie, & Miller, 2001). From either perspective, the literature clearly supports the notion that participating in volunteer activities facilitates a youth's self-actualisation and encourages the integration of community values; all of which contribute to the development of empowerment.

The engagement of youth in volunteer activities is noted throughout the literature (Hosty, 2005; Penner & Finkelstein, 1998; Safrit & Auck, 2003). As well, a variety of authors present discourse and report on youth involved in volunteer activities both as recipients of programme services as well as active participants in a variety of community-based initiatives (Johnson et al., 1998). For example, many youth who have been involved with the juvenile justice system are required to participate in volunteer activities. As part of their treatment, they participate in these activities to foster a sense of social responsibility and community. Some of the activities that they participate in have included delivering meals to elderly shut-ins and reading to children at the local homeless shelter.

Other youth may voluntarily participate in a wider range of traditional service programmes sponsored by community organisations, schools, and churches. One such programme known as Youth Leadership Athens, in Athens, Georgia, is sponsored by the local chamber of commerce. The youth, who voluntarily participate in this programme, not only engage in community service projects but also are exposed to meaningful training and education about economic issues and civic governance.

Additionally, there are a number of factors or components commonly cited that are associated with expressions of volunteerism, which underscore the development of youth empowerment (Johnson, et al., 1998; Safrit & Auck, 2003). Among others, these include youth participating significantly in the decision-making process; being involved and engaged in activities that have a genuine impact and meet a community need; fostering significant relationships with adults serving as mentors; and having the opportunity to integrate learning experiences into their personal identity (Safrit & Auck, 2003).

Blueprint for a Youth Empowerment Model (YEM) through Volunteerism

What has been presented previously is the notion that the convergence of empowerment through volunteerism reflects a reciprocal and interactive relationship that enhances the social and psychological development of youth. Moreover, the factors and processes identified and discussed associated with youth empowerment and volunteerism lend credence to the development of conceptual models. It is the synergy and relationship between empowerment and youth volunteering that allows us to distill core elements of a conceptual framework to inform and guide programmes which promote those two areas. Their relationship is described in Figure 3.1.

At its basic core, a conceptual framework for a YEM designed to support volunteerism should consider, at a minimum: a) the environmental context, b) the identified interactive processes, and c) the knowledge-based outcomes for stakeholders. Once established, this framework can serve as the blueprint to develop a YEM that is formulated to promote the desired programme goals and create processes to engage youth in volunteer activities.

Figure 3.2 provides an illustration of the three core elements of a conceptual framework for empowerment which will now be

Figure 3.1 How empowerment and youth volunteerism are interrelated

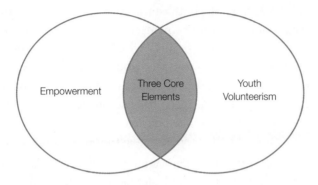

Figure 3.2 Core elements and blueprint for a Youth Empowerment Model (YEM)

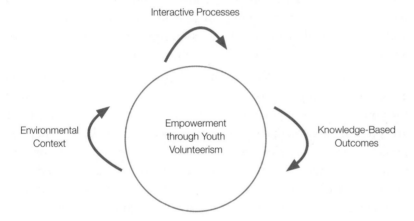

discussed. After a brief discussion of these, a series of process questions will be offered to assist in identifying how these elements should be considered for any initiative to have a relative degree of success in this process.

The Environmental Context of Empowerment

The environmental context considers the factors and mechanisms, which facilitate and promote the processes of youth empowerment.

These include: the cultural norms and attitudes toward youth; the community perception of youth status in the social structure; the socio-political view of youth themselves; and the resources and desired needs of the community which promote opportunities for volunteer service. For instance, youth should be valued and hold a voice in their culture and seen as a viable resource in their community. There should also be established institutions and resources in place that can make opportunities available for youth to engage in meaningful and empowering activities.

More importantly, the environmental context also serves to conceptualise the structure and define the relationships, which create the interactive circumstances for youth to become engaged in the empowerment process. The components and processes inherent within this configuration are readily identifiable, but primarily include the group setting and climate embracing participating youth and the relational involvement and commitment of significant adults. Some examples may serve to illustrate this point.

Typical programmes that create effective models for volunteerism are defined by a group setting and climate that provides a catalyst for youth to have opportunities to become empowered. Thus, there are programme incentives for youth to engage in decision-making processes in relationship to the establishment of opportunities for their involvement. Youth are motivated to volunteer when they believe they can impact a process, which shows a genuine concern or issue for their community. In turn, the climate in which this process occurs frames the identity of the group, promotes member affiliation, and contributes to the development of dynamic group cohesion and support. This is particularly true for the integration of a youth's mutual shared belief in the collective efficacy of the group. As such, youth value the group's purpose, and they believe in themselves as important members through this reciprocal belief.

Functionally, the involvement of adults and other supports establishes a focal point for the group setting and climate in this empowering process. Such programmes typically have adults attracted to them who are committed and invested in the empowerment of youth. Essentially, these adults set the contextual tone for the transactional processes for the development of youth empowerment to occur by coordinating networks of programmematic support with local community agencies and organisations. The leadership and mentoring demonstrated by the involved adults provides an anchor that facilitates the integration of learning experiences in the developmental processes of youth empowerment (Holosko et al., 2001).

The environmental context of empowerment designed to engage youth in volunteerism may be articulated in a variety of ways. The group setting and climate may be observed in groups that project a particular image promoting the members' identity. Examples could include: a physical structure that represents community values; articles of clothing which identify group affiliation, e.g. caps, T-shirts, etc.; established group norms of acceptance of others and inclusion within the group; and newsletters or web pages that communicate current events and the achievement of volunteer projects. Likewise, the group members and the volunteer activities achieve legitimacy when adults are significantly involved, openly committed, and provide supportive leadership to participating youth. Endorsements and support from institutional and agency organisations provide further legitimacy to the group in a similar fashion. As indicated in the previous chapters in this book (1 and 2), the synergy between the volunteer activities and community as a whole is a dynamic growth inducing relationship. Following (see p. 70) are not answers but a series of process questions for each element of YEM, in this case the first one, the environmental context.

Interactive Processes

Within the YEM, consideration is given to the synthesis of the interactive processes that occur at various levels between the youth, the group members, and participating adults while engaging in volunteer activities. Intrinsically, these are the very factors that facilitate change and promote the development of youth empowerment.

Environmental Context — Process Questions

1. What are the cultural norms and attitudes toward youth in this community?

2. What organisations provide opportunities and supports for youth to volunteer?

3. Are there mechanisms to promote group identity, inclusion, and affiliation in the volunteer experience?

4. What resources are available to provide supports for youth volunteer initiatives?

5. Are adult mentors available and accessible for the volunteer initiatives?

Conceptually, interactive processes of empowerment can be linked to the dynamic purpose, nature, and duration of involvement of the participants in this process. On a functional level, this refers to the sophistication of the group's level of involvement and degree of investment in volunteer activities. For example, some programmes have a specific purpose and a considerable history in involving youth in volunteer activities for long periods of time. A case would be the previously mentioned YES, Youth Committee (in Georgia), and the volunteer project targeting the school drop-out problem that took more than a year to plan and implement. Other volunteer initiatives (in this project) engaged youth for a brief period of time and focused on a single activity to address a specific issue, such as a school that organised youth to distribute refreshments to donors during a blood drive.

Pragmatically, indications of effective interactive processes can be evident in a variety of contexts that facilitate the development of empowerment. Systemically, these processes are reflected and emerge from the symbiotic relationship between the individual youth, the other members of the group, and the involved adults. Again the synergy and interrelatedness between empowerment and volunteerism, as well as the core elements is an inherent developmental feature of the YEM model (see Figures 3.1 and 3.2).

The interactive processes for the individual are centred on actualising the potential of the youth. This includes a mechanism for engaging and motivating youth in a purposeful manner and a process for the integration of learning, growth, and development. Programmes with effective interactive processes typically provide a welcoming social climate to engage and inspire youth participation. Such programmes promote community values and clearly express the opportunities and incentives for youth to participate in meaningful events and activities—that they consider meaningful!

The foundation here begins with the pre-disposing and unique characteristics of the youth. Youth who are involved in empowerment programmes are rarely socially, emotionally, and/or psychologically equal. For example, there are youth from other experiences that have fostered a higher level of personal empowerment, and are often viewed as leaders among their peers. Not surprising, such youth typically have some history of participating in organised volunteer activities. They generally exude confidence and have developed social, psychological, and relationship skills that make them able to effectively contribute to the overall group process and successfully involve in community activities.

By contrast, there are youth who are involved in specific programmes designed to address their therapeutic needs that present as less empowered. Usually, these youth have had some degree of difficulty in cultivating and developing healthy social and psychological relationships with peers as well as adults. Characteristically, they have low self-esteem, lack competence, struggle with the process of self-actualisation, and seldom feel a part of or engage in any community service. It is important to note here that these youth are not necessarily unwilling to do so, but simply may not have acquired the opportunity, developmental knowledge, or more specifically, interpersonal empowerment, to contribute. As such, they may have experienced failure socially and/or academically or may have been involved with anti-social activities, e.g. delinquency, substance abuse, etc.

Volunteer programmes that facilitate an interactive process of empowerment for youth are driven by the actualisation of individual potential achieved through two dynamic dimensions. First, there are specific processes that establish a level of acceptance for youth to commit to the process, i.e. an open and welcoming environment, which promotes their engagement. For example, rituals and symbols can be used to encourage a sense of belonging that reinforces the organisations' mission, values and purpose with which youth can readily identify. These may include: a mission statement, code of ethics, creed, poster, T-shirts to wear, or a pledge that all serve to empower and enhance the awareness of youth. Some recognisable illustrations of this are community organisations such as the Boy or Girl Scouts of America or the Red Cross, which have rituals and symbols recognised internationally.

Second, effective volunteer programmes that empower youth contain interactive and structured processes that enhance and motivate interpersonal growth. By design, these processes focus on enhancing one's self-esteem, confidence, and competence. Within this process, youth may experience respect, encouragement, and a sense of personal values, which they internalise developmentally when they interact with an environment. This is another way to foster empowerment. A community youth programme "Focusing On Children Until Success" (FOCUS) in Gainesville, Georgia, provides an example. This therapeutic programme was based on an empowerment model for services for youth that had been involved with the juvenile justice system. The youth participating in this programme were provided opportunities to participate in a variety of civic activities, e.g. driving for the food bank, maintaining a community park, which fostered the development of empowerment. Within this programme, youth were supported and mentored, and they received encouragement for their contributions. In addition, they were periodically acknowledged and awarded recognition for successful volunteer services performed in the community that contributed to the development of self-esteem and confidence.

The success of the actualisation of individual youth within such interactive processes is inherently dynamic and relational. Conceptually, this refers to the youth's involvement with both the other group members and supportive adults. Programmatically, there are structured processes for youth to have ownership in voicing opinions and making decisions, as well as taking responsibility and confronting issues that may challenge the group. For example, effective groups establish norms of behaviour and individual youth assume roles that emulate the programme's system of shared beliefs. Ultimately, this process creates the evolution of group cohesion and promotes a sense of collective efficacy that empowers an individual.

Adults play a critical role in supporting youth in this interactive process by role modelling and integrating the learning experiences for participating youth. Effective programmes are led by committed adults who recognise the global context of the developmental and dynamic growth of youth participating in volunteer activities which benefit the community. These adults create a transactional partnership with youth in the process of empowerment and typically serve as mentors or teachers to provide respectful encouragement and caring support. More importantly, they provide feedback and cultivate a cycle of constructive development through each successful volunteer experience (Larson, Walker, & Pearce 2005).

With each experience, adults help facilitate the integration of learning that enhances the empowerment of youth, which further promotes and motivates them. One example of this process would be an adult leader conducting a guided group discussion where youth had the opportunity to reflect on what the volunteer experience meant and how it impacted them individually. This process could also be achieved through the use of written journals, posters, murals, or other forms of art expression.

Consider a youth group that became concerned about graffiti in their neighbourhood. An adult mentor facilitates a discussion about how these youth and the community was affected by the problem, and permits them to process a constructive plan to address the issue. After much discussion and debate, these youth decide to voluntarily paint over the offensive graffiti with drawings and poetry that expressed their feelings. Once the activity was completed, the adults and the youth participate in a reflection on what the experience meant to them individually. Below are the process questions one needs to consider to plan for this stage in the YEM.

Interactive Processes — Process Questions

1. What are the purpose, nature, and duration of involvement of youth in this volunteer initiative?

2. Can youth become involved in active decision-making to plan their volunteer participation?

3. How welcoming and supportive is the host organisation/ community to the volunteer initiative?

4. Can different skills of different youth be accommodated in this learning experience?

5. What processes are available to help youth commit to this programme?

Knowledge-Based Outcomes

The final core element of the interrelated, dynamic, and ever changing empowerment ↔ volunteerism relationship (see Figure 3.2) is knowledge-based outcomes. Inherently, these outcomes highlight the actual results and efficacy associated with the interactive processes of empowerment. Ideally, they represent a level of empowerment and documented contextual changes in the individual youth, the group and its members, and the community.

For individual youth, this tangible evidence may be readily apparent. Typically over time, and often in a dramatic fashion, youth appear to be more self-actualised as well as socially and psychologically empowered. Their individual actions and behaviours reflect an integrated perception and value of overall community membership and worth. They demonstrate a committed intention to remain involved in the group, and often assume leadership roles within this process. As youth developmentally become empowered and their personal maturity increases, they ultimately are able to become agents of social change in the community.

Evidence of collective group empowerment can be seen as more developmentally pragmatic and dynamic in nature. Such empowered groups have a higher degree of satisfaction among their members. These groups are effective at mobilising community resources, and planning and achieving the desired outcomes of their activities. Indeed, additional successes at achieving group goals for different projects impacts cumulatively greater degrees of satisfaction overall (Holosko, Leslie, & Cassano, 2001). They also have structured processes that maintain and, if necessary, expand the membership of the group. Functionally, groups that are highly empowered create their own identity and history, and are able to sustain themselves with minimal adult supervision.

Community empowerment and change can be seen in a broader context as it is developmentally influenced by both individual and group outcomes. On the surface, the number of youth programmes and the types of activities achieved provide concrete and demonstrated evidence of the evolution of youth empowerment in the community. Empirical indictors pertain to changes in the perception and awareness of youth empowerment by the larger community membership. Youth are recognised, respected, and viewed as viable and important members in the achievement of community goals (Holosko et al., 2001).

In sum, effective models for youth empowerment should be based on a conceptual framework like the YEM blueprint presented herein, that minimally presents: a) the environmental context, b) a level of interactive, and c) identified knowledge-based outcomes for the individual youth, programme group, and global community. If such elements are meaningfully incorporated into youth volunteer programmes, the likelihood of empowerment through such programmes is greater than if such programmes ignore these elements. Here are the process questions for the final stage of the YEM, which should be considered.

Knowledge-Based Outcomes — Process Questions

1. What projects and accomplishments were achieved by the group?

2. What were some of the individual accomplishments achieved by youth in this experience?

3. What challenges were overcome by members through this volunteer experience?

4. What community resources were mobilised, procured, and/or leveraged to achieve the desired objectives of this volunteer initiative?

5. How satisfied were the individuals, groups, organisations, and/or communities with this experience?

Conclusion

These final remarks provide a bridge to understanding the dynamic application of the framework within a given context to maximise the process of youth empowerment.

A guiding principle of any model of empowerment is that it is fundamentally grounded on an initiated process of engagement that serves as the catalyst for change and development. The efficacy of any such model within an applied context is intrinsically dependent on maximising the process of engagement. The process of engagement can be viewed dynamically on a continuum from empowerment to disempowerment (Holosko et al., 2001). Between each pole on this continuum are contextual factors and processes, which either facilitate and support or conversely are impediments and barriers to the efficacy of the model of empowerment. Each component or level of the conceptual framework described herein can be applied and observed through this continuum. For example, the group setting and climate may be influenced by factors that impact the process of engagement such as a lack of support or community resources, or few opportunities for involvement. Another relates to factors that sway the engagement of the interactive processes including negative peer influences, societal norms, and/ or perceptions of youth. While some contextual factors are process related, others that fall on the continuum may be social and culturally based.

As noted at the beginning of this chapter, all societies and cultures have methods to educate and facilitate the developmental growth of youth so that they may socially integrate into their communities as mature adults. However, while similar in many respects, not all societies and cultures embrace the concept of empowerment or the processes of engagement in a comparable fashion. Kam-shing Yip (2004) suggested that empowerment within a cultural context may be influenced through stories and constructed by longstanding social and philosophical mores and traditions. Developing effective models of empowerment that involve youth in volunteer activities is intrinsically and significantly related to an understanding of this context.

At its core, the premise of disempowerment implies a lack of growth for the individual youth, the programme and group, as well as the community. Within a particular culture or society one could examine, on the above continuum, the positive and negative risk factors that could influence the efficacy of the three core elements presented: environment context, the interactive processes, and the knowledge-based outcomes, associated with developing successful models of youth empowerment.

Given our social work backgrounds and extensive experience in working at all levels of the practice continuum—micro/mezzo/macro—we offer an insight to close this chapter. We have taught our students for numerous years about the importance of self-awareness in order to be effective in assisting individuals. Indeed, the clinical adage "know thyself and you will know others" has been staid as well in our social work professional education and training for a number of years.

This chapter's main contention throws a bit of a different spin on this self-awareness contention. "Know others, do for your community, and you just may get to know yourself better!" And, it corroborates chapter 2 in espousing the role of community in motivating individuals to volunteer.

References

Altman, D. G., & Feighery, E. C. (2004). Future directions for youth empowerment: Commentary on application of youth empowerment theory to tobacco control. *Health Education & Behavior, 31*(5), 641–647.

Angelique, H. L., Reischl, T. M., & Davidson, W. S. (2002). Promoting political empowerment: Evaluation of an intervention with university students. *American Journal of Community Psychology, 30*(6), 815–833.

Bandura, A. (1997). *Self-efficacy: The exercise of control.* New York: Freeman.

Cargo, M., Grams, G. D., Ottoson, J. M., Ward, P., & Green, L. W. (2003). Empowerment as fostering positive youth development and citizenship. *American Journal of Health Behavior, 27*(Supplement 1), 66–79.

Clary, E. G., Snyder, M., Ridge, R. D., Copeland, J., Stukas, A. A., Haugen, J., et al. (1998). Understanding and assessing the motivations of volunteers: A functional approach. *Journal of Personality and Social Psychology, 74*(6), 1516–1530.

Cleary, T. J., & Zimmerman, B. J. (2004). Self-regulation empowerment programme: A school based programme to enhance self-regulated and self-motivated cycles of student learning. *Psychology in the Schools, 41*(5), 537–550.

Coble, J., Risler, E., & Nackerud, L. (1999). The effects of a behavioral intervention with five Hispanic children with school attendance problems. *School Social Work Journal, 23*, 60–71.

Curtis, J. E., Grabb, E., & Baer, D. (1992). Voluntary association membership in fifteen countries: A comparative analysis. *American Sociological Review, 57*, 139–152.

Erikson, E. (1950). *Childhood and society.* New York: W. W. Norton & Co.

Freire, P. (1970). *Pedagogy of the oppressed.* New York: Continuum.

Freire, P. (1973). *Education for the Critical Consciousness.* New York: Seabury Press.

Garst, B. A., & Johnson, J. (2005). Adolescent leadership skill development through residential 4-H camp counseling. *Journal of Extension, 43*(5), On-line # -5RIB5.

Gutierrez, L. (1995). Understanding the empowerment process: Does consciousness make a difference. *Social Work Research, 19*(4), 229–237.

Holden, D. J., Messeri, P., Evans, W. D., Crankshaw, E., & Ben-Davies, M. (2004). Conceptualizing youth empowerment with tobacco control. *Health Education & Behavior, 31*(5), 548–563.

Holosko, M. J., Leslie, D. R., & Cassano, R. D. (2001). How service users become empowered in human service organisations: The empowerment model. *International Journal of Health Care Quality Assurance, 14*(2,3), 126–132.

Holosko, M. J., Leslie, D., & Miller, D. (2001). *An evaluation of the outcomes of the Kid's Alliance Project in Windsor and Essex County, 2001.* Windsor, ON: The School of Social Work.

Hosty, M. (2005). 4-H wildlife stewards: A new delivery model for 4-H. *Journal of Extension, 43*(5), On line # - 51AW3.

Hyde-Hills, I. (1998). It is better to learn to fish: Empowerment in adventure education. *In exploring the boundaries of adventure therapy: International perspectives.* Proceedings of the International Adventure Therapy Conference, Perth, Australia, July 1997.

Independent Sector (2006). *Giving and volunteering in the United States* (On-Line). Available: http://www.independentsector.org/programmes/research/gv01main.html.

Johnson, M. K., Beebe, T., Mortimer, J. T., & Snyder, M. (1998). Volunteerism in adolescence: A process perspective. *Journal of Research on Adolescence, 8*(3), 309–332.

Keith, A., Nelson, B., Schlabach, C., & Thompson, D. (1990). The relationship between parental employment and three measures of early adolescent responsibility: Family-related, personal, and social. *Journal of Early Adolescence, 10*, 399–415.

Kohlberg, L. (1984). *Essays on moral development. Vol. II. The Psychology of Moral Development.* New York: Harper Row.

Larson, R., Walker, K., & Pearce, N. (2005). A comparison of youth-driven and adult-driven youth programmes: Balancing inputs from youth and adults. *Journal of Community Psychology, 33*(1), 57–74.

Leroy, L., Benet, D. J., Mason, T., Austin, W. D., & Mills, S. (2004). Empowering organisations: Approaches to tobacco control through youth empowerment programmes. *Health Education & Behavior, 31*(5), 577–596.

Lo, T. W. & Au, E. (2004). *Youth empowerment: International experiences.* Hong Kong: City University of Hong Kong.

Loughmiller, C. (1965). *The wilderness road.* Austin, TX: The Hogg Foundation, The University of Texas.

McWhirter, E. H. (1991). Empowering in counseling. *Journal of Counseling & Development, 69*(3), 222–227.

Moody, K., Childs, J., & Seeples, S. (2003). Interviewing at risk youth: Evaluation of the youth empowerment and support programme. *Pediatric Nursing, 29*(4), 263–270.

Nowicki, S., & Strickland, B. R. (1973). A locus of control scale for children. *Journal of Consulting and Clinical Psychology, 40*, 148–154.

Oesterle, S., Johnson, M. K., & Mortimer, J. T. (2004). Volunteering during the transition to adulthood: A life course perspective. *Social Forces, 82*(3), 1123–1149.

Omoto, A. M., & Snyder, M., (1995) Sustained helping without obligation: Motivation, longevity of service, and perceived attitude change among AIDS volunteers. *Journal of Personality and Social Psychology, 68*, 671–686

Penner, L. A., & Finkelstein, M. A. (1998). Dispositional and structural determinants of volunteerism. *Journal of Personality and Social Psychology, 74*(2), 525–537.

Piaget, J. (1957). *Construction of reality in the child.* London: Routledge & Kegan Paul.

Pipher, M. (1994). *Reviving Ophelia, saving the selves of adolescent girls.* New York: Ballantine Books.

Raffo, C., & Reeves, M. (2000). Youth transitions and social exclusion: Developments in social capital theory. *Journal of Youth Studies, 3*(2), 147–166.

Raskoff, S., & Sundeen, R. A. (1994). Volunteering among teenagers in the United States. *Nonprofit and Voluntary Sector Quarterly, 23*(4), 383–403.

Ribisl, K. M., Steckler, A., Linnan, L., Patterson, C. C., Pevzner, E. S., Markatos, E., et al. (2004). The North Carolina youth empowerment study (NC YES): A participatory research study examining the impact of youth empowerment for tobacco use prevention. *Health Education & Behavior, 31*(5), 597–614.

Risler, E., Sutphen, R., & Shields, J. (2000). Preceding delinquent behavior in youth: preliminary validation of the First Offender Risk Assessment Index. *Research on Social Work Practice, 10,* 111–126.

Rose, S. M. (2000). Reflections on empowerment-based practice. *Social Work, 45*(5), 403–412.

Safrit, R. D., & Auck, A. W. (2003). Volunteerism, community service, and service learning by Ohio 4-H'ers in grades 4–12. *Journal of Extension, 41*(4), 1–9.

Wallerstein, N. (2002). Empowerment to reduce health disparities. *Scandinavian Journal of Public Health, 30,* 72–77.

Wehmeyer, M. L., & Gragoudas, S. (2004). Centres for independent living and transition-age youth: Empowerment and self-determination. *Journal of Vocational Rehabilitation, 20,* 53–58.

Yip, K. (2004). The empowerment model: A critical reflection of empowerment in Chinese culture. *Social Work, 49*(3), 479–487.

YOUTH DISPOSITIONAL EMPOWERMENT: CULTIVATING HARDINESS AND RESILIENCE

4

Xiaodong YUE

Introduction

Empowerment has become increasingly popular in academic, political, and professional circles of social work, social psychology, and public administration (Lee, 1994; Lo & Au, 2004). This chapter attempts to define a new form of empowerment, called dispositional empowerment, in terms of two personality constructs, hardiness and resilience. It explores how they may be developed through promoting one's subjective well-being, dispositional optimism, positive cognitive re-appraisal, and coping effectiveness.

Dispositional Empowerment Defined

Empowerment, seen from a psychological perspective, means to enhance one's self-functioning and ego strength by promoting one's self-control, self-esteem, self-determination, and self-efficacy. Alternatively, empowerment more simply means to acquire a number of desirable dispositional traits or competencies that contribute to one's optimal self-functioning. Rappaport (1987) stated that empowerment conveys both a psychological sense of personal control or influence and a concern with actual social influence, political power, and legal rights. Gutierrez (1991) described it as "the ability to get what one needs; the ability to influence how others think, feel, act or believe; and the ability to influence the distribution of resources in a social system such as a family, organisation, community, or society" (pp. 201–202). DuBois and Miley (1999) stated that empowerment is acquired through life experiences, particularly experiences affirming efficacy, rather than from circumstances in which one is told what to do. Therefore, dispositional empowerment may be defined as a process of acquiring a number of personality traits or competencies that serve to empower the self-functioning of a person or a group of people.

Psychologically empowered individuals typically develop positive self-schemata (Markus, 1977), positive self-traits (Rosenberg, 1979), positive self-labels (Bem, 1978), and positive self-identity (Harter, 1983). Zimmerman (1990) proposed an empowerment model that included control variables within a person (intrapsychic), variables that address how people related to the environment (interactional), and variables that involve taking actions that are self-motivated and not dominated by helping professionals (behavioural). He argued that awareness of one's choices resulted in motivation that successfully exerted control over the environment (Zimmerman, Israel, Schultz, & Checkoway, 1992).

Dispositional empowerment may be achieved at societal or institutional levels. For example, participating in volunteer services may be empowering to people by enhancing their self-acceptance, self-confidence, social and political understanding, and self-assertiveness in controlling one's resources in the community (Zimmerman & Rappaport, 1988). Further, joining collaborative prevention programmes may empower people by facilitating their acquisition of resources to free self-correcting capacities (Rappaport, 1981; Servian, 1996). Thus, Kieffer (1984) regarded empowerment as a dynamic process, one of the developing insights and abilities which are best characterised as "participatory competence."

Dispositional empowerment, at the individual level, has been achieved primarily through the use of counselling or clinical services. There has been a lack of awareness and intervention programmes that promote dispositional empowerment of people facing stress and adversities in life. Nor has there been consensus about the core components of dispositional empowerment enhancing one's self-functioning. Having studied stress psychology and counselling psychology for over 15 years, I believe that people can be self-empowered by cultivating hardiness and resilience in themselves.

Dispositional Empowerment through Hardiness and Resilience

The Concept of Hardiness

Hardiness refers to a general quality that emerges from rich, varied, and rewarding childhood experiences and is "a general sense that the environment is satisfying" (Maddi & Kobasa, 1984, p. 50). It is defined in terms of one's personal control, commitment, and challenges that may influence both positive appraisal and behaviour in response to stressful events (Kobasa, 1979). Specifically: a) control includes such elements as nihilism, external locus of control, powerlessness, achievement, dominance, and leadership; b) commitment includes such elements as alienation from self, work, family, and interpersonal relation, and role consistency; and c) challenges include such elements as vegetativeness, security, cognitive structure, adventurousness, endurance, and interesting experiences (Kobasa, 1979).

Further, in everyday functioning, personal control enables one to exert influence over their surroundings such that s/he may re-frame problems as opportunities. Commitment enables a person to have full engagement in activities with a strong sense of purpose, direction, and self-understanding. Challenge enables a person to believe that change rather than stability, characterises life and to anticipate change as affording them conduits and opportunities for self-development (Crowley, Hayslip, & Hobdy, 2003).

In stressful situations, hardy individuals tend to approach adversity and re-adjustments with "a clear sense of values, goals, and capabilities, and a belief in their importance (commitment to, rather than alienation from self) and a strong tendency toward active involvement with one's environment (vigorousness rather than vegetativeness)" (Kosaba, 1979, p. 9). In turn, this may help one to approach life with more curiosity, enthusiasm, and commitment (Maddi & Kobasa, 1984). As such, Bergeman and Wallace (1999) identified hardiness as an attribute of psychological resiliency as it related to physical health and mental well-being. Thus, developing hardiness lies in its capacity to enable a person to develop optimistic cognitive appraisals and adaptive coping strategies that may transform the perception of stressful events in less stressful terms (Crowley et al., 2003).

Over the past few decades, the concept of hardiness has generated considerable interest among psychologists (Funk,

1992). Early studies primarily focused on its relationship with physical illness and some known stress moderators such as Type A personality characteristics (e.g. Kobasa, Maddi, & Zola, 1983; Nowack, 1986; Rhodewalt & Agustsottir, 1984; Schmied & Lawler, 1986), cynical hostility (Smith & Frohm, 1985), and social support (Ganellen & Blaney, 1984; Kobasa & Puccetti, 1983). The research literature generally indicated that stressful life events and adversities affect a strain reaction which may result in exhaustion and accompanying illness or psychological distress. Hardiness serves to modify the regular strain-exhaustion process by: a) altering perceptions of events to make them less stressful; b) leading to active or "transformational" coping; c) influencing coping indirectly through its reliance on social supports; and d) leading to changes in health practices that help reduce illnesses (Maddi & Kobasa, 1984).

In short, hardiness is a cultivatable personality trait that helps enhance one's self-functioning and ego strength by confronting changes, adversities, and challenges in life. It enables a person to constantly take a positive re-framing of stressful events in life and allows one to develop more effective coping strategies.

The promotion of hardiness has been shown to be empowered for individuals. For instance, Nowack (1989) reported that hardier individuals selected coping strategies that were more active and problem-focused, whereas less hardy persons tended to choose denial or avoidance to cope with threats (Williams, Wiebe, & Smith, 1992). Similarly, Huang (1995) reported that hardy people tended to be healthier and to perceive life changes as positive and challenging, as mediated by the appraisal of such changes. Clark and Hartman (1996) found that hardy family caregivers felt less distressed with demands for caring for an elderly relative.

In addition, hardy people tend to use transformational coping to change potentially stressful life events into opportunities for growth and make less threatening appraisals of stressors (Funk, 1992). For instance, compared with less hardy people, hardy people were found to view previous life events as more positive and controllable, in gereral (Rhodewalt & Agustsdottir, 1984; Rhodewalt & Zone,

1989). They also evaluated their life experiences as more challenging and less threatening (Pagana, 1990).

In sum, hardy people tend to develop social support networks that facilitate transformational coping in times of stress (Maddi & Kobasa, 1984). Moreover, hardiness reflects a fundamental perspective within psychology in that it emphasises mental health wellness over psychopathology (Funk, 1992; Pagaua, 1990). Thus conceived, it is no surprise that the depictions of hardy people are very similar to those of self-actualising people (Campbell, Amerikaner, Swank, & Vincent, 1989).

The Concept of Resilience

Resilience (also called resiliency) is defined as the process of adapting positively in the face of adversity, trauma, tragedy, threats, or even significant sources of stress, e.g. family and relationship problems, serious health problems, or workplace and financial stressors. It often means "bouncing back" from difficult life experiences.

Benard (1995) defined resilience as a "set of qualities" which develop out of an innate capacity. She divided these "qualities" into sub-categories of fine personal abilities and traits. They included:

1. social competence: responsiveness, the ability to elicit positive responses from others, flexibility, empathy, communication, and sense of humour;

2. problem-solving skills: ability to plan, resourcefulness, critical thought, creativity, reflectiveness;

3. critical consciousness: a "reflective awareness of the structures of oppression" plus strategies to overcome them;

4. autonomy: sense of identity, self efficacy, independence and detachment; and,

5. sense of purpose: aspirations, optimism, motivation, persistence, and "spiritual connectedness." (p. 4)

Later, Benard (1997) refined her definition to avoid a "blaming the victim" stance "with its concomitant focus on 'fixing kids', as she emphasised that a child's resilient qualities are developed through interactions of the child with the environment. She started that: "personality and individual outcomes are the result of a transactional process between self, agency, and environmental influences" (p. 169). Benard also emphasised the developing, fluid nature of these qualities: "resilience... is not a trait or even a set of traits. It is, instead, the accumulating matrix of capacities, resources, talents, strengths, knowledge, and adaptive skills that continues to grow over time" (p. 171).

Resilience is also a composite construct consisting of positive personal characteristics including extraversion, optimism, internality, purpose in life, active coping, and positive re-interpretation and growth (Russell & Richards, 2003). For instance, the Michigan Psychological Society suggested that factors of resilience include minimally: confident optimism, productive and autonomous activity, interpersonal warmth and insight, and skilled expressiveness. Other studies have shown that a major factor in developing resilience is having caring and supportive relationships within and outside the family. Relationships that create love and trust, provide role models, and offer encouragement and reassurance to help bolster one's resilience. Additional factors associated with resilience, include: a) the capacity to make realistic plans and take steps to carry them out; b) a positive view of yourself and confidence in your strengths and abilities; c) skills in communication and problem solving; and d) the capacity to manage strong feelings and impulses. In brief, resilience, similar to hardiness, serves to enhance one's self-functioning or ego strength in stressful conditions through positive thinking, feeling, and acting.

Resilience factors have been shown to exert many positive effects on people's self functioning. For instance, Smith (2002) reported that although resilience factors could not predict pain, affect, and the pain-affect relationship, resilience factors such as HIV/AIDS knowledge, self-esteem, and hopefulness may be an especially salient component of HIV prevention in incarcerated adolescents. McKnight and Loper (2002), having investigated the effects of risk factors including poverty, single parent status and sexual abuse reports, and resilience factors such as school involvement, drug abstinence, and religious belief on predicting delinquency in adolescent girls (aged 10–19 years), argued that resilience factors improved prediction of delinquency beyond risk factors alone.

From another perspective, Jennison and Johnson (1997) studied dyadic cohesion in marital communication (i.e. frequency of interaction and agreement on substantive issues that may affect couples), discovering that an imputed transmission of risk for drinking vulnerability in women who were adult children of alcoholics (ACAs), controlling for non-ACA status, was effectively moderated by positive dyadic interaction. Alternatively, resilience factors may help one deal with alcoholism.

Yonke (2000) examined how a group of students with personal resiliency functioned at high school. The author found that students interpreted their school experiences through a combination of factors including the people, events, and experiences which worked, in coordination with their personal resiliency, to help them succeed in school. Some longitudinal studies have consistently shown that between one-half and two-thirds of children growing up in families with mentally ill, alcoholic, abusive, or criminally involved parents or in poverty-stricken or war-torn communities, do overcome their initial traumatic life experiences. As such, they can essentially reverse a life trajectory of risk into one that manifests "resilience." In such a way, resilience is "the ability to deal with adversity without becoming overwhelmed by it" (Grotberg, 1999, p. 67).

Resilience factors may also change according to situations which emerge in life. For instance, when an accident happens, unit cohesion and habitual coping styles may emerge as resilience factors; whereas previous exposure to critical incidents and the personal experience of not coping in accident situations emerge as vulnerability factors (Eid & Johnsen, 2002). Perceptions of hope and social support were hypothesised to serve as resilience factors against distress in mothers of children with chronic physical conditions (Horton & Wallander, 2001). In another study, the hardiness dimensions of commitment, challenge, and control were examined as resilience factors in adaptation among persons with symptomatic HIV disease and AIDS. Results suggested that higher hardiness was significantly related to: a) lower psychological distress levels; b) higher perceived quality of life in physical health, mental health, and overall functioning domains; c) more positive personal beliefs regarding the benevolence of the world and people, self-worth, and randomness of life events; and d) lowered belief in controllability of life events (Folkman, 1997).

The Relationship between Hardiness and Resilience

It may be posited that hardiness and resilience are two interrelated constructs of dispositional empowerment, and they share a number of fundamental assumptions to optimal self-functioning. First, advocates of the two constructs believe that to successfully cope with stress and remain healthy is a decided "personality style" that may be perfected through one's life experiences (Maddi & Kobasa, 1984). It may also be enhanced through the cultivation of core "personal abilities and traits" (Benard, 1995). Alternatively, both constructs are defined in dispositional terms that aspire people to achieve optimal self-functioning. Thus, hardiness and resilience reflect a fundamental perspective within psychology that emphasises mental health over psychopathology, and optimal over abnormal functioning (Funk, 1992; Keyes, 2002).

Second, both constructs emphasise having a positive reappraisal of the many changes, adversities, and challenges of life. As such, they serve to cultivate, enhance, and reinforce the dispositional optimism in a person such that s/he will learn to habitually treat all forms of stress as opportunities of self-growth instead of threats of self-worth. Moreover, hardier or more resilient people are capable of approaching stressful situations with curiosity, enthusiasm, and commitment (Funk, 1992).

Third, both constructs emphasise keeping a positive outlook or subjective perceived well-being, such that a person will try to feel happy no matter what happens to him or her, in life. In other words, hardier or more resilient people are capable of maintaining the belief that life is generally worth living, and change is just a normal aspect of life (Funk, 1992). They are also capable of ridding themselves quickly of various negative mood states in times of stress (Crowley et al., 2003).

Fourth, both constructs emphasise the active use of effective coping strategies to deal with stress that are both problem-focused (e.g. confrontative coping, self-controlling coping, accepting responsibility, positive reappraisal, planful problem-solving, seeking support, etc.) and emotion-focused (e.g. positive affect, sense of humour, etc.) (Crowley et al., 2003). Taken together, these two terms may actually be hyphenated to describe and prescribe an optimal state of self-functioning that can be cultivated and learned through life experiences.

With regard to their differences, it is worth noting that hardiness originated from studies of business personnel and university students and is defined primarily in social-psychological terms. Resilience, on the other hand, originated from studies of health or stress psychology and is defined primarily in dispositional terms. Further, hardiness appears to emphasise more motivational input to self-empowerment whereas resilience seems to pay closer attention to character formation of optimal self-functioning.

In conclusion, hardiness and resilience share much more than they differ. What is common to both constructs is shown in Figure 4.1.

A Hardy-Resilient Personality Style

Hardiness and resilience have been shown to be overlapping personality styles (see Figure 4.1) that empower individuals to confront life changes, adversities, and difficulties with interest, enthusiasm and commitment. It is important that young people, either individually or collectively, should try to orient themselves to be hardy-resilient such that they will always be adaptable to the environment and be optimistic about their future. It is also critical

Figure 4.1 How empowerment and youth volunteerism are interrelated

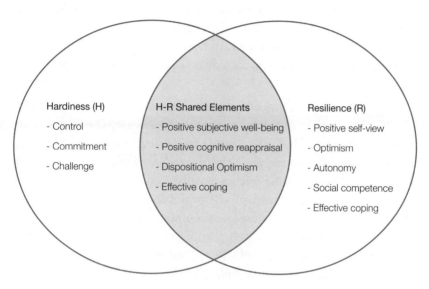

that such self or group efforts enhance the following elements of optimal self-functioning: subjective well-being, dispositional optimism, positive cognitive reappraisal, and coping effectiveness. A brief discussion of the nature, composition, and significance of each of these elements is now presented.

Enhancing Subjective Well-being

Subjective well-being (SWB) is a phenomena that includes people's emotional responses, domain satisfactions, and global judgments of life satisfaction (Diener, Suh, Lucas, & Smith, 1999). As a self state, SWB is an overriding emotional sense of well-being and serves as a global index of one's life satisfaction (Fordyce, 1977).

Generally, four inner traits make happy people: self-esteem, a sense of personal control, optimism, and extraversion (Myers & Diener, 1995). In other words, happy people, who value themselves (Campbell, 1981), feel in control and empowered (Campbell, 1981;

Larson, 1989) are usually optimistic (Dember & Brooks, 1989; Seligman, 1991) and tend to be extraverted (Costa & McCrae, 1980; Headey & Wearing, 1992). Additionally, personal strivings for achievement (e.g. goal setting and commitment) and intimacy (e.g. loving and caring for others) also delight people (Colby, Emmons, & Rabin, 1994; Emmons, 1997).

For example, happy people are found to be less self-focused, less hostile and abusive, and less vulnerable to disease, compared with depressed people. They are also more loving, forgiving, trusting, energetic, decisive, creative, helpful, and sociable (Myers, 1993; Veenhoven, 1988). People with a positive sense of well-being focus on personal growth instead of self-protection and are able to have emotional resources to pursue autonomous and challenging goals (McAuley, Bond, & Ng, 2004). People with a positive disposition sometimes even use more self-deception, which in turn, increases one's SWB (Erez, Johnson, & Judge, 1995).

Fredrickson (2003) argued that positive emotions broaden an individual's momentary mind-set, allowing people to think differently and develop enduring personal resources. Specifically, when people feel good, their thinking becomes more creative, integrative, and open to new information. Feeling good can transform people for the better, making them more optimistic, resilient and socially connected. Thus, Fredrickson (2003) suggested that by cultivating positive emotion through finding positive meanings within current circumstances, people will generally enjoy life more.

In brief, SWB contributes to one's dispositional empowerment and optimal self-functioning. Happiness is, "an imaginary condition, formerly attributed by the living to the dead, now usually attributed by adults to children, and by children to adults" (Lyubomirsky & Abbe, 2003, p. 133). Happiness is, according to Benjamin Franklin, "produced not so much by great pieces of good fortune that seldom happen, as by little advantages that occur everyday" (Myers & Diener, 1995, p. 17). Therefore, satisfaction is less a matter of getting what you want, than wanting what you have.

Enhancing Dispositional Optimism

Optimism represents a generalised tendency to expect favourable outcomes in one's life (Scheier & Carver, 1985). This belief leads to accomplishments of more successes by optimists than by pessimists. As a personality style, optimism represents an optimal self-functioning state that persistently and consistently makes people feel hopeful about the meanings of their lives. Studies have shown that the need for optimism regarding oneself is intimately linked to life satisfaction (Dember & Brooks, 1989) and influences physical as well as mental well-being (Scheier & Carver, 1992; Taylor & Aspinwall, 1996).

Recently, with the awareness of positive psychology, individuals wonder the best way is to achieve optimal self-functioning. Keyes (2002) proposed that by "flourishing," which is the epitome of healthy mentality, people are able to keep higher levels of emotional well-being: they are happy and satisfied with life; they tend to see their lives as having purpose; they feel a certain degree of mastery, accepting all parts of themselves. Flourishing adults also have a sense of personal growth—as they are always growing, evolving, changing. They also have a sense of more autonomy—as they choose their fate in life, rather than see themselves as victims of fate. In this regard, the opposite of flourishing is "languishing" which means having low or little emotional, psychological or SWB even though individuals are not depressed. Studies have shown that languishing adults have the same number of chronic diseases as those who are depressed. Conversely, flourishing adults are fairly better in physical health.

In short, the construct of dispositional optimism is rooted in the long traditions of expectancy-value theories of psychology, and is based primarily on positive outcome expectancies (Lai & Yue, 2000). Enhancing optimism, at the dispositional level, means to identify ways to keep a person goal-oriented, no matter what happens. This is in accordance with what Lyubomirsky and Abbe (2003) described for the goal of positive psychology which "is committed to investigating the factors that allow individuals, families, and communities to flourish, to thrive and to function in an optimal way" (p. 132). Indeed, dispositional optimism makes people flourish and thrive.

Enhancing Positive Cognitive Reappraisals

Positive cognitive reappraisal represents one's assessment of changes or adversities in life in a positive light. As a cognitive state, it emphasises a positive attributional or judgmental bias. Taylor and Brown (1988; 1994) described a set of beliefs or cognitions regarding one's sense of worth, control, and optimism that are held at positive levels in general populations. Perceptions of health are more important than objective health indicators in their impacting SWB (Diener et al., 1999).

For instance, Cummins and Nistico (2002) proposed that positive-cognitive biases (PCBs) have two distinct properties: they are non-specific and empirically unfalsifiable. Taken together, they foster a robust and reliable mechanism by which people maintain positive self-cognition resulting in self-satisfaction as well as life satisfaction. Furthermore, PCBs of optimism may enable people to believe that they live in a world where good things are more likely to happen to oneself, rather than to hypothetical others (Cummins & Nistico, 2002). In conditions of adversity, PCBs may also motivate people to re-frame a bad situation into one of optimism for the future. In fact, PCBs of optimism have been reported for both normal populations and those experiencing adversity (Cummins & Nistico, 2002; Taylor, 1983).

For instance, Tabachnik, Crocker, & Alloy (1983) found that non-depressed college students described a set of positive self-attributes as more true of themselves than the "average" college student. Thus, these students viewed themselves as more cheerful, enthusiastic and confident when compared with their college peers. Similarly, Brown (1986) found that students rated positive personality adjectives as more true indicators of themselves, when compared with non-descript "others," and negative personality adjectives as less true of themselves compared with "others".

Summing up, positive cognitive reappraisal facilitates one's optimistic thinking as well as positive outcome expectancy. The PCBs of control, optimism, and other dimensions of self-functioning act as buffers to reality. Ultimately, positive cognitive reappraisal serves to maintain one's SWB within an optimal range of functioning.

Enhancing Coping Effectiveness

Coping represents one's cognitive and behavioural efforts to handle the internal or external demands for a person-environment encounter, appraised as exceeding one's own resources (Lazarus & Folkman, 1984). Coping effectiveness represents one's skilled competencies, and/or abilities to manage stress to the utmost optimal self-functioning and involves using the most appropriate coping method(s) or skill(s) that are induced by stressful conditions.

Coping effectiveness involves using transformational coping. For instance, Nowack (1989) reported that hardier people tended to use more problem-focused coping, such as planful problem-solving and active action while less hardy people tended to use more avoiding or denying coping. Crowley et al. (2003) concluded that hardier people characteristically used optimistic cognitive reappraisals and adaptive coping strategies that served to transform the perception of stressful events in less stressful terms. Folkman (1997) found that spiritual beliefs, positive reappraisal, giving meaning to ordinary events, and problem-focused coping were all related to positive states in HIV caregivers. Use of such transformational strategies contributes not only to SWB and PCBs but to coping efficacy as well.

Coping effectiveness also incorporates effective social support seeking. For instance, Maddi and Kobasa (1984) remarked that hardiness affected coping directly or indirectly through social supports. Specifically, hardier people tended to have relationships that supported transformational coping in times of stress, whereas less hardy people tended not to seek such relationships which increased their tendency to use regressive coping. For example, Horton and Wallander (2001) reported that perceptions of hope and social support served well as resilience factors against distress in mothers of children with chronic physical conditions.

It is worth noting that humour contributes a great deal to one's SWB and effective coping (Carroll, 1988; Henman, 2001; Nezu, Nezu, & Blissett, 1988). Humour represents a positive affect state and embodies creativity and wisdom. Humour can be divided into two kinds: verbal and visual. It has been shown by research that humour, especially laughter, helps your body relax and your mind feel better (Cetola, 1988). When laughing, one's endorphins, which are brain released chemicals, give an individual a feeling of well-being, better thinking skills, and relief of pain. Humour also reduces stress and rids of anger and tension (Decker & Rotondo, 1999). Particular cells in one's immune system are activated when you laugh. These cells help kill germs, and new cells are produced faster.

In Chinese society, humour has traditionally been neglected as a desirable trait of creativity and personality (Rudowicz & Yue, 2002; Yue & Rudowicz, 2002). Chinese people should learn to use humour effectively to generate optimism and SWB in one's self-functioning as well as positive cognitive reappraisal or PCBs to cope with stress. To enhance one's sense of humour is to promote his or her creativity in thinking, as well as appetite for life.

Enhancing coping effectiveness improves a person's coping skills, interpersonal repertoire, and human resources and ultimately consolidates his or her hardy-resilient personality style as well. And as indicated, in developing one's coping effectiveness, we need to pay greater attention to the empowering effect of humour.

Conclusion

This chapter argues that dispositional empowerment is based on the assumptions of positive psychology which, according to Seligman and Csikzentmihalyi (2000), is "a science of positive subjective experiences, of positive individual traits, and of positive institutions which promise to improve the quality of life, and also to prevent the various pathologies that arise when life is barren and meaningless" (p. 5). Specifically, positive psychology deals with optimal self-functioning at three levels: the subjective, the individual, and the group level. At the subjective level, it deals with valued subjective experiences: well-being, contentment, and satisfaction (past), hope and optimism (future), and flow and happiness (present). At the individual level, it deals with positive individual traits—the capacity for love and vocation, courage, interpersonal skill, aesthetic sensibility, perseverance, forgiveness, originality, future-mindedness, spirituality, high talent, and wisdom. At the group level, it deals with civic virtues and the institutions that move individuals toward better citizenship: responsibility, nurturance, altruism, civility, moderation, tolerance, and work ethic (Seligman & Csikszentmihalyi, 2000). Dispositional empowerment, as advocated here, deals with one's optimal self-functioning at these three levels. It is thus advisable that individual or group programmes of self-empowerment should be developed to enhance young people's optimism, subjective well-being (SWB), positive-cognitive biases (PCBs), and the like at these levels.

It is also posited that present dispositional empowerment adopts a humanistic view of human potentials and competencies, believing that all people can become increasingly hardy and resilient as long as they are determined to modify or perfect their personality styles. Alternatively, people may obtain personal flourishing or thriving when they develop personal abilities or competencies which constitute a hardiness-resilience disposition. As a result, they will more likely feel a sense of control over events and anticipate life changes as exciting and/or challenging (Funk, 1992).

It is worth noting that hardiness and resilience do not constitute the whole spectrum of dispositional empowerment. Other personality traits may also be relevant, such as assertiveness, sociability, creativity, etc. The present dispositional empowerment model generally applies to perception of, and adaptation to, various stressors and conditions in one's life. A broader concept of dispositional empowerment needs to incorporate other conditions of life, as well as other goals of living.

This chapter assists in helping people to understand how these often "talked about" yet important concepts are integral to the growth and development of youth in any society. They are deemed as cornerstone concepts to fulfilling one's development. The assumption put forward is that youth who participate in volunteer activities are likely to accrue more hardiness and resilience not by internal awareness but by the altruistic acts of volunteering to help those in need. Thus, doing for others as such results in doing for oneself.

In conclusion, this chapter proposes to empower young people by cultivating such dispositional traits as hardiness and resilience, so that they may perform at their optimal levels. Compared with other forms of empowerment, the present dispositional approach calls for greater initiative-taking and motivational input from young people themselves. After all, empowerment is as much as societal matter as an individual matter.

References

Bem, S. L. (1978). *Bem sex-role inventory: Professional manual*. Palo Alto, CA: Consulting Psychology Press.

Benard, B. (1995). *Fostering resilience in children*. Retrieved May 3, 2004, from http://www.ed.gov/databases/ERIC_Digests/ed386327. html.

Benard, B. (1997). Fostering resiliency in children and youth: Promoting protective factors in the school. In D. Saleebey (Ed.), *The strengths perspective in social work practice* (pp. 167–182). New York: Longman.

Bergeman, C. S., & Wallace, K. A. (1999). Resiliency in later life. In T. L. Whitman, T. V. Merluzzim, & R. D. White (Eds.), *Life-span perspectives on health and illness* (pp. 207–225). Mahwah, NJ, US: Lawrence Erlbaum Associates.

Brown, J. D. (1986). Evaluations of self and others: Self enhancement biases in social judgment. *Social cognition, 4*, 353–376.

Campbell, A. (1981). *The sense of well-being in America*. New York: McGraw-Hill.

Campbell, J. M., Amerikaner, M., Swank, P., & Vincent, K. (1989). The relationship between hardiness test and the Personal Orientation Inventory. *Journal of Research in Personality, 23*, 373–380.

Carroll, J. M. (1988). Modularity and naturalness in cognitive science. *Metaphor and Symbolic Activity, 3*(2), 61–86.

Cetola, H. W. (1988). Toward a cognitive-appraisal model of humour appreciation. *Humour: International Journal of Humor Research, 1*(3), 245–258.

Clark, L., & Hartman, M. (1996). Effects of hardiness and appraisal on the psychological distress and physical health of caregivers to elderly relatives. *Research on Aging, 18*, 379–401.

Colby, P. M., Emmons, R. A., & Rabin, N. (1994, August). *Intimacy strivings and well-being: The role of social support*. Poster presented at the 102nd Annual Convention of the American Psychological Association, Los Angeles, CA.

Costa, P. T., & McCrae, R. R. (1980). Influence of extraversion and neuroticism on subjective well-being: Happy and unhappy people. *Journal of Personality and Social Psychology, 38*(4), 668–678.

Crowley, B. J., Hayslip, B., & Hobdy, J. (2003). Psychological hardiness and adjustment to life events in adulthood. *Journal of Adult Development, 10*(4), 237–248.

Cummins, R. A., & Nistico, H. (2002). Maintaining life satisfaction: The role of positive cognitive bias. *Journal of Happiness Studies, 3,* 37–69.

Decker, W. H., & Rotondo, D. M. (1999). Use of humor at work: Predictors and implications. *Psychological Reports, 84*(3, Pt 1), 961–968.

Dember, W. N., & Brooks, J. (1989). A new instrument for measuring optimism and pessimism: Test-retest reliability and relations with happiness and religious commitment. *Bulletin of the Psychonomic Society, 27*(4), 365–366.

Diener, E., Suh, E. M., Lucas, R. E., & Smith, H. L. (1999). Subjective well-being: Three decades of progress. *Psychological Bulletin, 125*(2), 276–302.

Dubois, B., & Miley, K. (1999). *Social work: An empowering profession* (3rd ed.). Boston, MA: Allyn and Bacon.

Eid, J., & Johnsen, B. H. (2002). Acute stress reactions after submarine accidents. *Military Medicine, 167*(5), 427–43.

Emmons, R. A. (1997). Motives and life goals. In R. Hogan & J. A. Johnson (Eds.), *Handbook of personality psychology* (pp. 485–511). San Diego, CA: Academic Press.

Erez, A., Johnson, D. E., & Judge, T. A. (1995). Self-deception as a mediator of the relationship between dispositions and subjective well-being. *Personality and Individual Differences, 19*(5), 597–612.

Folkman, S. (1997). Introduction to the special section: Use of bereavement narratives to predict well-being in gay men whose partner died of AIDS—Four theoretical perspectives. *Journal of Personality and Social Psychology, 72*(4), 851–854.

Fordyce, M. W. (1977). Development of a programme to increase personal happiness. *Journal of Counselling Psychology, 24*(6), 511–520.

Fredrickson, B. L. (2003). Value of positive emotions. *American Psychologist, 91,* 330–335.

Funk, S. C. (1992). Hardiness: A review of theory and research. *Health Psychology, 11*(5), 335–345.

Ganellen, R. J., & Blaney, P. H. (1984). Hardiness and social support as moderators of the effects of life stress. *Journal of Personality and Social Psychology, 47*(1), 156–163.

Grotberg, E. H. (1999). *Tapping your inner strength: How to find the resilience to deal with anything.* Oakland, CA, US: New Harbinger Publications, Inc.

Gutierrez, I. G. (1991). Motivacion de logro, diferencias relacionadas con el genero y rendimiento. [Achievement motive, differences associated with gender and productivity]. *Revista de Psicologia General y Aplicada, 44*(4), 405–411.

Harter, S. (1983). To smile or not to smile: Issues in the examination of cross-cultural differences and similarities. *Monographs of the Society for Research in Child Development, 48*(5), 80–87.

Headey, B., & Wearing, A. (1992). *Understanding happiness: A theory of well-being.* Melboune: Longman Cheshire.

Henman, L. D. (2001). Humor as a coping mechanism: Lessons from POWs. *Humour: International Journal of Humour Research, 14*(1), 83–94.

Horton, T. V., & Wallander, J. L. (2001). Hope and social support as resilience factors against psychological distress of mothers who care for children with chronic physical conditions. *Rehabilitation Psychology, 46*(4), 382–399.

Huang, C. (1995). Hardiness and stress: A critical review. *Maternal Child Nursing Journal, 23*(3), 82–89.

Jennison, K. M., & Johnson, K. A. (1997). Resilience to drinking vulnerability in women with alcoholic parents: The moderating effects of dyadic cohesion in marital communication. *Substance Use and Misuse, 32*(11), 1461–1489.

Keyes, C. L. M. (2002). The mental health continuum: From languishing to flourishing in life. *Journal of Health and Social Behaviour, 43*(2), 207–222.

Kieffer, C. H. (1984). Citizen empowerment: A developmental perspective. *Prevention in Human Services, 3*(2–3), 9–36.

Kobasa, S. C. (1979). Stressful life events, personality, and health: An inquiry into hardiness. *Journal of Personality and Social Psychology, 37*(1), 1–11.

Kobasa, S. C., & Puccetti, M. C. (1983). Personality and social resources in stress resistance. *Journal of Personality and Social Psychology, 45*(4), 839–850.

Kobasa, S. C., Maddi, S. R., & Zola, M. A. (1983). Type A and hardiness. *Journal of Behavioural Medicine, 6*(1), 41–51.

Lai, J. C. L., & Yue, X. D. (2000). Measuring optimism in Hong Kong and mainland Chinese with the revised Life Orientation Test. *Personality and Individual Differences, 28*(4), 781–796.

Larson, R. (1989). Is feeling "in control" related to happiness in daily life? *Psychological Reports, 64,* 775–784.

Lazarus, R. S., & Folkman, S. (1984). *Stress, appraisal, and coping.* New York: Springer.

Lee. J. (1994). *The empowerment approach and social work practice.* New York: Columbia University Press.

Lo, T. W. & Au, E. (2004). *Youth empowerment: International experiences.* Hong Kong: City University of Hong Kong.

Lyubomirsky, S., & Abbe, A. (2003). Positive Psychology's Legs. *Psychological Inquiry, 14*(2), 132–136.

Maddi, S. R., & Kobasa, S. C. (1984). *The hardy executive: health under stress.* Homewood, IL: Dow Jones-Irwin.

Markus, H. (1977). Self-schemata and processing information about the self. *Journal of Personality and Social Psychology, 35*(2), 63–78.

McAuley, P. C., Bond, M. H., & Ng, I. W. C. (2004). Antecedents of subjective well-being in working Hong Kong adults. *Journal of Psychology in Chinese Societies, 5*(1), 25–50.

McKnight, L. R., & Loper, A. B. (2002). The effect of risk and resilience factors on the prediction of delinquency for adolescent girls. *School Psychology International, 23,* 2.

Myers, D. G. (1993). *The pursuit of happiness.* New York, NY: Avon Books.

Myers, D. G., & Diener, E. (1995). Who is happy? *Psychological Science, 6*(1), 10–19.

Nezu, A. M., Nezu, C. M., & Blissett, S. E. (1988). Sense of humour as a moderator of the relation between stressful events and psychological distress: A prospective analysis. *Journal of Personality and Social Psychology, 54*(3), 520–525.

Nowack, K. M. (1986). Type A, hardiness, and psychological distress. *Journal of Behavioural Medicine, 9*(6), 537–548.

Nowack, K. M. (1989). Coping style, cognitive hardiness, and health status. *Journal of Behavioural Medicine, 12*(2), 145–158.

Pagana, K. D. (1990). The relationship of hardiness and social support to student appraisal of stress in an initial clinical nursing situation. *Nursing education, 29,* 255–261.

Rappaport, J. (1987). Terms of empowerment/exemplars of prevention: Toward a theory for community psychology. *American Journal of Community Psychology, 15*(2), 121–148.

Rappaport, J. (1981). In praise of paradox: A social policy of empowerment over prevention. *American Journal of Community Psychology, 9*(1), 1–25.

Rhodewalt, F., & Agustsdottir, S. (1984). On the relationship of hardiness to the Type A behaviour pattern: Perception of life events versus coping with life events. *Journal of Research in Personality, 18*(2), 211–223.

Rhodewalt, F., & Zone, J. B. (1989). Appraisal of life change, depression, and illness in hardy and nonhardy women. *Journal of Personality and Social Psychology, 56*(1), 81–88.

Rosenberg, M. (1979). *Conceiving the self.* New York: Basic Books.

Rudowicz, E., & Yue, X. D. (2002). Compatibility of Chinese and creative personalities. *Creativity Research Journal, 14*(3–4), 387–394.

Russell, G. M., & Richards, J. A. (2003). Stressor and resilience factors for lesbians, gay men, and bisexuals confronting antigay politics. *American Journal of Community Psychology. 31*(3–4), 313–328.

Scheier, M. F., & Carver, C. S. (1985). Optimism, coping and health: assessment and implications of generalised outcome expectancies on health. *Journal of Personality, 4,* 219–247.

Scheier, M. F., & Carver, C. S. (1992). Effects of optimism on psychological and physical well-being: Theoretical overview and empirical update. *Cognitive Therapy and research, 16,* 201–228.

Schmied, L. A., & Lawler, K. A. (1986). Hardiness, Type A behaviour, and the stress-illness relation in working women. *Journal of Personality and Social Psychology, 51*(6), 1218–1223.

Seligman, M. E. P. (1991). *Learned optimism.* New York, NY: Random House.

Seligman, M. E. P., & Csikszentmihalyi, M. (2000). Positive psychology: An introduction. *American Psychologist, 55*(1), 5–14.

Servian, R. (1996). *Theorising empowerment: Individual power and community care.* Bristol: Policy Press.

Smith, B. W. (2002). Vulnerability and resilience as predictors of pain and affect in women with arthritis. *Dissertation Abstracts International: Section B: The Sciences and Engineering, 63*(3–B), 1575.

Smith, T. W., & Frohm, K. D. (1985). What's so unhealthy about hostility? Construct validity and psychosocial correlates of the Cook and Medley Ho scale. *Health Psychology, 4*(6), 503–520.

Tabachnik, N., Crocker, J., & Alloy, L. B. (1983). Depression, social comparison, and the false-consensus effect. *Journal of Personality and Social Psychology, 45*(3), 688–699.

Taylor, S. E. (1983). Adjustment to threatening events: A theory of cognitive adaptation. *American Psychologist, 38*(11), 1161–1173.

Taylor, S. E., & Aspinwall, L. G. (1996). Mediating and moderating processes in psychosocial stress: Appraisal, coping, resistance, and vulnerability. In H. B. Kaplan (Ed.), *Psychological stress: Perspectives on structure, theory, life-course and methods* (pp. 71–110). San Diego, CA: Academic Press.

Taylor, S. E., & Brown, J. D. (1988). Illusion and well-being: A social psychological perspective on mental health. *Psychological Bulletin, 103*(2), 193–210.

Taylor, S. E., & Brown, J. D. (1994).Positive illusions and well-being revisited: Separating fact from fiction. *Psychological Bulletin, 116*(1), 21–27.

Veenhoven, R. (1988). The utility of happiness. *Social Indicators Research, 20*(4), 333–354.

Williams, P. G., Wiebe, D. J., & Smith, T. W. (1992). Coping processes as mediators of the relationship between hardiness and health. *Journal of Behavioural Medicine, 15*(3), 237–255.

Yonke, L. C. (2000). School effects on student resiliency at York High School: A case study (Illinois). *Dissertation Abstracts International Section A: Humanities and Social Sciences, 62*(6–A), 2074.

Yue, X. D., & Rudowicz, E. (2002). Perception of the most creative Chinese by undergraduates in Beijing, Guangzhou, Hong Kong, and Taipei. *Journal of Creative Behaviour, 36*(2), 88–104.

Zimmerman, M. A. (1990). Toward a theory of learned hopefulness: A structural model analysis of participation and empowerment. *Journal of Research in Personality, 24*(1), 71–86.

Zimmerman, M. A., & Rappaport, J. (1988). Citizen participation, perceived control, and psychological empowerment. *American Journal of Community Psychology, 16*(5), 725–750.

Zimmerman, M. A., Israel, B. A., Schulz, A. J., & Checkoway, B. (1992). Further explorations in empowerment theory: An empirical analysis of psychological empowerment. *American Journal of Community Psychology, 20*(6), 707–727.

From Social Control to Empowerment: Toward a Youth Empowerment Approach in Services for Young People

Ping Kwong KAM

5

Introduction

Youth is a critical transitional period. Services for young people are to help them cope with their difficult developmental tasks in this transitional stage, realise their potential, learn to take charge of their lives, and develop their capacities to face personal challenges. However, it has been noted that services designed for young people have either put too much emphasis on a deficit-oriented model (Kim, Crutchfield, Williams, & Helper, 1998), or problem-oriented approach (Lee, 1999). All these focus on the pathologies and problems of youth rather than their potential. As a result, more societal resources are directed to reducing risk behaviours of young people.

In Hong Kong, one of the main goals of youth services is to reduce young people's anti-social and deviant behaviours (Hong Kong Government, 1991). This is related to the historical development of youth services in Hong Kong. Services for young people emerged and developed rapidly after the occurrence of two riots in 1966 and 1967. It was determined that a significant number of participants in these riots were youth and the Hong Kong government held the view that there was a need to channel their discontent and guide them to more "proper social behaviours". From then onward, the government has offered significant resources to develop youth services, i.e. children and youth centres, outreach youth work, school social work, integrated youth services, annual territory-wide summer youth programmes, etc. All of these services were expected to alleviate the problems faced by young people and promote healthier youth development, overall in Hong Kong. However, the main assumption behind these services was to protect, and/or encourage young people to refrain from engaging in anti-social or socially unacceptable behaviours. Thus, the main objective of services like the annual summer youth programmes in Hong Kong, is to help youth properly spend their leisure time, ventilate their feelings and channel their energy in positive and appropriate ways. As such, services for young people in Hong Kong have long been criticised for operating to fulfil a social control function (Chiu, 1999; Chung, 2002).

Under a social control model, youth services tend to become more reactive, leisure-orientated and remedially focused (Lee, 1999). Youth are often regarded as a group "at risk" and not as a resource (Delgado, 1998). This tends to control young people's behaviours and development, resulting in fostering a more passive, dependent and powerless youth. However, in the light of present social and political changes, young people need to become more prepared to take up the challenges in their ever-changing environments. They should also be regarded as individuals with something to offer and better equipped to become the decision-makers not only of tomorrow, but also of today (Foster, Naidoo, & Akuhata-Brown, 1999).

Positive youth development and youth empowerment should become the central focus of youth services (Lo & Au, 2004). To effectively promote proper development of young people and to address youth disempowerment issues, there should be a shift in the traditional and longstanding practice in youth services from the focus on social control to the development of youth empowerment. This chapter examines how empowerment theory may be applied to working with young people. Disempowered situations of young people are identified and factors leading to youth disempowerment are also discussed. Finally, an eight-step youth empowerment approach is offered to assist young people to become well prepared and better equipped to be at the forefront of global changes.

Empowerment and Empowerment-oriented Practice

Before examining how empowerment is applied to working with young people, empowerment needs to be defined. Empowerment is usually a process and an ability to gain, control, and/or develop power. It means having access to power which refers to the ability and capacity to cope constructively with forces that undermine and hinder coping, and the achievement of some reasonable control over one's destiny (Pinderhuges, 1983). Lord and Hutchison (1993) defined empowerment as "processes whereby individuals achieve increasing control of various aspects of their lives and participate in the community with dignity" (p. 7). Whitmore (1988) identified empowerment as "an interactive process through which people experience personal and social changes, enabling them to take action to achieve influence over the organisations and institutions which affect their lives and the communities in which they live" (p. 13). It refers to a process of reducing, eliminating, combating, and reversing negative valuations, so as to achieve a state of mind such as feeling worthy and competent, perceiving power and control (Payne, 1991).

Empowerment defined by Solomon (1976) is when social workers or other professionals engage in a set of activities with a client who belongs to a stigmatised collective, aimed at reducing powerlessness, stemming from an experience of discrimination or stigmatisation. Stigmatised groups can be helped to gain, develop and increase particular skills, knowledge, and sufficient power to influence their lives and exercise interpersonal influence and the performance on valued social roles (Solomon, 1976; Torre, 1985 as cited in Cox & Parsons, 1994). Empowerment-oriented practice is defined by Cox and Parsons (1994) as a model which focuses on utilising people's strengths, abilities and competence in order to mobilise their resources toward problem-solving and ultimately, toward empowerment. Torre (1985) stated that "empowerment is a process by which people become strong enough to participate within, share in the control of, and influence events and institutions which affect their lives" (p. 61). Browne (1995) viewed empowerment as "both the possession of control, authority, or influence over others and as the help provided to assist a person to gain control over his or her life" (p. 359).

The levels of intervention of empowerment-oriented practice are broad. It does not focus on one dimension or level only (e.g. at an individual level). According to Gutierrez, Parsons and Cox (1998), empowerment-oriented practice combines individual, interpersonal, and institutional elements. As such, empowerment must encompass all three of these and focusing on any one of them is insufficient. Cox and Parsons (1994) also stated that there should be four dimensions in empowerment-oriented practice, including: personal, interpersonal, micro-environmental and organisational, and macro-environmental or socio-political. As indicated by Solomon (1976), it is not sufficient to empower people individually without enhancing power in the collective group. Hence, empowerment-oriented practice addresses both individual and collective empowerment. For example, a worker assists an elderly person to re-define himself/herself as a capable and worthy individual, to feel better, and have an increased sense of personal dignity, self-respect, and self-esteem. Reciprocally, workers help the elderly as a collective group to eliminate negative public perceptions, to promote collective bargaining power, to combat structural problems, attain social equality, and negotiate the challenges of social structures. Empowerment-oriented practice affirms that individual empowerment increases an individual's capacity and contribution to the individual's empowerment as a group. Reciprocally, collective empowerment also fosters empowerment of the individual (Staples, 1990).

Disempowerment Among Young People

To fully understand empowerment, an examination of powerlessness or disempowerment is required. Typically, target groups of empowerment-oriented practice are those who are disempowered or feel powerless. Interventions are specifically aimed at counteracting disempowered situations. The problems of powerlessness are thus the focal concerns of empowerment. Solomon (1976), based on her work with minority groups, conceived powerlessness as created by negative valuations based on membership of a stigmatised group. She called attention to the relationship between social roles and powerlessness, and she defined powerlessness as "the inability to obtain and utilise resources to achieve individual or collective goals" (Solomon, 1976, p. 28). Powerlessness more specifically, refers to some objective vulnerable conditions people hold. Holdsworth (1991) also pointed out that powerlessness can be seen as "essentially a social construct which should be tackled by working on its social rather than its individual causes" (p. 5).

Solomon (1976) identified two "power blocks" which cause the problem of powerlessness. The first one is indirect power block which "represents internalised negative valuations (of the oppressor) which are incorporated into the developmental experiences of the powerless individual" (p. 30). The second are described as direct power blocks which "are applied directly by some agent of society's major social institutions" (Lee, 1991, p. 8). The former is the self-devaluation of powerless people themselves, and the latter refers to the barriers, restrictions, and discrimination existing in society. Based on this understanding of powerlessness, the following sub-section examines the disempowered situations typically experienced by young people.

Negative Stereotypes

Many people hold the perception that young people do not belong to a stigmatised or vulnerable group. Society conveys the message that young people are expected to be healthy, energetic, active, creative, trendy, and full of potential. In the past, there were some adages about the image of young people, such as—"they are the masters of tomorrow" and "young people are the pillars of the society," etc. However, public attitudes toward young people have become increasingly negative. Indeed, there exist many negative stereotypes among young people nowadays. Unlike the past, young people are often perceived as immature, irresponsible, impulsive, self-centred, having poor work attitudes, lacking knowledge, having poor language proficiency, unconfident, and incompetent (Chung, 2002; Lee, 2002). One of the ubiquitous popular negative sayings is: "compared with the last generation, the performance of young people of this generation has become poorer and poorer."

These negative public attitudes have affected the morale and self-images of young people. Due to the existence and prevalence of such negative stereotypes, young people nowadays de-value themselves, have lower self-esteem and lower self-images. In turn, some have feelings of powerlessness and helplessness. As such, they become more dependent and incompetent to manage their own life events and lack confidence to deal with various personal challenges. Young people are increasingly regarded as a vulnerable group that requires care, guidance, protection, and control.

Youth Voices are Unheard and not Respected

Young people are typically discouraged to express their needs, aspirations, or "their voices". In schools, at the workplace, at home and in social organisations, their voices are easily ignored and not respected. Adults seldom show their respect for youth's voices by acknowledging youth ideas, seeking their input, keenly listening, and responding with seriousness (Cargo, Grams, Ottoson, Ward, & Green, 2003). They are not considered to be a priority social group to be consulted with regard to public issues, and/or social development. Youth views are often regarded as immature, shallow, and/or insensible. They are often thought to be disinterested in social affairs and lacking in analytical ability for any relevant social analyses.

They are also assumed to be incapable of making any significant suggestions or influential ideas for the betterment of society. Even though young people are sometimes invited to express their views on selected issues, the extent to which their views are actually listened to, is questionable. Often, there is a lack of open communication in which adults listen and young people given a voice, resulting in genuine and constructive dialogue (Foster et al., 1999). Their voices are rarely brought to the attention of the political venues, and/or decision-makers. A remark by an ex-senior official of the Education and Manpower Bureau of the Hong Kong government at a public occasion in 2004 vividly reflected this disempowered reality. The remark made was: "young people are beneficiaries of an educational system put in place by the Chief Executive of the Hong Kong government, so they are the least qualified to criticise him" (Ming Pao Daily News, 11 April 2004). This quote frustrated members of local students' bodies and youth organisations. Many young people had the resultant feeling of being denied their right for freedom of speech.

Policies and Services Based on Adult Views

Existing social policies and services for young people are designed and implemented based on adult, rather than youth's perspectives. Decisions about policies and services are almost all adult-driven, often resulting in youth having no role to play in affecting any significant decisions. Since society is also adult-dominated, the main consideration for planning and developing youth services and policies is not to meet young people's needs, but rather to fulfil the adults' expectations of youth needs. As such, choices and alternatives in services are not the real choices of young people, but are confined within the limits set by the adult world and perspective. Adults' views of young people pre-dominate in decision-making processes. As pointed out by Foster et al., (1999, p. 75), "in many adult-dominated civil society organisations and processes, while a notion of youth participation in decision-making exists, all it amounts to, in effect, is a rubber-stamp of adult-driven decisions." Since young people are expected to enter the adults' world in the future, adults' views are "taken-for-granted" but young people's views are considered as inferior, in general.

Rolelessness

A sense of rolelessness is prevalent among many young people. Chinman and Linney (1998) pointed out that "the adolescent role is defined mostly by what it is not" (p. 397). Young people are typically asked not to do something, rather than encouraged to take up meaningful social roles. It is not uncommon to find that young people usually cannot give a concrete answer to the question about their relationships with the community, and/or society. For many, they are not schooled or taught to care about what is happening in their community and thus, in their mind, the issues or events happening in a community are "the business of adults." As such, they generally assume a passive role and are isolated or segregated from their community. Even though they are active consumers of community facilities and services, they typically lack awareness about the importance of community concerns and their ability to exert influence on community changes. Without the identification of meaningful social or community roles, young people may easily feel lost and have feelings of incompetence and inefficacy to master the changes in social environment. Rolelessness or the lack of meaningful roles has been identified as one cause impacting social and behavioural problems among adolescents (Chinman & Linney, 1998).

Shouldering the Responsibility for Building the Future—but not Given Power

Young people are generally expected to be contributing members in society. They are asked to develop or prepare themselves to shoulder the responsibility for building the future of our society. However, this expectation does not carry the corresponding power given to young people. They are expected to learn social responsibility but are not offered the necessary supports, power, and/or opportunities to make decisions for themselves. Young people feel confused and incompetent to face this reality. Without real opportunities to exercise power, young people tend to lack the ability to make decisions and take responsibility as a potential contributor to the betterment of the society. It should be noted that if young people are not granted legitimate power and are rarely involved in processes that affect them, they should not be expected suddenly to emerge as full-blown empowered adults (Nessel, 1988). One should note that if young people do not have opportunities to be included in legitimate ways, they may seek to gain power through more accessible means, such as involvement in negative or dysfunctional behaviours.

According to Seligman (1972), people can learn to become helpless and powerless. If young people are not offered power, and/or feel unable to control what happens to them, they may form an expectation that their actions will not produce useful results. If they are often exposed to a social environment over which they have little control, a deficit may be created in their motivation to respond and affect positive change. As such, they come to expect that any effort to improve their situation is useless and meaningless. In the absence of positive experiences, any response is likely to cease altogether and young people may virtually give up or accept the disempowered situation.

Marginalisation of Vulnerable Youth

Another form of disempowerment facing young people is the increasing marginalisation of vulnerable and "at risk" youth. Due to the economic downturn, more and more young people are becoming unemployed and under-employed. They find it increasingly difficult to obtain a permanent or stable job in the labour market. Choices for jobs are limited and they are often marginalised to occupy jobs with low wages and typically unfavourable working conditions. The situation is even worse for those who are regarded as school failures, dropouts, or underachievers. Other vulnerable youth groups who are generally ignored or neglected in society, such as ethnic minorities and new arrivals from mainland China, face multiple deprivations resulting from a lack of personal, social, political, or financial opportunities (Barry, 1998). Their marginalisation creates a further problem of alienation or social exclusion which deprives them of the resources required for participation in the social, economic, and political activity of society as a whole. Through this process, vulnerable young people are alienated from institutions and services, social networks, and developmental opportunities that a great majority of society enjoys (Pierson, 2002).

Public and existing social policies tend to take a "blaming the victim" mentality in dealing with the problems of marginalisation and social exclusion among vulnerable youth groups. This perspective attributes a problem to the characteristics of the victims of that problem. It focuses on efforts to deal with the problem by changing the characteristics of the victims themselves rather than changing the social conditions that cause that problem (Ryan, 1971). Vulnerable and marginal young people, like other disadvantaged groups, are often described as having characteristics that cause such problems. They are said to be the victims of their own personal failures, not the victims of society. In turn, their problems are often regarded as the result of their own inadequacies, culture, or failure to acculturate (Delgado, 1998) which require professional intervention. The limitations and constraints of the social environment and social structures, such as the problems and deficits in the educational system and labour policies, the lack of racial equality policies, the existence of racial discrimination, are seldom examined. This "blaming the victim" attitude camouflages their disempowering situations. What vulnerable youth have to do, accordingly, is to accept the situation and, as a result, they seldom request societal resources or benefits to solve their problems.

Excluding Youth Participation

Apart from being denied opportunities for voicing and exercising power, youth are also often excluded from processes in which they could be meaningfully engaged. As previously indicated, adults tend to negate their ability and participation in providing input into decisions that affect their well-being. In schools, in the community, and in society as a whole, young people are often discouraged in deciding about services and policies that may affect them. They are typically placated and afforded limited opportunities to participate in defining their own problems, deliberating on what might be possible to solve the problems, and engaging in relationships with professionals who consider them as pre-adults, waiting to be invited to participate in decision-making processes (Nessel, 1988). It has been noted that in Hong Kong, youth were denied participation in discussion and the formulation of many important social policies and social programmes which have direct impact on them e.g. educational reform, review of the children and youth services, improvements in the employment assistance scheme for young people, social integration programmes for minority youth, etc. There was also no mechanism initiated by the government or decision-making bodies to systematically or comprehensively invite and collect young people's views on these policy considerations. These experiences clearly demonstrate the fact that young people's participation in local decision-making is not considered as important in the process of formulating social policies.

A paternalistic mode of practice (Beresford & Croft, 1993) which emphasises the active professional/passive young service receiver working style is prevalent in the current educational system and in different kinds of social services for young people in Hong Kong. Thus, an unequal power relationship between young people and social service or teaching professionals is still maintained. They are in a relationship in which the professional is "the expert authority" with decision-making power and young people come to depend solely on the power resources of these professionals (Miley, O'Melia, & DuBois, 1995).

Even social work services for youth have been criticised for "not doing enough" to involve their participation in the overall service delivery process (Chung, 2002; Fan, 2002). Social work practitioners are still found to be unwilling to share power with young service users and to release sufficient information (to them) in order to involve them in monitoring service implementation (Wong, 2002). The following factors have been identified as having the inducing effect on social workers' hesitation and resistance to user participation: 1) young people do not want to be involved in user participation and they like to depend on workers; 2) it is not easy to keep control if young people are allowed to participate; 3) workers' workload and pressures will be increased if channels are open for young people's participation; 4) misunderstandings may easily happen as young people find it difficult to understand the administrators' consideration; and 5) young people lack the ability to participate.

Toward a Youth Empowerment Approach

Following the previous analysis of powerlessness among young people, it is clear that in order to counteract youth disempowerment, one should move away from a social control model to the adoption of a youth empowerment approach. Nessel (1988) pointed out that a youth empowerment approach should aim at enhancing youth's control of their lives and the systems that have impact on them. Chinman and Linney (1998) identified active participation, awareness of the surrounding world, and identification of strengths as key components of a youth empowerment process. They also suggested that under this empowerment approach, young people should be given the opportunity to participate in meaningful roles, learn new skills, and be recognised for their involvement. Cargo et al. (2003) defined youth empowerment as the process of transferring power to youth as responsibility for voicing, decision-making and action. The aim is to actualise youth potential through developing esteem, gaining confidence, building competencies and raising consciousness. To effectively apply empowerment to working with young people, one needs to pay attention to the following common features which provide significant elements of an eight-step youth empowerment approach.

Step 1—Empowerment Goals

Step 1 calls for an emphasis on counteracting young people's internal negative valuation and assisting them to develop on-going capacities, competencies, and rights to act on their own behalf—to achieve a greater measure of control over their lives and destiny. The ultimate goal of empowerment is to help young people perceive themselves as capable individuals who are willing and able to gain control of their lives and to become active participants to exert influence on policies, decisions, and processes which affect them (Kam, 1997). This approach should not be perceived as asking social workers to give or return power to young people. It is young people who are assisted by workers to seek power as well as to discover the considerable power within themselves (Saleebey, 1992). It is a process of a young person's internal transformation from a state of powerlessness to a state of self-efficacy, self-worth, and self-esteem. It should be a process through which young people feel confident and competent to act on oppressive social structures or institutions which are presently disempowering them.

Step 2—Recognise the Heterogeneity of Young People

To effectively empower young people we need to recognise that young people do not belong to a unified monolithic group (Foster et al., 1999). They are very heterogeneous rather than homogeneous (Wong, 1999). Different youth groups are facing different kinds of disempowerment although some of them enjoy high levels of commonality. If we consider youth as only one unified group, we lack a clear understanding of the unique and diverse range of issues relating to their disempowerment. As such, the problems of some minority youth groups may become invisible. The recognition of heterogeneity helps identify different and appropriate strategies to empower different disempowered youth groups. An appropriate youth empowerment approach requires one to recognise diversity but at the same time acknowledge and build on the substantial common ground that exists (Foster et al., 1999).

Step 3—De-Label Young People by Emphasising Their Strengths

As discussed previously, negative stereotypes are found to have significant impacts creating negative valuation and powerlessness among young people, and disrespecting their voices. Generally, adults deny young people's participation and are unwilling to share power with them. A youth empowerment approach should, therefore, focus their efforts on first de-labelling young people in society. The public's negative attitudes toward young people need to be challenged and the stigmatised labels imposed by the adult world have to be de-constructed. The best way to de-label is to adopt a strengths perspective (Saleebey, 1992). We need to shift the public's view at young people from a "fix the deficit" perspective to a strengths perspective (Chinman & Linney, 1998). According to Saleebey (1992), a strengths perspective conceives that all people have strengths and there is natural power within every person that can be released. The presence of this strength (for continued growth) means that people must be accorded the respect that this power deserves. From this perspective, youth service workers should develop a positive attitude toward young people, and recognise that young people also have a distinctly individual, innate capacity for growth and change, and still have a reservoir of resources and competencies to draw upon in their efforts to create change (Miley, O'Melia, & DuBois, 1995).

As such, young people should be viewed as assets and resources to our community, rather than social problems or community liabilities (Kim et al., 1998). We need to pay more attention to identifying and building upon existing youth strengths and potential, rather than focusing on their limitations and pathologies. As long as young people continue to be regarded as a negatively valued stigmatised group, there is less a likelihood of any positive change of the disempowering effects. Youth service workers should have a belief that young people are capable of making positive changes and existing strengths can be mobilised to build new resources (Miley, O'Melia, & DuBois, 1995). We need to help young people address the problems facing them as life challenges and opportunities. We need to encourage them to use a strengths perspective to look at themselves and help them understand that they are the best resources for promoting their own development.

Step 4—Focus on Asset-Based, Capacity-Building Development

Based on the above strengths perspective, a youth empowerment approach should also focus on asset-based and capacity-building development (Kretzmann & McKnight, 1993). This shifts the focus from the traditional needs-driven approach to a capacity-oriented one. Young people should no longer be perceived as those with special needs that can only be met by outsiders, or as deficient people who are incapable of taking charge of their own lives and future. The focus here should be on making an account of and discovering assets (see Chapter 9), capacities, and resources available in young people themselves. We should not start with what is absent or problematic, but start with what is present and what is going on within, what assets are available, and what individual capacities exist in young people. With this focus, a youth empowerment approach "views youth as community assets and resources with an increasing call for their participation in the processes of socioeconomic, public, and political affairs of the community than hitherto has been" (Kim et al., 1998, p. 6).

This approach helps young people identify and develop their on-going capacities and make use of their existing assets to gain control over their lives and influence the social conditions that affect them. By focusing on an asset-based and capacity-building development, young people can be induced with confidence, hope, and motivation for change. Young people who feel helpless and powerless begin to think that they have more resources and ability to think anew and act anew, and feel more competent to transform their problems and disempowered situations into an opportunity for rebirth and true renewal (Brueggemann, 2002; Saleebey, 2002).

Step 5—Become an Ally with Youth

In a youth empowerment approach, a worker needs to become an ally (Bishop, 2002) with young people. An ally means "being there" to face the numerous disempowered situations and to work with them, rather than to work for them in an empowerment process. To become an ally, a worker needs to be aware of the problem of power imbalance and the power-dependency relationship between workers and young people. A worker needs to avoid the trap of "knowing what is good" for youth. A worker also needs to be sensitive to the possible disempowering effects of professional practice due to the exercising of their professional power to control clients (Kam, 2002). As suggested by Cargo et al. (2003), "youth empowerment requires a shift in programming from a top-down to a partnering approach where professionals welcome youth and assume an active enabling role" (p. S76–S77). Yowell and Gordon (1996) also suggested a re-conceptualisation of professionalism among youth service providers by emphasising strong youth-professional relationships and moving young people "from dependence on institutional supports to dependence on their own intrinsic powers and capacity to access resources" (p. 20).

The working relationship between young people and workers should transform from an unbalanced power relationship to an egalitarian one, based on partnership, collaboration, and sharing of power. Workers should minimise their expert power and recognise that young people themselves are experts with regard to their own problems, capacities, and potential resources (Dodd & Gutierrez, 1990). Young people have to be treated as full partners and resources in the helping process, rather than as bearers of problems. We should assist them to experience a sense of personal power within the helping relationship. Helping young people become actively involved in identifying and defining their problems and needs is essential to placing them in a position of power and control in the helping relationship.

In daily encounters with workers, young people should be encouraged to express their opinions and ideas openly and to learn how to share power with their workers. An important aspect of this partnership is to discourage over-protection and over-reliance on workers and to avoid the replication of the powerless situations which young people experience in their everyday lives. Workers also need to try their best to avoid limiting the choices and alternatives for young service users. We need to recognise that choosing and making choices is an element of power (Rees, 1991). Providing youth with more choices in service provision and helping them exercise their right to choose, are both necessary and important. We need to assist them to deliberate on what might be possible and to look for possible alternatives to tackle their problems. Through these experiences, their ability to choose and decide for themselves can be enhanced. Thus, they can identify that there are areas in their lives over which they can exercise control.

Step 6—Anti-Oppressive Practice

A youth empowerment approach should also include anti-oppressive practice. Chiu (1999) called for our attention to the fact that youth empowerment work needs to raise young people's consciousness of anti-oppressive issues and concerns. According to Dominelli (2002), anti-oppressive practice aims at reducing the negative effects of social divisions and structural inequalities in people's lives. Dalrymple and Burke (1995) pointed out that anti-oppressive practice deals with power imbalances and works toward the promotion of change to redress the balance of power. An empowering approach directs our attention to helping marginal and vulnerable youth groups confront oppression and discrimination. Workers need to help vulnerable youth groups break their silence and make oppression and discrimination issues visible.

We should also help them understand how oppression comes about; how it occurs; and how the existing social, economic, and political structures interact to construct oppressive situations. A focal concern is to confront inequalities of power and hierarchies, to challenge oppressive legislation, and to break the cycle of oppression. It helps marginal youth groups value inclusiveness rather than separation, equality rather than hierarchy, and cooperation rather than competition (Bishop, 2002).

Step 7—Involve Youth in their Communities

Young people need to be encouraged and mobilised to become more involved in their communities and political participation. Research has demonstrated that community participation enhances young people's self-perception, social competence, sense of responsibility, and commitment to the overall community (Chinman & Linney, 1998). Delgado (1998) found that empowerment effects are evident when ethnic minority youth are involved in community asset assessment programmes. Workers need to spend more effort linking young service users on having more contact with their community, by organising them to provide community volunteer services, and becoming concerned with disadvantaged groups in their community.

Youth can also be organised to form "community concern groups" which can function as a vehicle to raise young people's awareness of and concerns with community problems and policy issues. Thus, it can help unite them together, identify community issues that they need to, express their views and voice their opinions as a collective, elucidate request, and take group actions. As a result, young people can strengthen their contacts within their community, obtain a better understanding about their living environment, identify their potential roles in the community, and make contributions to the well-being of their community.

Community participation should be regarded as an ongoing empowerment process which may produce the following: reduce youth's isolation from the community; change the public's negative image toward young people; enhance self confidence and self-esteem in order to express their views and act on social structures; enlarge youth exposure; bring youth voices to decision-making processes; and help young people learn the knowledge, skills, and attitude to take up a life-long and contributing future citizen role.

Youth should also be assisted in becoming involved in political participation. They need to be equipped with knowledge about the functions, roles, and operations of political parties and different existing political structures in their communities. Political forums can be organised regularly in order to encourage them to express their concerns about political affairs, and have elected councillors and politicians listen to their views. In addition to casting votes in elections to assert their political power, young people can also hold elected councillors more accountable for their actions. Thus, their views, requests, and demands need to be regularly channelled to elected councillors. Public meetings can be held to ask politicians to report on what they have done for their interests and allow them to indicate the extent to which they have kept the promises made during an election. By becoming involved in political participation as such, they can be empowered and feel that they have political voice and power to affect the political system. Political participation helps them learn to become politically significant and competent.

Step 8—Promote User Participation in Services for Youth

A culture of user participation or user involvement has to be promoted for a successful empowerment approach. It has been shown that an environment which encourages involvement/participation is useful in helping disempowered groups to be empowered, learn skills, and gain competence in asserting their influence (Gutierrez et al., 1998). Workers need to involve youth participation in planning processes, to obtain their feedback on service provision, to enable them to speak up for themselves, and to take an active role in assisting the delivery of services. It should be noted that there are two competing approaches to user participation: the consumerist versus the democratic or empowerment approach (Barnes & Walker, 1996; Beresford & Croft, 1993). The basic philosophy of the consumerism is to directly involve user participation in order to improve the efficiency, economy, and effectiveness of the service with an emphasis on confining involvement to information-seeking or consultation. Here, service users are perceived as consumers or customers. This approach is seen as service-centred or provider-led, and is primarily concerned with meeting the needs of services (Beresford & Harding, 1993). As stated by Croft and Beresford (1995), "power and control remain with services and their providers and purchasers. People can feed in their views and experience, but agencies still make the decisions" (p. 62).

Contrarily, a more democratic or empowerment approach is a user-orientated, needs-driven, and power sharing approach (Barnes & Walker, 1996). Its aim is to foster empowerment in the sense that users can speak directly for themselves and have a right to a direct say in community agencies and services leading to greater control over their lives (Croft & Beresford, 1990). Users are provided with a range of opportunities to define their own needs and the services they require. Payne (1995) noted that participation as a "citizen", is different from participation as a "consumer". The consumerist approach has been criticised as a token effort to involve users. It is sometimes also, regarded as "managed-user" participation (Braye & Preston-Shoot, 1995). In empowerment-oriented practice, user participation should adopt the democratic or empowerment approach rather than the consumerist approach, making the involvement as true user-managed participation (Braye & Preston-Shoot, 1995). Support and access are two important components in user involvement/participation (Beresford & Croft, 1993). One cannot expect young service users to initiate active participation automatically. There should be sufficient support, both material and personal, for facilitating and encouraging young people's involvement. There should also be adequate and suitable forms or channels for participation within community service organisations. Without adequate access, incentives and motivation to participation will be largely undermined.

Conclusion

This chapter examined the application of the concept of empowerment to working with young people. If one wants to find out the difference between youth empowerment and other empowerment forms, there is one area which requires our attention. This is the reluctance of making the actual process work. When discussion occurs about the application of empowerment approaches to other target groups, queries are rarely raised about the necessity or suitability of this application. Rather, more concerns are usually expressed about the difficulties in actual implementation. Unfortunately, this is the case in true youth empowerment models. Thus, there is likely to be more reluctance among service providers to apply a youth empowerment approach.

There are many queries, worries, or challenges regarding whether it is suitable or appropriate to empower young people. Concerns often raised include: young people may not be able to properly use power; young people easily get uncontrolled if power is in their hands; young people have already had power to do whatever they like to do; it is better to help young people learn what responsibility or obligation is rather than helping them obtain power. All of these reiterate the fact that we still do not trust young people and their abilities. We still hold fears or subscribe to the myth that their empowerment will result in irresponsible actions and uncontrollable social behaviours. To counteract such reluctance and make the youth empowerment work applicable, we need to examine our views toward young people and develop a stronger belief in their abilities and strengths. Only by genuinely believing in young people; trusting and respecting them; providing them with a welcome and empowering environment; and offering them opportunities for voicing, taking responsibilities, making decisions, and taking actions can youth empowerment be practised authentically and effectively.

References

Barnes, M., & Walker, A. (1996). Consumerism versus empowerment: A principled approach to the involvement of older service users. *Policy and Politics, 24*(4), 375–93.

Barry, M. (1998). Social exclusion and social work: An introduction. In M. Barry & C. Hallet (Eds.), *Social exclusion and social work.* Dorset: Russell House Publishing Limited.

Beresford, P., & Croft, S. (1993). *Citizen involvement: A practical guide for change.* London: Macmillan.

Beresford, P., & Harding, T. (1993). *A challenge to change: Practical experiences of building user-led service.* London: National Institute for Social Work.

Bishop, A. (2002). *Becoming an ally: Breaking the cycle of oppression in people* (2nd ed.). London & New York: Zed Books.

Braye, S., & Preston-Shoot, M. (1995). *Empowering practice in social care.* Buckingham: Open University Press.

Browne, C. V. (1995). Empowerment in social work practice with older women. *Social Work, 40*(3), 358–363.

Brueggemann, W. G. (2002). *The practice of macro social work* (2nd ed.). Belmont, CA: Brooks/Cole.

Cargo, M., Grams, G. D., Ottoson, J. M., Ward, P., & Green, L. W. (2003). Empowerment as fostering positive youth development and citizenship. *American Journal of Health Behaviour, 27,* S66–S79.

Chinman, M. J., & Linney, J. A. (1998). Toward a model of adolescent empowerment: Theoretical and empirical evidence. *The Journal of Primary Prevention, 18*(4), 393–413.

Chiu, W. S. (1999). Youth work and empowerment: Concept exploration. In W. S. Chiu & C. W. Wong (Eds.), *Youth work and empowerment* (pp. 3–24). Hong Kong: Hong Kong Policy Viewers. (in Chinese)

Chung, K. W. (2002). Youth services in Hong Kong from an empowerment perspective. In Chinese YMCA of Hong Kong (Ed.), *Youth empowerment in Hong Kong: Collection of theories and cases* (pp. 65–70). Hong Kong: Chinese YMCA of Hong Kong. (in Chinese)

Cox, E. O., & Parsons, R. J. (1994). *Empowerment-oriented social work practice with the elderly.* California: Brooks/Cole.

Croft, S., & Beresford, P. (1990). *From paternalism to participation.* London: Open Service Project.

Croft, S., & Beresford, P. (1995). Whose empowerment? Equalising the competing discourses in community care. In R. Jack (Ed.), *Empowerment in community care.* London: Chapman and Hall.

Dalrymple, J., & Burke, B (1995). *Anti-oppressive practice: Social care and the law.* Buckingham: Open University Press.

Delgado, M. (1998). Community asset assessments by Latino youths. In P. L. Ewalt, E. M. Freeman, & D. L. Poole (Eds.), *Community building: Renewal, well-being and shared responsibility* (pp. 202–212). Washington, DC: NASW.

Dodd, P., & Gutierrez, L. (1990). Preparing students for the future: A power perspective on community practice. *Administration in Social Work, 14*(2), 63–78.

Dominelli, L. (2002). Anti-oppressive practice in context. In R. Adams, L. Dominelli, & M. Payne (Eds.), *Social work: Themes, issues and critical debates* (2nd ed.) (pp. 3–19). New York: Palgrave.

Fan, Y. C. (2002). Practice of youth empowerment in children and youth centres. In Chinese YMCA of Hong Kong (Ed.), *Youth empowerment in Hong Kong: Collection of theories and cases* (pp. 105–116). Hong Kong: Chinese YMCA of Hong Kong. (in Chinese)

Foster, J., Naidoo, K., & Akuhata-Brown, M. (1999). Youth empowerment and civil society. In COVICUS (Eds.), *Civil society at the Millennium* (pp. 69–83). Connecticut, USA: Kumarian Press, Inc.

Gutierrez, L., Parsons, R., & Cox, E.O. (1998). *Empowerment in social work practice: A source book.* Pacific Grove: Brooks/Cole.

Holdsworth, L. (1991). *Empowerment social work with physically disabled people.* Norwich: Social Work Monographs.

Hong Kong Government (1991). *Social welfare into the 1990s and beyond (White Paper).* Hong Kong: Government Printer.

Kam, P. K. (1997). Towards empowerment and advocacy: Practice and policy in social services for old people in Hong Kong. *Asia Pacific Journal of Social Work, 7*(2), 46–62.

Kam, P. K. (2002). From disempowering to empowering: Changing the practice of social service professionals with older people. *Hallym International Journal of Aging, 4*(2), 161–183.

Kim, S., Crutchfield, C., Williams, C., & Helper, N. (1998). Toward a new paradigm in substance abuse and other problem-behaviour prevention for youth: Youth development and empowerment approach. *Journal of Drug Education, 28*(1), 1–17.

Kretzmann, J. P., & McKnight, J. L. (1993). *Building communities from the inside out: A path towards finding and mobilising a community's assets.* Evanston, IL: Institute for Policy Research.

Lee, F. F. L (1999). Empowerment model in youth work. *Asia Pacific Journal of Social Work, 9*(2), 96–103.

Lee, H. W. (2002). Youth empowerment: Limited and unlimited. In Chinese YMCA of Hong Kong (Ed.), *Youth empowerment in Hong Kong: Collection of theories and cases* (pp. 81–88). Hong Kong: Chinese YMCA of Hong Kong. (in Chinese)

Lee, J. A. B. (1991). Empowerment through mutual aid groups: A practice grounded conceptual framework. *Groupwork, 4*(1), 5–21.

Lo, T. W. & Au, E. (2004). *Youth empowerment: International experiences.* Hong Kong: City University of Hong Kong.

Lord, J., & Hutchison, P. (1993). The process of empowerment: Implications for theory and practice. *Canadian Journal of Community Mental Health, 12*(1), 5–22.

Miley, K. K., O'Melia, M., & DuBois, B. L. (1995). *Generalist social work practice: An empowering approach.* Boston: Allyn and Bacon.

Nessel, L. (1988). A coalition approach to enhancing youth empowerment. *Social Policy, 19*(1), 25–27.

Payne, M. (1991). *Modern social work theory.* London: Macmillan.

Payne, M. (1995). *Social work and community care.* London: Macmillan.

Pierson, J. (2002). *Tackling social exclusion.* London: Routledge.

Pinderhuges, E. B. (1983). Empowerment for our clients and for ourselves. *Social Casework, 64*(6), 331–338.

Rees, S. (1991). *Achieving power: Practice and policy in social welfare.* North Sydney: Allen and Unwin.

Ryan, W. (1971). *Blaming the victim.* New York: Vintage.

Saleebey, D. (1992). *The strength perspective in social work practice.* New York: The Haworth Press.

Saleebey, D. (2002). Community development, neighbourhood empowerment, and individual resilience. In D. Saleebey (Ed.), *The strengths perspective in social work practice* (3rd ed.). Boston: Allyn and Bacon.

Seligman, M. E. P. (1972). Learned Helplessness. *Annual Review of Medicine, 23*, 407–412.

Solomon, B. (1976). *Black empowerment: Social work in oppressed communities*. New York: Columbia University Press.

Staples, L. H. (1990). Powerful ideas about empowerment. *Administration in Social Work, 14*(2), 29–42.

Whitmore, E. (1988). *Empowerment and the process of inquiry.* A paper presented at the Annual Meeting of the Canadian Association of Schools of Social Work, Windsor, ON, Canada.

Wong, C. W. (1999). The political dimension of youth empowerment. In W. S. Chiu & C. W. Wong (Eds.), *Youth work and empowerment* (pp. 119–134). Hong Kong: Hong Kong Policy Viewers. (in Chinese)

Wong, C. W. (2002). How to implement youth empowerment work at the agency level. In Chinese YMCA of Hong Kong (Ed.), *Youth empowerment in Hong Kong: Collection of theories and cases* (pp. 43–52). Hong Kong: Chinese YMCA of Hong Kong. (in Chinese)

Yowell, C. M., & Gordon, E. W. (1996). Youth empowerment and human service institutions. *The Journal of Negro Education, 65*(1), 19–29.

part two

Youth Empowerment and Volunteerism:
Selected Examples in Countries around the World

This part presents six chapters from six countries in the world spanning the East and West hemispheres. Here, examples make theories, models, and concepts come alive. They clearly exemplify that youth who volunteer in timely and altruistic ways not only assist those with needs which vary from traumatic to in-home care, but also indicate the impact that their volunteering effort has made in the lives of individuals who are usually vulnerable. The altruism of volunteering rings true in each chapter. Despite the very different cultures in which these creative initiatives take place, the message is clear, that giving is better than taking in the big picture of life. These examples are about the gifts of time, compassion, understanding, and often times, just being there for other individuals who are often estranged or marginalised. Another unique feature of these chapters as a set is that the youth of the world hold the keys to our future. Indeed, they are the shapers of a caring and compassionate future and with their initiatives, they demonstrate that an individual can make a difference in the lives of others if they simply care.

In Search of Youth Empowerment in England

6

Malcolm PAYNE

Introduction

It is clear from any examination of the literature on empowerment that its meaning is to say the least, contested. Baistow (1994) suggested that it has both regulatory and liberatory potential, reflecting both how power itself is conceptualised, and the social, professional, or governmental context in which it is applied. Others have pointed to the potential for even well-intentioned "participatory" intervention to have disempowering effects (see for example Gilbert, 1995). Its potential to be used as a "conceptual deodorant" (Ward, 1998) to mask social divisions, or to blame those felt not to be "in control of their lives" (Baistow, 1994) further underlines both the complexity and difficulty associated with the term and its use.

The most authoritative recent statement of the principles of youth work in England is as follows:

- Young people choose to be involved, not the least because they want to relax, meet friends, and have fun.

- The work starts where young people are—with their view of the world and their interests.

- It seeks to go beyond where young people start, in particular by encouraging them to be critical and creative in their responses to their experiences and the world around them, and supporting their exploration of new ideas, interests, and creative ability.

- It takes place because young people are young people, not because they have been labelled or categorised as deviant.

- It recognises, respects, and is actively responsive to the wider network of peers, communities, and cultures which are important to young people.

- Through these networks, it seeks to help young people achieve stronger relationships and collective identities—for example, as black people, women, men, disabled people, gay men, or lesbians—and through the promotion of inclusivity, particularly for minority ethnic communities.

- It is concerned with how young people feel and not just with what they know and can do.
- It is concerned with facilitating and empowering the voice of young people.
- It is concerned with ensuring that young people can influence the environment within which they live.
- It respects and values differences by supporting and strengthening young people's belief in themselves and their capacity to grow and change.
- It works with other agencies which contribute to young people's social and personal development, and
- It complements and supports school and college-based education by encouraging and providing other opportunities for young people to achieve and fulfil their potential. (Department for Education and Skills, 2002)[1]

Although they have not been the subject of widespread debate, it is likely that many of these principles would command general support amongst professional workers. It would, of course, be naive to expect anything other than broad agreement. They should be seen perhaps, rather like a treaty or constitution: sufficiently general and pluralist to enable different points of view to sign up to them. Differences in opinion or approach would be expected to emerge in their implementation.

Principles and Values

Underlying these statements are a number of connected principles which warrant being drawn out if one is to examine their capacity to promote young people's empowerment (Lo & Au, 2004). These are: a) a belief in the intrinsic value of education and learning; b) a belief in human agency; c) commitment to equality and social justice; d) valuing the place and voice of young people in a democratic society; and e) a belief in the voluntary participation of young people.

Youth Work as an Educative Activity

In the United Kingdom, youth work's adherence to being an essentially educative activity remains paramount, at least in its own professional literature. Informal education, which is the method through which youth work is pursued, is not intended simply to be instrumental (i.e. a means to an end), but an assertion of learning in its own right, as a "fully human" attribute: "being and becoming are not only what living is about, but also the chief object of learning" (Kidd, 1978, in Smith, 1994, p. 33).

As Smith (1994) observed, educators "make a commitment; have a vision of how relationships can be and what might make for human flourishing; and some feeling of liking for those they work with" (p. 34). It is clear from this that the practice of youth work is not just a cognitive or intellectual pursuit. It engages the worker in the affective domain—both in terms of the emotional commitment that s/he brings to it, and in the pursuit of the activity of doing the work. What do I want for these young people? And why?—are questions which cannot be answered without recourse to beliefs and values that I hold to be important. And in doing the work, I bring those values to bear in the ways in which I relate to young people: relating itself has an essentially emotional dimension. In pursuing young people's growth—their personal and social development—youth work attends to the affective domain of their lives.

Alongside a fundamental belief in education as a human activity, Young (1999) asserts other values for youth work's relationship with young people. It is, she suggests, based upon honesty, trust, respect, and reciprocity, and:

> *enables and supports young people to ask and answer the central questions of self—"what sort of person am I?", "what kind of relationships do I want to have with myself and others?", and "what kind of society do I want to live in?" (Young, p. 81)*

Informal education is a dialogical activity which involves a youth worker and young person in exploration of:

relationships with friends, families, teachers, bosses
... and the way in which people place themselves with
respect to wider collectivities. What sense do people make
of their living in a particular neighbourhood; of being
members of a particular (social) class or culture; of being
male or female; of being white, African, Punjabi or Irish,
and so on? What is their attitude and behaviour towards
people they see as different from themselves? (Smith,
1994, p. 35)

It is a way to engage young people in "sense making" as a "process of continuous self discovery and re-creation" (Young, 1999, p. 1). The educative process here then is, for the young person, about discovering "me" and "me-in-the-world." Not just "who am I?" but, to do so by asking "what is my world like?" and "how do I, and should I, act within it?"

Human Agency

Underlying a belief in education lays a commitment, not always clearly stated, in young people's capacity for choice and action, in human agency.

We seek to: "engage with young people in the deliberate and purposeful process of experience, reflection, and learning through which they gain the motivation and capacity to:

- examine their values;
- deliberate over the principles of their own moral judgements; and,
- develop the skills and dispositions to make informed decisions and choices that *can be sustained through committed action."*

(Young, 1999, p. 5)

Human agency implies not just that the young people with whom we work are agents themselves, but that others are also agents who are acting upon them. And at another level, that many other things will also be influencing them including: others' beliefs, experiences, norms, ideologies, demands, and expectations. The focus here is on young people's reciprocal relationship with their world: the ways it acts upon them and they upon it, how their world shapes them, and how they interact with and can shape that world.

This is not intended to imply some naive or absolute freedom of choice. Rather, it is to point to the potential for young people to understand themselves as "selves in interaction" as "connected beings" (Smith, 1994, p. 38). They do and can make choices and decisions, and which are increasingly understood as complex, reflexive events: a world in which they are neither free agents, nor simply victims of others' actions.

Equality and Social Justice

All helping professions, whether in the United Kingdom or elsewhere, would wish to assert that a belief in the equality of people, a commitment to human rights, and the pursuit of social justice inform the principles on which they work. As well as a belief in learning for its own sake, the words used to describe that belief also begin to point toward its intended outcomes: "human flourishing" suggests the pursuit of common good; "honesty," "trust," and "respect" assert a strong belief in fundamental human values as the basis of a just society.

Over the past 30 or more years in the United Kingdom, a developing professional consensus about the structural causes of inequality and injustice has served to define youth works' position. This has increasingly focused upon the power relations and the mechanisms (i.e. prejudice, stereotyping, discrimination, etc.) which bring about such inequalities, and which serve to limit human flourishing (cf. Banks, 1999). Those arising from gender, poverty and social class, race and ethnicity, and the ways in which these intersect, have all been central to professional discourse and practice. Religion, disability, and sexual identity have also, more recently perhaps, informed practice. Each of these dimensions has been the subject of a search for "informed and committed action" (praxis) intended to bring about collective human well-being.

In the past ten years, however, the twin concepts of social exclusion and inclusion have come to dominate political and social policy discourse, and have increasingly affected the ways in which youth work has come to be deployed by the state. This will be discussed later in this chapter.

Young People's Voice

Although young people are the subject of increasing public policy, and attract widespread media attention, their own authentic voices are rarely heard. This applies not just to young people as a whole who, until they are 18, are not considered to be adults, but to different groups of young people too. So, it is still common to find that in the key institutional arenas in which their interests are discussed, their own wishes, opinions, or aspirations are usually absent (see Chapter 5).

When young people are consulted at all, there is a tendency for this to happen "on adult terms," and in ways which may alienate or intimidate them. Frequently, adult solutions fail to take account of their perspectives, and are impoverished or unjust as a result.

Youth work's belief in enabling young people's voices to be heard has long been a central tenet of practice: young people as "creators not consumers" (Smith, 1987). This has led to: working with groups of young people to support them to express their views; bringing them together so that a sense of collective identity can be developed; helping them gain the skills and confidence to express themselves; acting as advocates on behalf of young people; and developing the means for their participation in decision-making.

Voluntary Participation

The consent of young people, their choice as to whether to be involved in youth work, is held by youth workers as central to their practice. This is not intended to imply a "take it or leave it" attitude, for workers may spend many weeks gaining young people's consent. But, it does imply that the relationship between youth worker and young person is one which is freely chosen, not one which comes about as a result of coercion or intimidation. Whilst recognising that such a choice may arise from some external force (e.g. the young person may be in trouble with the police), a youth worker will nonetheless offer an opportunity for the young person to explore and decide for themselves whether, how much, and on what terms, they will be involved. This is a reciprocal activity as it does not simply give the young person freedom to choose, but allows them to negotiate and, ultimately, to say "No".

A General Principle of Empowerment

These five broad principles are the cornerstones of much of contemporary UK youth work practice. One might suggest that, on the basis of these, a general principle of empowerment can be sketched out as:

Empowerment of young people arises when:

- we believe in and respect their value as human beings who can, individually and collectively, make choices and act upon them. We offer them, on their terms and in ways they feel comfortable, opportunities for learning, growth, and development.

- we encourage them to reflect upon their experiences and beliefs, find their own authentic voice, and hear the voices of others, and

- we join them in the pursuit of a fairer, more just and more democratic society.

Whether and how such broad principles are borne out in the practice of youth work in England, and bring benefits to young people, are the questions addressed in the remainder of this chapter.

Ambiguity and the Social Policy Context

With a century or more of history and different traditions in religious, philanthropic, charitable, and social-political work with young people in the United Kingdom, one might expect to find that the practice of youth work, now increasingly sponsored and controlled by the state, carries with its deep ambiguities, not to say contradictions. It is a history of many narratives and motives which, in its formative periods reflects how its early pioneers saw the world during the late 18th and early 19th centuries as the United Kingdom experienced rapid industrialisation and urbanisation.

Was it a world which needed a response which, based on Christian values, could "turn the city's outcast population into respectable, independent citizens through an invigoration of family life?" (Prochaska, 1988, p. 49, quoted in Jeffs & Smith, 2002). Or, one in which "the ideas of service, comradeship, and esprit de corps should be in the forefront" of a movement to promote a more socialist world, as in the Federation of Miners' Boys' Clubs? (quoted in Russell & Russell, 1932, p. 16, in Jeffs & Smith, 2002). Or a little later perhaps, a world which required "clubs and projects fostering democracy and a sense of community," as in the approach adopted by those who promoted community centres, community schools, and settlements? (Gordon & White, 1979, in Jeffs & Smith, 2002).

Any examination of youth work's capacity for empowerment will find such ambiguities played out in current day practice. In the English context, two contemporary themes are of particular relevance to this discussion. First, an ideological tension between the state and what might broadly be called the helping professions; and second, closely connected, deep divisions about the nature of social justice and the role of social welfare professionals. Both of these can be seen in the accommodations which are reached in the policy and practice arena of social work, youth work, and similar state-sponsored welfare.

Certainly, in the second half of the 20th century in Europe, social work became acutely aware of the danger of "falling prey to, or actively putting itself at the disposal of, ideological misuses" (Lorenz, 1994, p. 59). Whilst there is no suggestion that the current struggle in the United Kingdom is of the same order, for it is not, this nonetheless serves to illustrate that tension. The helping professions cannot avoid the fact that their task is a political one: at one and the same time, to be the servant of the state which sponsors them; and to assert a professional independence from it. However, much we strive for a body of "scientifically" derived professional skills and knowledge, we will always operate within the particular social conditions, social policies, and laws which prevail. The state will wish to marshal the resources which the helping professions represent in order to further its current project. And for their part, the helping professions will seek an accommodation with the state.

It is not simply the state's influence that requires critical examination. The pursuit of social justice confronts the helping professions with other ideological forces which serve to reinforce and structure injustice: e.g. in relation to the distribution of wealth; in the position of women; toward minority ethnic communities and other vulnerable groups. This gives rise to a concern to combat disadvantage, counter prejudice and discrimination, and uphold human rights. To do so, we are forced to subject prevailing values and ideologies (including our own) to continuing critical examination.

Contemporary narratives, unlike those which we can examine with the benefit of hindsight, are not so easily assessed. Doubly so if we take seriously post-modern accounts of a world in which competing knowledge domains are symbolised by ideas and language which reinforce power relations. Which version should we believe of young people's criminal activity, for example? Is it primarily a failure of the family to properly educate and control its (mostly male) children (Murray, 1990)? Or an inevitable consequence of the fragmented, uncertain "risk society" in which some, perhaps many, young people will make wrong choices as "rootless new cosmopolitans" (Beck, 1999). Or, the understandable behaviour of a new (under)class of young people whose status and wealth has been removed by economic uncertainty and society's lack of care and support (Williamson, 1997)?

How we construct our version of young people's social conditions will not only determine our analysis of need and the nature of "the problem," but also our intended solution. For youth workers, a new version of the old agency structure question emerges: a search for practice which can reinforce agency, the capacity of young people individually and collectively to make their own (different) choices, be who they wish to be, find their own paths; and at the same time, to attempt to recognise and direct our [and their] attention to the economic, cultural, social, and political conditions (structures) which serve, positively or negatively, to influence, limit, or determine their choices and decisions.

The Prevalence of the Social Exclusion Discourse

The so-called "third way" of the New Labour government, reflecting Giddens's sociological perspectives (Giddens, 1998), has given rise to a raft of reform initiatives aimed at young people (and more widely), which have, at times, been likened to a moral crusade (Jordan, 2000). The forces which gave rise to impetus for reform in UK youth policy are well documented. Williamson (1993), for example, has suggested that policy through the 80s and early 90s, which was set against a background of recession and unemployment, had:

> *polarised choice and opportunity for the young —*
> *while the "social condition" of many young people has*
> *remained relatively positive for the past two decades, a*
> *significant minority has been steadily marginalised and*
> *increasingly disadvantaged. (p. 33)*

He further argued that youth policy had impinged most detrimentally on young people who are black, female, poorly qualified, with disabilities, from "broken homes" and with criminal careers (1993, p. 35) leading to young people's increasing demoralisation and alienation and, in turn, to their disaffection from "conventional opportunities to participate in a democratic society." For those who found themselves at the margins of education, training and employment opportunities, criminality may even seem an "attractive option;" these young people had developed a "nothing to lose" mentality. There was, he said, "a growing population of homeless and rootless young people whose stake in the social order is precarious." (1993, p. 44).

The findings of the Non-aligned Working Group (1997) resonated with Williamson's view. It identified the risks associated with contemporary youth. Among them were: unstable and incomplete family structures; reduced parental and neighbourly care and supervision; earlier physical maturity; extended dependency; more choices but less opportunity and job security. This had led to a "heightened crisis of identity, of meaning and purpose" for young people, whose "risky reactions" it characterised as numbing (use of drugs, alcohol); party excess (hedonistic highs); over-work (workaholism and competitive achievement as routes to self-value); relational cynicism (distrust of attachments); withdrawal (fantasy video, lonely privacy); or unplug (suicide or drop out) (Non-aligned Working Group, 1997, p. 15).

The Group's analysis saw contributory factors present across much of UK youth policy in the 80s and 90s. Recognising that young people are not a homogeneous group, however, the report concluded that:

> *There is some evidence of widening gaps between the successful and unsuccessful—in education, qualifications, jobs, health and recorded crime—evident in some ethnic minority groups and in specific localities. Some have become disconnected from the democratic process, neither voting nor registering to do so. Many . . . feel*

surplus to requirements, yet most will all too soon parent the next generation. A decent society cannot function in the modern era by even unintended processes which (lead to) exclusion, and the creation of a permanent or semi-permanent "underclass" early in life. (1997, p. 29)

The costs of exclusion, in social and economic terms then, were seen to be immense—and the divisions this reflects, to have social, cultural, and moral consequences.

Reforms since 1997

The economic conditions which had given rise to large scale youth unemployment in the 1980s had changed significantly and for the better by the time of the New Labour government's election in 1997. But the dominance of social exclusion in the political discourse remained. Thus, the project, Bridging the Gap (Social Exclusion Unit, 1999), focused its attention on the 9% (161,000) young people between 16 and 18 who were found to be outside of education, work, or training at any one time, and the "obstacles" they were seen to face.

According to Social Exclusion Unit (1999, p. 8),

"At worst, these years involve no education or training, but some combination of short term, poor quality jobs with no training, a lack of any purposeful activity and, all too often, a descent into the hardest end of the social exclusion spectrum—a variety of relationship, family and health problems, including homelessness, persistent offending or drug use problem."

Those most at risk (of non-participation in education, employment or training, and by implication, of social exclusion) face "multiple disadvantages" associated with one or more factors such as their parents' poverty or unemployment; their minority ethnic status; or circumstances such as having been in care, having a disability, mental illness, drug or alcohol use, or criminal activity.

In this analysis, social exclusion was seen to be a result of the failure of education and training, and associated support systems, to overcome social disadvantage. The central aim of the new support service was to follow being to work with all young people "but giving priority to those at most risk of underachievement and disaffection, to support them between the ages of 13 and 19 through education and the transition to adulthood" (SEU, 1999, p. 11). Thus, the government's aim, in the increasingly globalised, flexible, and knowledge-based economy of the imminent 21st century, was to "enable everyone to stay in learning . . . until they are at least 18" (SEU, 1999, p. 51).

Reforms since 1997, as Davies has recorded (Davies, 1999, Chapter 9) have been focused on a number of fronts:

- education in schools, where successive measures have been introduced to raise standards, and to overcome longstanding problems such as disaffection, truancy, and the exclusion of students;
- a range of reforms of post-school education;
- the introduction of the New Deal programme for young people not in work, promising "high quality" job preparation, training, and work opportunities;
- co-ordinated programmes for young offenders, leading to the introduction of the 1998 Crime and Disorder Act;
- investment in youth volunteering initiatives;
- a strategy for tackling drug misuse amongst young people, emphasising information, education, and support;
- initiatives to address a number of other social concerns: teenage pregnancies, homelessness, mental ill-health, and to improve the experience of young people in the care of the state.

Reform has continued at a brisk pace since. While the focus here is not simply on those who are excluded, social inclusion as the leitmotiv of youth policy is inescapable, and has served as a main thrust of continuing initiatives. It has also given rise to a new breed of welfare professional modelled on the idea of the mentor, someone who can support and guide young people, and particularly those seen to be "at risk" of exclusion. At the same time, measures have been put in place to "track" all young people who may be in danger of escaping, or who have fallen through the net of welfare support, thus intending to ensure that arrangements for their co-ordinated care and support are in place in order to keep them in education or training until they are 18. This is the core of the new Connexions Service for young people in England.

It would be unfair to focus attention only upon the government's intentions for individual young people's welfare. A balanced picture also needs to acknowledge the efforts being made to regenerate the poorest communities, and in parallel, to direct albeit on a relatively small scale, income support to poor people. There is then, recognition that exclusion is directly related to poverty: at least a nod toward redistribution.

At the same time, however, and increasingly focused in areas of the highest poverty, welfare professionals are expected to intervene in people's lives: to support them to change their attitudes and behaviours so that they can "benefit" from the opportunities that the modern economy and welfare state has to offer. Indeed, Jordan (2000) argued, those benefits are often conditional upon compliance with the "agreements" struck with this new breed of what he calls "enforcement counsellors" in whom the state vests authority. There is a danger of overstatement here: we must be careful not to harp back to some mythical golden age of client autonomy. But toughness and pressure to comply are certainly part of the armoury of the new welfare professional and the programmes they inhabit.

It is against this background that youth workers in England now operate. Unlike social workers, probation officers, youth justice workers and teachers, they are without any statutory powers or responsibilities. Traditionally, they and the organisations for whom they work, are free to make contact with young people, by offering clubs, projects, activities, friendship, support, information, etc. on the basis that young people themselves are free to take them up, reject, or negotiate. This has not meant that youth work has been unconcerned with disadvantage or under-privilege. Much of the history of its work is with young people in deprived areas, and over the past 20 or more years, with groups who occupy a marginalised position in society. Our recent research underlines that this approach has given youth workers a particular position in many young people's lives: "He's more like a friend really," or "They're not like other adults: they don't shout at you and tell you what to do" are typical of the ways young people describe youth workers with whom they are in contact.

An Offer Youth Work Could Not Refuse?

That position in young people's lives has meant that it has been able to contact, make and maintain relationships with young people whom other services often label as the "hard to reach." This has not gone unnoticed by the state. Nor by youth services themselves. After 30 or more years of declining resources for youth work, and being seen as a discretionary and largely peripheral activity, from 1997 the youth service was in Davies's words "made an offer it could not refuse" (Davies, 1999). In the theatre of youth policy, where previously youth workers had only a walk-on part, now they were being offered a chance to speak for the first time. But of course, where before there were no words, now someone else had written their lines. The script, in the words of Charles Clarke, Secretary of State for Education and Skills, was: "we expect reform in the way the service is developed, delivered and managed" (DfES, 2002). The speaking role on offer was to act as "the key partners in the Connexions Service . . . in contributing to cross-cutting preventive strategies including identification, referral, and tracking of young people."

The intention is that all young people who are "at risk" should be known by the key education and welfare agencies so that appropriate intervention can be targeted to them. Once known, they should be referred to the agency best placed to deal with their problems or risks. And because of the complexities of their lives (and the attendant risk that they will "disappear"), ongoing contact should be maintained (tracking) so that intervention can continue.

Is this a benign safety net, or something more sinister? Its depiction by Jordan as "tough love" may be nearer to the truth: a recognition that the "law of the jungle" had resulted from previous free-market approaches.

> *There was simply no way to get poor people off benefits and back into the mainstream economy, or to live within the rules of mainstream society, so long as the cash-in-hand and petty criminal sectors prospered. (Jordan, 2000, p. 32)*

Where Jordan departs from Murray is that he sees this to be a consequence of a lack of financial security and support, instead of a result of such support being too easily available in the form of benefits. Nonetheless, there is some agreement that tough measures would be required, and that a proportion of young people need help and support in their development, as some will be "at risk."

But a problem for youth welfare agencies is that, even if they are able to contact excluded young people, this does not, on its own, lead to change. Young people may be supported or coerced to comply, to take part in education or training, even to get a job; their drug use or criminal behaviour may be challenged, but this does not lead to change unless they choose. Compliance is not enough: for those young people whose alienation, and often, sense of failure, has become deeply ingrained, thus, re-building their confidence and trust is a first and critical step to any progress. Wanting a change implies young people seeing the benefits to them, and feeling that they can change. Often however, welfare agencies lack the tools and resources, and the relationships with young people.

Case Study 1 (below) illustrates how a local youth project has worked with such a group of young people.

Case Study 1

The project which is the subject of this case forms part of provision in a local youth centre on a housing estate in a north midlands city. Its origins lie in the attempt by the centre's youth worker to respond to the needs of local school age young people who she found "out and about" on the streets and around the supermarket during the school day. This was a very needy group of young people, all excluded from school, and for whom formal education provision had not worked. She offered them a once a week drop-in session where they could come and cook food for themselves. A dozen or more young people began to attend, got involved in the cooking and, subsequently, wider activities available at the centre and beyond.

The success of the project in attracting and holding onto a group of young people who had either been excluded from school, or who had excluded themselves, led to recognition of its value by the local authority support service for young people with special education needs. Funding was provided to expand the project to five mornings a week. In return, the service refers to it young people aged 11 to 16 for whom it has responsibility. Young people from across the city also began to hear about the project from their friends, and began to attend. On some days as many as 35 young people are present although it formally caters for only eleven.

The project is staffed by a full-time youth worker and a part-time worker. They have drawn their own friends in as volunteers. All are local to the area. In addition, as the project gained recognition, teachers have been appointed to work alongside the youth workers.

A subtle negotiation between different agencies with apparently different agendas[2] is being played out here. The history of the project is telling, and will have had a strong influence on the approach the project takes. First, its origins lie in the initiative of a youth worker who drew local young people into something new and as yet unformed. It was their choice to be involved. Perhaps just as critical to begin with was that this was small-scale and informal: not threatening to the young people; not "smelling of school"; not coercion. From the first minute, they could feel in control, not in the sense of having absolute power to do whatever they liked, but were free to leave, and able to influence what went on. Project workers talk of building trust and young people's involvement over time. The project's practice model is described as:

> . . . *we recognise that when a young person first joins the project, education is probably the last thing on their mind and that attending the project is entirely voluntary. We use an empowering and holistic approach that allows young people to engage with the project and education at their own pace and at a level they feel comfortable with. (Youth Worker)*

The local dimension was also a feature of this project. There is a long history suggesting the importance of locality as a practice principle in youth work (see Smith, 1994). Here, staff and volunteers were drawn from the local population, and the project was located in the neighbourhood that young people knew. Once established, young people were drawn from a wider area, but into something already known and located by their peers. More important perhaps, was locality in the sense of "giving voice to," or validating locally derived meaning and shared experiences. Young people, and subsequently, their parents and carers, became part of a network of social support. This was not a project which was being imposed upon them, but one which they were involved in devising. And as each new step was negotiated (e.g. bringing tutors in to work with the young people), these could be accommodated. One youth worker said: "We talk and discuss. Everything is discussed. There's a lot of responsibility on the young people. If there's a fight it's resolved before we leave the building. Not tomorrow, but sorted now." Another said that the project: ". . . does not fit young people into the system but helps fit the system to them." *Everything is discussed* are the key words.

At the time of our research visit, the project was about to change. It was to become a formal part of education provision for young people excluded from school. Will that sense of working together, of negotiating the way ahead, be retained? Can formal education provision, which works with a very different ethos, accommodate the project's way of working? Youth workers in the project were nervous about the future.

To begin with, no doubt, the project will negotiate a way forward on the basis of its own ethos. But experience elsewhere suggests that steady (and perhaps stealthy) pressure will build: "at their own pace" will become, over time, "at our pace." Young people who do not want to be there will be referred; the "entirely voluntary" principle may be eroded. The danger is that the youth work will be lost, leaving only the youth workers, now unable to approach the work in the "way that young people feel comfortable with." That is the danger facing the project. If it is to avoid this it will need to assert the essential value of what it does—and how it does it.

Youth Work in Partnership

There have been examples during our research of youth work successfully negotiating and collaborating with other services. Because of policy pressure to reduce social exclusion, and the recognition that youth workers are able to reach young people where other services fail, they are increasingly asked to work in new ways or with new partners. Case Study 2 began as an experimental piece of work in a city hospital, at the request of hospital staff.[3]

This is an example of health services and youth work objectives combining well. A key issue for the hospital is the young person's

Case Study 2

Research undertaken in a city hospital showed that many young people arrived at Accident and Emergency with e.g. symptoms of self-harm or overdose but, after the admissions procedure, did not wait to be treated. This was seen as a "cry for help" which was going unheard. Feedback from young people was that they were being treated as "cases" rather than as individuals. The report argued for a young person's advocate to support and empower them with information and support during clinical encounters so that they were able to take responsibility for their health. Discussion led to the recognition that the hospital was too heavily focussed on medical intervention, failing to take account of the other issues in young people's lives: their home situation, housing, emotional stability—and therefore, their ability or readiness to engage with medical professionals.

Four youth workers now form the Hospital Youth Work Team and after initial cynicism about what was an untried approach, it is now an integral part of the hospital's service to young people. All young patients aged 11 upwards are contacted by youth workers. They offer support, information and activities, including taking young people out for a break, to the shops, or for a game of pool. Frequently they are involved intensively with young people who are distressed and fearful. Alongside such casework support, a central concern is to be advocates on behalf of young people, to "de-mystify" medical language so that they can understand and be more actively involved in their own health care. The team runs training sessions with medical staff about communicating with young people, young people's issues and perspectives.

Youth workers have made a significant difference within the hospital. "I can see the transition of the young people. They are healthier; they are taking responsibility for themselves; they are empowered; they are able to vocalise their views; elements of contentment/satisfaction in their lives—you can see that in the way they engage with professionals".

health, and their compliance with treatment. At the same time, all public services are expected to be more responsive to the needs and wishes of those they provide for. What might the obstacles be to success? An adult medical perspective might well blame young people for their failure, or be impatient with their unwillingness. It is in these circumstances that the young people here talked about being "treated as children." Sibeon (1990) might refer to this as a pathological perspective. Youth workers tell us that they begin from a different place which rejects pre-judgement, gives validity to, and allows young people's distinctive voices to be heard. Critically, these are young people first, not patients or clients. Conversation with, liking for, and a concern for their well being are the youth worker's starting points. By attending to these first, their medical needs can be met.

For example, the way in which the young person leaves the hospital was not explored before. Their medical needs would be accounted for so that they knew when to come back for their next appointment, or what to do with their medication. But assumptions were made about the environment to which that young person was returning. There was no time for nurses to consider the holistic needs of the young person. Youth workers have apparently bridged that gap. They work with young people by helping them understand their medical conditions; consider and negotiate their treatment options; and manage their illnesses, both when they are in the hospital, and subsequently. All of these are seen in the context of their overall social and family circumstances.

There are echoes here of Solomon's (1976) model of empowerment, developed in very different circumstances. She saw worker and client as "peer and partner" in solving problems. This meant working both with the client themselves, in helping them understand what might be getting in the way of their own progress (e.g. their "negative valuations" of themselves); and, at the same time influence institutions in order to remove the power blocks (and their negative valuations) that prevent effective services from being offered. By influencing the hospital and its staff, some of these blocks are being removed. And, as a result, clinical staff are beginning to utilise some of the methods of working with young people demonstrated by the youth workers; in particular, enabling young people to learn at their own pace, and treating the young person as a young adult and not as a child. It was felt by medical staff that the practice was "moving from telling the young person toward enabling the young person."

Power is a central issue here. Young people are relatively powerless in the hospital environment. As Illich, Zola, McKnight, Caplan, & Shaiken (1977) observed, the authority of the medical establishment (also perceived by adults), reflected in its specialist knowledge and language, serves to create a professionalised barrier which reinforces hierarchy and distance, and acts against the real interests of patients. It is the antithesis of dialogue and reciprocity. For young people, this combines with their age and lack of knowledge, to reinforce their relatively powerless position.

Furthermore, passivity is encouraged. In the hospital environment they are also isolated from any support networks in their "outside" lives, yet they will have brought with them all of the social issues which may have contributed to their situation. Expecting young people to "take responsibility for their own health" is unrealistic when their identity as social beings is so compromised, and so little attention is paid to who they are, beyond a set of medical symptoms.

Often, when asked what their relationship with youth workers meant to them, young people said to us: "They don't tell you what to do, they listen and respect you." As a result, they said, they feel that they are somebody with an opinion worth hearing, with experience to be valued, and with needs, interests, and aspirations to be taken seriously. Such young people can begin to "take responsibility" for themselves because they can now make informed choices.

Community Settings and Youth Work

Alongside the state's preoccupation with social exclusion, two other related dimensions of policy concern are evident: first, what has become known as "community cohesion," which is the term adopted by the government to refer to its aspiration for harmonious social relations between different ethnic, religious, or racial groups. It gained particular significance after street disturbances between different racial groups in northern English cities in 2001.[4] This is not a new policy concern since race equality has been enshrined in UK law since the Race Relations Act of 1976, and has long been a central concern of the helping professions, including youth work.

The Cantle Report (Community Cohesion Unit, 2002) into the disturbances of 2001 drew new attention to what it saw to be the causes of declining social cohesion in local communities. Different racial and cultural groups had, as it suggested, experienced social and economic change in different ways. As a result, they had become effectively segregated from one another and there was often "little interaction between individuals of different cultural, religious, and racial backgrounds." Communities had become socially and culturally polarised so that they were leading "parallel lives." The report called for, amongst other things, educational initiatives with young people, and particularly those who might be "disaffected" and thus more likely to express the "deep-seated frustrations and divisions" they experience.

The second area of increased policy concern is crime and disorder—particularly though not exclusively by young people. The Crime and Disorder Act 1998 saw a major re-focusing of youth justice—away from "keeping young people out of care and custody to community safety" (Jordan, 2000, p. 134). This approach emphasised localised planning and co-ordination of stringent measures such as curfews for children under 10 in "hot-spots," where there is a high incidence of what is referred to as anti-social behaviour, and, at the same time, there is localised negotiation and mediation to reduce tension and conflict.

Common to both of these policy concerns is the question of locality as identified earlier. As Jordan (2000) points out, formal measures can only go so far:

> *It demands negotiation with local people, mediation between victims and offenders, and sensitivity to local tensions and conflicts . . . young people are in and of these communities and their actions reflect the social relations of these neighbourhoods with all their . . . elements of bonding, loyalty, fear, loathing, violence and reconciliation—the solidarities and the feuds of the informal, local order. (p. 134)*

The following case studies[5] illustrate some of these themes.

Case Study 3

Councillors in a midlands city passed a new bye-law prohibiting skating around the civic centre, a favourite place for young people with skateboards and skates. Young people's activities were unpopular with local adults who preferred to use the piazza as a sitting area. From their point of view, they were a danger and a nuisance.

The police were keen not to enforce the bye-law without an alternative place for young people to go. After discussion between different council departments, detached youth workers were asked to engage with skateboarders in an attempt to divert them toward the skateboard areas then being designed and built around the city.

Over time, workers built relationships with a group of skateboarders who were supported to make their views known to the council. This had the effect of transforming the problem in the eyes of council members and officials so that, rather than simply being seen as diverting young people away from street activity, it was seen as a project to consult them and enable the council to respond more sensitively and effectively. As a result the council understood that "herding" young people into skate parks would not work: they would simply stay away since they felt that street skating was more interesting. Skate park designs—which young people began to feel that they now "owned"—were changed alongside the council's own perceptions.

A database of some 500 young people across the city has developed as a result of the initiative, with young people able to be contacted and consulted through a website. Of more importance perhaps, youth workers recognised that many of the young people skateboarding in the city centre were quite vulnerable — particularly in terms of their health, education, and in relation to crime. For example, it was recognised how many young people were becoming involved in crime through very minor offences which could then lead onto more serious issues. These could be avoided through sensitive intervention.

Workers have also responded by setting up peer education projects, health events, DJ initiatives; and by working with local projects to whom young people could be referred. They report that young people themselves now feel that they can have an influence on local services.

Case Study 3 illustrates the conflicting positions of young people and the local adult population. As Notten has pointed out, local politicians tend to "steer by the compass of civic commotion, incidentalism,[6] and even moral panic." This is what gave rise to the new bye-law. Did youth work's intervention serve further to regulate (Baistow, 1994) young people's behaviour, by acting primarily in the political interests of the local state, and in so doing, extending Foucault's "governmentality?" Or should we take the view that intervention resulted in a "transformation" in Moreau's terms (1990) in which conflicts of (power) interests are resolved in the interests of the less powerful group. What is inescapable is that youth work here plays a decided political role.

What might be seen as "local meaning" is changed during the process. Young people are seen before the intervention as a cause of nuisance by some adults, who take it upon themselves to regulate their behaviour, and provide an alternative outlet which they (adults) believe to be "suitable." This kind of action by adults is experienced by young people as authoritarian. But there is space within this action-reaction equation which can be exploited. Young people can be offered the chance to gain a collective voice where previously, if they were heard at all, it was likely to be as irresponsible children. In gaining a voice, they learn not only how to influence adult-led institutions, but that there is benefit for them in doing so. And, at the same time, those institutions also begin to learn about young people's perspectives, and that it is worthwhile to hear them.

In order for youth workers to intervene effectively, they had to learn from young people how they experienced it, rather than accept the adult-led perspective with which they were presented. If they had entered this arena as the council's officials, doing its bidding, (and they are employed by the council), this would be seen by young people as the "soft policing" it may well have been; and further evidence of the adult world treating them as a "nuisance" to be moved on and controlled.

Instead, youth workers gained young people's trust by listening, being concerned for, and valuing their world so that young people could feel that their opinions counted: "I know I can talk to these guys and together we can do something" is how one young man described it. Youth workers could, as Jordan (2000) suggests, combine authority with street credibility, challenge with empathy (p. 135); that enabled young people to gain power and influence over a situation which, previously, disallowed any legitimate means of influence. In describing what youth workers did in advocating for young people and mediating between them and adult institutions, one police officer said: "They have the ability to access young people (in ways we can't because our uniforms act as a barrier) and translate what they say into adult words acceptable to bureaucrats." A young man said: "Without it we wouldn't have so much fun here."

Case Study 4 (see p. 164) represents a different kind of intervention.

The threads of social cohesion within communities are easily tangled or broken. Young people from different ethnic backgrounds can begin to live the separate or "parallel" lives that the Cantle Report identified. With little informal social interaction, and exacerbated by localised poverty which leads to few outlets for

Case Study 4

Following the racial disturbances in northern cities in 2001, tensions between different racial groups were also evident in other towns and cities. In one, a white teenager was assaulted and killed by four Asian young men. The youth work team set out to develop a programme designed to generate greater understanding and mutual respect between young people from different areas of the city, and from different racial backgrounds. A specific aim was to reduce the number of "racial incidents" (fights, assaults, gang violence and so on which have racial origins). Police data indicated that 70% of racial incidents occurred in the four areas also experienced the highest levels of deprivation.

To begin with, the programme responded to a request from a school in the area to help them tackle a racialised gang dispute. This became known as Project Unity. Subsequently it has been extended to include the Unity Youth Crew and, in 2003, the Unity Football Club.

Project Unity supports schools to resolve conflict between individuals and groups from different racial backgrounds, using conflict resolution approaches. A programme is devised in each school, using youth workers and selected teachers. Individual and group work is undertaken away from the school, and negotiated with participants.

Unity Youth Crew recruits and trains young people so that they can support local youth projects and other work across the city. Involvement is "earned" through an application and interview. Workers encourage "street youngsters—the movers and shakers in different areas" to be involved. 25 young people were selected. They are offered an accredited training programme, work placements and 1:1 support by youth workers as they develop their role as "apprentice" youth workers.

Alongside its school work and Youth Crew, the project also undertakes other initiatives—outdoor activities, residential experiences and sports, all designed to promote positive racial messages to young people.

The underlying theoretical perspective of all of the project's work is the idea of racial unity—maximising understanding and interaction across different geographical and racial groups, and decreasing distance and polarisation.

entertainment, groups formed around perceived cultural identity can easily come to feel antagonistic toward one another. If one adds in the "testosterone factor" among young males (as it was referred to by one of the youth workers), the potential for more violent confrontation is present. This was the situation confronting schools in these areas where serious fighting occurred between large groups of young men. "This was a feud which got out of hand," was how one young man described it.

The youth work response was to work on a number of fronts. First, workers of similar ethnic backgrounds (to the young people) went into schools to resolve conflicts between individuals and groups. Young people who had been involved were, with their agreement, taken out of the school for two days. Through mediation and conflict resolution, "contracts" were agreed to allow them to return to school. The threat of being excluded by the school was averted. One young man said: "You can see past the colours now. It's not a problem any more. Girls and boys got to know one another." This not only had the effect of resolving the immediate problem, but had more far reaching impact: "It's increasing mutual tolerance and respect." "The children of today are the parents of tomorrow" as the school's deputy head teacher observed.

Conflict resolution was seen only as a first step, however. The second approach was to begin to build interaction between different groups outside of the schools. Youth Crew brings young people themselves into the work so that its effects become more widespread, as well as being rooted in the different backgrounds from which they come. Small multi-racial teams of young people were recruited and trained, with each team supported by a worker. They help in local clubs, organise activities, make contact with other young people, and help shape the future of the overall project. Youth Crew has then become the catalyst for a much wider range of action: a football club, activities weeks, residentials, and workshops. These serve to increase the recreational and social opportunities available to young people while, at the same time, propagating the two central messages: racial unity and giving young people a voice. Analysis of the project captures a number of the themes which illustrate empowering approaches to working with young people.

First there is the question of what Jeffs & Smith (2002, p. 39) have referred to as individualisation of risk. The problem confronting schools was not seen by youth workers as one which could be approached simply through casework. While each young person who was involved brought with them their own background, motivations, and history, the social dynamic was seen as the key issue to work on. So, individual pathology was rejected in favour of a community development approach. The problem was not the young people themselves, but the ways in which they were susceptible to being influenced by wider social and economic forces. Youth work could begin to change the social dynamics by building the social capital of young people: creating new relationships and networks; offering activity which extends choices; and enabling young people to find ways to become involved in their communities in new ways.

The use of peers as youth workers was also of importance. It had the effect not just of increasing the numbers of those involved, but more importantly, served to embed the work within young people's identity groups. It legitimised the work in young people's eyes. At the same time, for those young people directly involved as peer workers, it offered real opportunities for their personal growth.

Then there is the dimension of young people's voice and influence. Too often, young people are asked to become involved in councils or forums which are externally imposed. Usually, only those who are confident and eloquent take part. Here, similar also to Case Study 3 (see p. 161), the representative voice of young people is embedded in the ongoing work: they are involved in defining the nature of the "problem" confronting them and their peers; a means is found to engage them in devising the solutions by gaining control of, or at least resisting, the forces at work; and they are, individually and collectively, the direct (but not the only) beneficiaries of the interventions.

Have there been lasting change as a result? For these young people, there is clear evidence of changed relationships, perceptions, and behaviours, and that this is likely to continue: "I didn't mix that much with different people" said one young person. "They're not that bad. I want to do more." Another said: "We went bowling the other night and I went up to some white people and got chatting. I would never have done that before." There is also impact on their friends: "We tell them, it's not worth fighting." And there seems to have been impact on these young people's parents too: "Before, (my dad) didn't want to listen. After I got involved in Unity I think he takes my views a bit more seriously." As for impact in the arena of community cohesion—the invisible social and cultural threads that connect people—here, evidence is more difficult to assess. But the indicators of its absence—social tension, racial incidents, crime by and on young people, and school exclusions arising from racial conflict—may be able to be measured over time.

There is recognition however that the economic and social forces which continue to give rise to fragmentation and deteriorating social relations cannot be eradicated by educational initiatives alone. The need to build social cohesion will continue.

Conclusion: Youth Empowerment is Alive

This chapter began by suggesting that the notion of empowerment is contested. Drawing on Baistow (1994), the concept's regulatory and liberatory potential was noted. She pointed out that the term is often psychologically laden: that the "problem" to which empowerment is seen as the "solution" is frequently individualised. Cognitive strategies and behavioural skills are seen to offer the "client" the opportunity to "gain control of their lives." By implication then, the further down the casework (individualisation) road that youth work in the United Kingdom travels, the more likely it is perhaps, that it will be drawn into a pathological conception of empowerment. Thus, while the "empowered self" has clearly liberatory overtones, it lays us open to forms of professional intervention in which the personal and the structural are conflated. Public ills are translated into private troubles (Mills, 1970) for which a dose of empowerment may be the best medicine. The wider social forces at work are in danger of being ignored.

But perhaps this is to overstate the case by creating polarisation between liberation and regulation; and between the individual and the collective. Jordan (2000) suggested that "tough love" (deterrence and enforcement on one hand, supportive intervention on the other) is necessary to counter the forces of social fragmentation which were promoted during the later part of the 20th century. In this approach, human agency is encouraged at the same time as seeing problems in their structural forms. Is "tough love" the ground that youth work occupies now? Certainly, from our research, there are examples of youth workers being able to create close, understanding relationships with young people whom other professionals were unable to reach (the love in tough love) and negotiating (the tough element perhaps) with them to enable change to take place.

According to Jordan (2000), "supportive intervention" cannot simply be directed at individual pathologies, but must attend to "the bonds of trust, co-operation, mutuality, and community on which society relies for its prosperity and quality of life" (p. 36). And in this domain, youth work's approaches may be endangered.

The four case studies which form the focus of this chapter each illustrates that the locus of youth work lies beyond the individual "client." Young people who are excluded from school, young patients in hospitals, skaters in the city centre, and those involved in racial violence are each seen as reacting to social, cultural, or institutional influences which limit the choices available to them, and over which they feel little control. Legitimate influence by young people in the situations we presented, is apparently unobtainable.

In order to enable young people to find the means to influence (the adult world, other young people), youth workers work in two connected ways. First, they enable young people to reflect upon their experiences, develop a view, and act upon it through committed, often collective, action (as in the case of the city centre skateboarders). Second, and often in conjunction with the first, they may act on behalf of young people by enabling them to gain access to influential adults (doctors, councillors) who may be able to provide the resources they need; or they may advocate on their behalf by, for example, representing their views, training or advising other adults so that they can begin to hear young people's perspectives.

This is not to avoid the individual situations of young people and the "tangle of pathologies" each represents. As the case studies show, that individual young people should be helped to find a way back into mainstream if they are outside it, or to sustain their medical treatment if they are ill, is not at issue. Why they are in that position and what might help are the key questions. The reciprocal relationship between the young person's view of themselves and the external forces acting upon them, as in Solomon's (1976) model, is youth work's starting point. Attending to the individual or group is always the first step. Through the research, this is what young people themselves began to make a difference to their lives. But it is never the last step if we are not simply to repeat the cycle.

Attending to young people simply because they are "marginalised," "disaffected," or "excluded", also risks youth work becoming cut off from the very communities which serve to locate it. Only as workers with bases in youth clubs, centres and projects, and the "social tentacles" these provide, could Unity, begin to develop the networks of activity and opportunity which sustain the overall project. In Case Study 1 (see p. 154), without a local presence, the project would have been seen by young people as just one more attempt to get them to go to school. In a policy climate which measures inclusion in narrow and instrumental terms, the benefits of what we might call "soft participation" (belonging to groups, making relationships, spending time with friends) become devalued. The imperative is to tackle the (apparent) problems rather than to build social capital, to ignore young people's needs to "relax, meet friends and have fun" (Department for Education and Skills, 2002).

In pursuing the imperative, we risk having no means available to us beyond becoming the enforcement counsellors that Jordan (2000) feared.

To protect its position in young people's lives, youth workers have held hard to the principle of choice: that young people choose to be involved; that coercion or compliance is incompatible with learning. Each of the case studies demonstrates the importance of this. But the voluntary principle is also not secure in the current policy climate. It takes time to make relationships and negotiate consent. Public services are often impatient to meet external targets. Shouldn't young people just "do as they are told?" Youth workers are often portrayed as precious in holding on to choices. Yet, it remains fundamental to the nature of the relationship between youth workers and young people: for youth workers, it is a mark of their belief in and respect for them that we acknowledge their right to say "No." As a principle, it has stood the test of time. And for young people, belief and respect, often experienced for the first time from an adult world more used to exerting its authority, provide a foothold previously unavailable in what is often a precarious world.

End Notes

1. In July 2007 government policy has resulted in youth services in England becoming a part of a new 10 year youth strategy. The policy can be downloaded at: www.dfes.gov.uk/publications/tenyearyouthstrategy.

2. In English law, the local authority has a duty to provide for these young people when they are not in school but finds it notoriously difficult to do so.

3. I am grateful to my research colleague, Linda Deazle, for this case example.

4. This policy area is the responsibility of the Home Office in England. Further information can be obtained via its webpage: www.homeoffice.gov.uk

5. I am grateful to my research colleague Hilary Comfort for these case studies.

6. The term incidentalism in this context is intended to mean reacting to incidents.

References

Baistow, K. (1994). Liberation and regulation? Some paradoxes of empowerment. *Critical Social Policy, 42*(14), 35–46.

Banks, S. (1999). Ethics and the youth worker. In S. Banks (Ed.), *Ethical issues in youth work* (pp. 3–20). London: Routledge.

Beck, U. (1999). *Schöne Neue Arbeitwelt*. Frankfurt: Campus Verlag.

Community Cohesion Unit. (2002). *The report of the Independent Review Team chaired by Ted Cantle*. Retrieved 24 April 2004, from http://www.homeoffice.gov.uk/comrace/.

Davies, B. (1999). *A history of the youth service in England: Volume 2: From Thatcherism to New Labour*. Leicester: Youth Work Press.

Department for Education and Skills. (2002). *Transforming youth work: Resourcing excellent youth services*. Nottingham: DfES Publications.

Giddens, A. (1998). *The Third Way: The renewal of social democracy*. Cambridge: Polity Press.

Gilbert, T. (1995). Empowerment: issues, tensions and conflicts. In M. Todd & T. Gilbert (Eds.), *Learning disabilities: Practice issues in health settings* (pp. 111–137). London, Routledge.

Gordon, P., & White, J. (1979). *Philosophers as education reformers: The influence of idealism on British educational thought and practice*. London: Routledge and Kegan Paul.

Illich, I., Zola, I. K., McKnight, J., Caplan, J., & Shaiken H. (Eds.) (1977). *Disabling professions*. London: Marion Boyars.

Jeffs, T., & Smith, M. (2002). Individualisation and youth work. *Youth and Policy, 76*, 39–65.

Jordan, B. (2000). *Social Work and the Third Way: Tough love as social policy*. London: Sage.

Kidd, J. R. (1978). *How adults learn* (3rd ed.). Englewood Cliffs, NJ: Prentice Hall Regents.

Levitas, R. (1998). *The inclusive society? Social exclusion and new labour*. Basingstoke: Palgrave.

Lo, T. W. & Au, E. (2004). *Youth empowerment: International experiences*. Hong Kong: City University of Hong Kong.

Lorenz, W. (1994). *Social work in a changing Europe*. London: Routledge.

Merton, B., Smith, D.I., Payne, M., et al (2004) *An evaluation of the impact of youth work in England*. Department for Education and Skills. Available at: http://www.dfes.gov.uk/research/data/uploadfiles/RR606.pdf.

Mills, C. W. (1970). *The sociological imagination*. Harmondsworth: Penguin.

Moreau, M. J. (1990). Empowerment through advocacy and consciousness-raising: Implications of a structural approach to social work. *Journal of Sociology and Social Welfare, 17*(2), 53–68.

Murray, C. (1990). *The emerging British underclass*. London: Institute of Economic Affairs.

Non-aligned Working Group. (1997). *Young people as citizens now*. Leicester: Youth Work Press.

Notten, A. L. T. (undated). *Regulating the youth. Three decades of youth policy in the Netherlands*. Retrieved 3 April 2004, from http://www.cetadl.bham.ac.uk/ hes/abstract/NottenP.doc.

Prochaska, F. (1988). *The voluntary impulse: Philanthropy in modern Britain.* London: Faber and Faber.

Russell, C. E. B., & Russell, L. (1932). *Lads' Clubs: Their history, organisation and management.* London: A & C Black.

Sibeon, R. (1990). Comments on the structure and forms of social work knowledge. *Social Work and Social Sciences Review, 1*(1), 29–44.

Smith, M. (1987). *Creators not consumers.* Leicester: National Association of Youth Clubs.

Smith, M. (1994). *Local education: Community, conversation, praxis.* Buckingham: Open University Press.

Social Exclusion Unit. (1999). *Bridging the Gap: New Opportunities for 16–18 year olds not in education, employment or training.* The Stationery Office.

Solomon, B. (1976). *Black empowerment: Social work in oppressed communities.* New York: Columbia University Press.

Ward, D. (1998). Groupwork. In R. Adams, L. Dominelli, & M. Payne (Eds.), *Social work: Themes, issues and critical debates.* London: Macmillan.

Williamson, H. (1993). Youth policy in the UK and the marginalisation of young people. *Youth and Policy, 40,* 33–48.

Williamson, H. (1997). Status Zero Youth and the underclass: Some considerations. In R. MacDonald (Ed.), *Youth, the Underclass and Social Exclusion.* London: Routledge.

Young, K. (1999). *The art of youth work.* Lyme Regis: Russell House Publishing.

MISTAKEN IDENTITIES: CANADIAN YOUTH AND THEIR SEARCH FOR A PLACE IN THEIR COMMUNITIES

7

Michael UNGAR, Marc LANGLOIS, and Melissa HUM

Acknowledgements

The authors would like to thank Camille Dumond, Estair Van Wagner, and Lynn MacDonald for their assistance with drafting this chapter as well as acknowledge the generous support of the Social Sciences and Humanities Research Council of Canada and the Nova Scotia Health Research Foundation.

Introduction

Like youth all over the world, Canadian youth seek for a place in their communities and among their families where they are seen as both healthily and meaningfully involved. Both require that youth share access to the resources that support healthy growth and they have a voice in decision-making processes that decide how they are distributed. These resources include a long list of factors that have been linked to children's optimal development. For instance, at the level of the community, these may include access to education, health care, meaningful rites of passage, a contributing role in the community, and a sense of one's cultural heritage. At the level of intimate relationships with their families and other caregivers, children need parents who monitor their activities, mentors who model healthy behaviour, meaningful relationships with peers, and a safe environment free of violence. Finally, at an individual level, resources for health include the nurturing of individual capacities to be assertive, problem-solving, optimistic, have a sense of duty to others, self-awareness, and the ability to exercise control over one's life. There are, of course, many more factors than these that contribute to children's well-being. Youth who have a voice in the decisions that affect their access to these resources will be those who are most likely to report feelings of positive health. Therefore, health among children and youth is closely linked to their experiences of empowerment (Lo & Au, 2004).

Oddly, while the situation for many youth in Canada today continues to improve, a collective panic about youth is leading Canadian families and communities to deny youth their place, their purpose, and their power. In doing so, we are denying youth opportunities to access the very resources that form a foundation for actualisation and well-being. In turn, we are also denying them opportunities for empowerment. We typically overlook the capacities of our young people to not only survive, but to thrive despite the challenges they may face. With a sense of place and purpose comes the power to make decisions that affect their lives.

If we look carefully at the lives of Canadian youth overall, we note that adolescents today are doing far better than ever before. However, despite their relative success, some communities continue to deny them voice in decisions affecting them. In this chapter, we explore what empowerment means for youth, examining how access to health resources and participation in decision-making processes that build the competencies for youth to succeed. If empowerment is about having a place, purpose, and power, then one can expect that empowered youth will be those who have the capacity to overcome barriers to participate in their respective communities, changing how they are positioned in relationships with adults, addressing the constant pressure they feel to measure up, all leading to the creation of a space for them in their communities that is more "youth friendly".

When youth lack place, purpose, and power, the actual roots of empowerment, they are more likely to assume social roles that do not serve them well. Below, we examine three roles that youth are forced to adopt as a consequence of adults misunderstanding them and denying them access to the resources they need for personal health and fulfilment. Marginalised, youth are most likely to be seen as: 1) vulnerable and in need of protection; 2) clients of systems designed to meet their needs; or 3) adults-in-waiting, of whom little is expected. None of these roles are truly empowering. In contrast, youth argue they want to be seen as resilient (rather than vulnerable), participants (rather than clients), and community members in full standing (rather than adults-in-waiting). This chapter will explore how Canadian youth search for empowerment and two exemplary community programmes that contribute to their success.

The Story of Joanie

At age 16, Joanie had proven herself to be competent and able to survive a chaotic and dangerous home. She is an example of a child who succeeded in exercising control over those around her. As the domestic violence she witnessed increased, at one point resulting in her father being jailed for an assault he committed on Joanie's mother, Joanie herself acted out more and more violently in school. Her behaviour succeeded in bringing her to the attention of the Children's Aid Society at age 11. At age 12, Joanie was removed from her family and placed in a foster home under a voluntary care agreement.

Although it was a rough transition at first, the result was a more stable home and an opportunity for Joanie and her family to get the help they needed. It took some time, but with a series of interventions at school, which included a mental health counsellor, Joanie eventually brought her grades up, stopped her violence, and began to make decisions for herself. By age 16, she was doing well in school, working part-time at McDonald's, and then she had decided to return home to live with her parents.

Joanie's life story could easily be seen as one of a troubled child who just needed counselling to help her address her violence, encourage her academically, and build her coping capacity. In other words, Joanie could be seen as a vulnerable and disempowered child who was the victim of abuse and the product of neglect.

That story however, would not account well for Joanie's actual life experience. Far from vulnerable and disempowered, Joanie managed to use the resources she had to make her life work better. Even as young as age 11, she was asking her Social Service workers to provide her information on how to cope with her alcoholic and violent father. Later, her angry outbursts served her purposes better as: she drew attention to herself and her family, resulting in her removal from her home, intervention by the police to stop her father's violence, and the provision of counselling, an important health resource, for the entire family.

By age 14, Joanie had impressed her caregivers with her spirit to survive and won a Youth Achievement Award for her success at school and her contribution to other children in care, whom she regularly supported as friends and mentors. In fact, although supports were offered to Joanie to return home, she refused to say that she would do better at least temporarily where she was placed.

Through all these decisions, Joanie moved from a self-definition as a "problem child" blamed by her as the cause of her father's drinking and violence, to a young woman who is articulate and expressive of what she needed and what she wanted for her family. Even more, Joanie found a place in her community where she is safe, has a purpose to her life, and most importantly, the power to exercise a say over decisions that affect her. She lives at home now, by her own choice, is doing well in school, and is contributing to her own financial support.

Danger and Misunderstanding

Behind the facade of a "problem child," Joanie survived. Many Canadian youth are doing the same, but their communities generally misunderstand them and their behaviours. Ironically, many Canadian adults remain convinced that our children are doing worse than ever before. It is a claim without fact or substance. In fact, because of our social welfare safety net, programmes of early intervention and children's own entrenched rights, we are witnessing a burgeoning population of children who are coping better and better. What we have here is a case of mistaken identities: adult perceptions of problem youth in Canada are easily refuted by the anecdotal evidence of lives lived well, like Joanie's, and the statistics which tell us that collectively, teens are healthier than ever before.

What are the elements of an empowered youth in the Canadian context? Empowerment is a multi-dimensional construct. According to Swift and Levin (1987) empowerment refers both to the phenomenological experience of feeling powerful, competent and worthy of the esteem of others, as well as the capacity to modify the structural conditions that surround us in order to reallocate power to those who are marginalised. Empowerment is, therefore, both an internal and external event, in which individuals feel empowered when their worlds are shaped to meet their needs. Empowerment and well-being have been shown to be linked (Cowen, 1991; Ungar, 2006; Ungar & Teram, 2000). Aspects of well-being such as perceived control (Zimmerman, 1990), self-efficacy (Bandura, 1998), the reduction of self-blame (Ryan, 1976), and better coping (Dumont & Provost, 1999; Garmezy, 1983), all are synonymous with the experience of empowerment.

Structurally, we also understand that when individuals participate in their communities and influence decisions regarding the distribution and access of resources that support health, people experience a sense of empowerment (Kieffer, 1984). This combination of feeling and doing is similar to Freire's (1970) praxis in which action and reflection go hand in hand, to stimulate personal and collective growth. Thus, by definition, empowerment is a construct that focuses on capacity building, self-determination, participation, collective action, distributive justice, and social transformation (Prilleltensky, Peirson, & Nelson, 2001).

As Figure 7.1 shows, empowerment as a concept provides a way to understand the process by which individuals and communities take action that contributes to their sense of skilled competence.

Figure 7.1   A model of the empowerment process

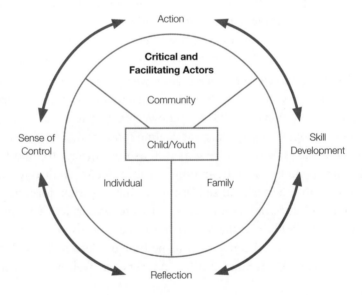

This in turn, leads to reflection by individuals on their capacities, and contributes to the creation of an identity as competent. From these positive identity constructions come feelings of control which motivate individuals to take further action. Individuals, their families, and communities contribute to each part of this cycle, adding resources such as social and instrumental support. It all adds up to a dynamic process in which action and reflection combined result in an empowered young person (Ungar, 1995; Ungar & Teram, 2000).

Health through Empowerment

Achieving a sense of place, purpose, and power, the three contributing factors to youth empowerment require:

1. Sustained relationships that provide them access to experiences of power with others;

2. Access to formal social and health care programmes, e.g. medical services, counselling, education, and recreation;

3. Experiences of competence and recognition for their talents through opportunities for work, volunteer services, meaningful contributions to their communities, and rites of passage.

Looking at Joanie's life, we see clearly that these three factors were present. For example, actions to get herself noticed and eventually removed from her home led to her feeling skilled as a child who could keep children like herself safe. In the group and foster homes where she was placed, she thrived, making friends, succeeding at school, and enjoying contact with her caregivers. Although throughout, Joanie never relinquished the control she felt over the decisions that affected her.

What's more, her community (and to some extent her family) came to realise that Joanie was doing well and recognised her as much more than just another troubled youth. Significantly, Joanie's process of empowerment was not hers alone. It was based upon a community of concern that helped invest Joanie with a sense of herself as empowered. Her subsequent empowerment was the result of her actions and those of a team of social workers who opened space for Joanie to make decisions for herself. It was also the result of her family acknowledging they had problems.

Too often, we deny youth opportunities to become empowered because we (adults) are afraid of doing this. Fuelled by our popular media that is always looking for the bad and sensational news story, we have created a moral panic about youth that is without substance (O'Reilly & Flemming, 2001). Take for example, a couple of issues relevant to a child like Joanie. First, as a sexually active teen, Joanie was less likely than teenagers in the mid-to-late 1900s to have a child. Better reproductive health information and better decision-making among teens is making it far less likely for them to become either pregnant or to give birth (Vanier Institute of the Family, 2000).

Second, we might look at the statistics relevant to youth crime in Canada and specifically the violent kinds of behaviour that Joanie was displaying at school. What is clear is that despite perceptions to the contrary, there is no epidemic growth in youth crime. In fact, although incidence of crime among juveniles increased over the 1970s and 1980s by as much as 50%, the incidence of crime among juveniles has steadily decreased since 1991. What has changed however, are the charge rates, with a 27% increase over the past 25 years (Carrington, 2001). In part, we can explain this as a consequence of our changing legislation that continues to offer more resources to divert youth from the justice system to other forms of help (Carrington, 2001).

Not surprisingly, we now have the capacity as a system of care to look after children like Joanie better (see Sykes & Palmer, 2003). In fact, we are also better at identifying children deemed at risk. For example, 135,000 investigations of child abuse occurred in 1998 across Canada, a rate of 21.5 investigations per 1,000 children, with 56,547 investigations finding substantiated claims of emotional, physical, sexual abuse and neglect. While we do not know if this number represents an improvement over past years, we do know that a substantial portion of children in any one year comes to the attention of the Children's Aid Societies who are there to protect them (Trocme, Phaneuf, Scarth, Fallon, & MacLaurin, 2003). Furthermore, a child like Joanie is in fine company, as some 16% of all children who are investigated for abuse are likely to be diverted to out-of-home placements.

All these tell us that children are surviving in difficult situations (better) because of the many different resources, we as Canadians, have historically committed to our children. And yet, this is still not enough. We still have zero tolerance for children living anything but orderly, healthy lives. Any signs of trouble and we typically resort to the rhetoric of fear, panicked by what we see. There is of course, still cause to be concerned about the well-being of many of our children without necessarily feeling that things are getting worse. For instance, only one sixth of all children with a need for mental health services receive intervention (Offord et al., 1987). Canadian youth continue to show many signs of mental illness and stress (Davidson & Manion, 1996). And as many as 32% of males and 25% of females are still classified as vulnerable and likely to experience developmental problems, if we rely on data from the *Canadian National Longitudinal Survey of Children and Youth*, a large multi-phased study of over 20,000 Canadian children (5,374 youth) now in its 10th year (Willms, 2002). What is unclear from these data is whether children today are better than or worse off than their parents? Regardless, statistics about our youth show that the more we provide positive relationships, access to social and health services, and opportunities to experience competence, the more likely children's lives will be improved in ways synonymous with empowerment.

More Pressure, Less Place

Children can be gloomy about their prospects for empowerment. Overall, the combination of more pressure (to perform) and less place has meant fewer opportunities for youth in Canada to feel empowered. This is due primarily to three forces at work in Canadian society. First, some fear that youth are dangerous, even out of control. Under the illusion of danger, we have become hesitant to pass to youth the rights and responsibilities that are their due. Second, working against youth, are adult perceptions that they are immature and require longer periods of time to develop and learn the skills necessary to make a contribution in a complex world. Third, we hesitate to permit youth to experience risks, even reasonable risks that are the basis for rites of passage. This fear and mistrust has meant many youth are unable to make the transitions to meaningful roles in their communities.

Such was not the case for Joanie who, lacking parents who worry about her, was forced to take command of her own life. She may just be a better person for it, although one would never wish such abuse on any child.

This fear then has made many Canadians view our children through one of three lenses, depending on our level of panic and our perception of the child's level of need:

1. **The Vulnerable Child**: This child is seen as having rights that are being denied and is therefore, in need of protection and advocacy.

2. **The Child Client**: From a service perspective, this child has a right to be provided with formal services (e.g. education, child welfare, medical care, correctional services) that can address the problems s/he faces.

3. **The Adult-in-Waiting**: This child is seen as needing recreation, amusement, and diversion that substitute for real inclusion and participation while s/he is getting training and education in how to function as an adult.

None of these three roles are experienced as empowering for the child. They may provide some health resources, but only under the terms set by those who provide them. There is no accountability to the children served, nor do children find a sense of place, purpose, or power when they adopt these roles.

Our "Response-ability" to Share Power

A preferred way to help youth experience empowerment is to look at the "response-ability" of adults to share with children and youth our actual power, creating places for them to express their purposes. Achieving this requires responsive programming and the provision of resources at all levels, including families and communities. When adults respond with opportunities for youth to have a voice and access resources, children change from disempowered to empowered. In the transformation process, vulnerable children become resilient, capable of exercising their rights and negotiating for resources; clients become participants in the process of designing and implementing services tailored to their needs; and adults-in-waiting become full community members, with roles and responsibilities tailored to their capacities to make a meaningful contribution.

Children and youth alike, navigate their ways into these preferred roles through a variety of different programmes. In particular, we will discuss two programmes that have provided opportunities for youth to experience empowerment and achieve a sense of place, purpose, and power. The first, the Phoenix Youth Programmes, provided an identifiable at-risk population (vulnerable youth and child clients like street youth) a voice in services tailored to their needs. The second, the HeartWood Centre for Community Youth Development, which stimulates community youth development, gives youth who are less at-risk (adults-in-waiting) an opportunity to demonstrate that they can contribute to the well-being of others in their communities while giving themselves a voice in the political process.

Phoenix Youth Programmes

Phoenix Youth Programmes have been providing services to homeless and at-risk youth in the Halifax, Nova Scotia, area since 1987. This non-profit organisation consists of 7 programmes that provide a continuum of care to support youth aged 16 to 24 in their transition from adolescence to adulthood and independence. These programmes include:

1. **Phoenix Prevention Programme** (opened in 2002)—a community education and therapeutic response service to at-risk youth and their families.

2. **Phoenix Centre for Youth** (opened in 1994)—a street-front, walk-in service offering counselling, crisis intervention, health services, referral to community resources, and advocacy.

3. **Phoenix Youth Shelter** (opened in 2001)—a 20-bed shelter offering a range of services including emergency accommodations, clothing, food, counselling, and therapeutic support to enable youth to move forward to a safer, healthier lifestyle.

4. **Phoenix House** (opened in 1987)—a 10-bed, residential facility for males and females that provides longer-term supportive housing to youth in their transition towards self-sufficiency.

5. **Supervised Apartment Programme** (opened in 1992)—three separate homes that provide nine youth with an independent, but supervised, living environment.

6. **Follow-up Programme** (established in 1998)—an outreach service designed to provide support to youth who are living independently within the community.

7. **Phoenix Learning and Employment Centre** (opened in 2002)—a programme aimed at providing youth with information and opportunities for pre-employment, life-skills, and academic development.

The Phoenix organisation receives support and funding from the provincial and federal government combined with fundraising efforts and local community supports. The development and growth of Phoenix programmes has been designed to address gaps in service identified by youth and care providers and provides a continuum of services. The voluntary nature of Phoenix programmes allows for youth to access services through self-referral or referral from other agencies.

Services are rooted in a strengths-based perspective that enables the 70 staff to focus on positive attributes and resilience in each individual youth. Youth tend to come to the Programme in crisis. Phoenix staff feels privileged to accompany with youth on their journey toward developing life long strength, independence, and adulthood. The continuum of services offered aims to break the cycle of homelessness by meeting the diverse needs of young people.

Youth Empowerment and the Special Initiatives Project

In 2001, Phoenix Youth Programmes received funding for the Special Initiatives Project that has, as its goal, to enhance youth development initiatives across all Phoenix Youth Programmes. Youth development is defined as "a process which prepares young people to meet the challenges of adulthood through a co-ordinated, progressive series of activities and experiences which help them to become socially, morally, emotionally, physically, and cognitively competent. Positive youth development addresses the broader developmental needs of youth, in contrast to deficit-based models which focus solely on youth problems" (National Youth Development Information Centre, 1998). Since its inception, the Special Initiatives Project has integrated a youth development approach across all of the various service-delivery programmes. This has been accomplished through research and consultation with youth using Phoenix services, thereby assisting programmes to move effectively, beyond traditional resource-provision.

At the core of this empowerment approach is the facilitation and fostering of youth skills and competencies (see Chapter 9 for a similar orientation). In contrast to deficit-based models, Special Initiatives Project has been the catalyst to fully integrate a youth development approach into all Phoenix Programmes. Phoenix has been a leader in addressing the problem of youth homelessness in Canada. The work done to date, highlights the importance of shifting away from traditional reactive approaches that are oriented toward "fixing problems." Instead, a youth development approach recognises that developing assets and competencies are pivotal to promoting resilience and youth empowerment.

The intention of the Special Initiatives Project has been to establish innovative programming that empowers youth to make a healthy transition to adulthood through skill and competency development. Creativity and self-expression, experiential education, capacity building, therapeutic recreation, and youth leadership have been the cornerstones of the programming. Special Initiatives draws on individuals as youth leaders, resources, and facilitators. It also strives to create empowering environments to enable positive change in the lives of the young adults involved with the project.

Community partnerships, committed staff, and volunteers complement the collaborative process by facilitating and ensuring that programming reflects a youth development perspective. Special Initiatives provide a rare opportunity for youth to connect with caregivers, both formal and informal, outside of their regular routines and roles. This serves to enrich the relationship between Phoenix staff and youth and provides an alternative context for engagement. As well, community partnerships with volunteers and community organisations have helped youth bridge the gap between their (low) sense of entitlement and accessing the many resources in their community. This is essential in supporting their transition to becoming both independent and positively engaged within their communities, re-establishing these youth at the centre of our community rather than on its margins.

Specifically, Special Initiatives provides innovative programming through four main streams: Arts and Culture, Therapeutic Recreation, Capacity Building, and Youth Involvement. The programming encourages youth to take "ownership" over Special Initiatives activities and participate in planning, promotion, organisation, and evaluation.

I.   Arts and Culture (Music, Drama, Art, Photography, Creative Writing, Pottery, Dance)

Creativity and self-expression positively engage youth while fostering skills, interests, and creative thinking. The arts and cultural activities play a key role in skill building and promoting feelings of confidence, self-worth, and pride. This stream has proven to be an excellent opportunity for positive engagement, enhancement of communication skills, and interrupting negative self-perceptions. Participants learn transferable skills such as teamwork, commitment, focus, and communication.

II.   Therapeutic Recreation (Hiking, Camping, High Level Physical Challenges, Sports, Kayaking)

Therapeutic Recreation improves or enhances self-esteem, interpersonal skills, and can promote healthier living through physical activities. This helps youth see themselves as capable and powerful, and is important for developing trust and understanding of individual, and shared responsibility. Utilising an experiential education model, therapeutic recreation enables youth to enter new roles.

III.   Capacity Building (Pre-Employment training, First Aid, CPR, Workplace Safety Training, Computer Skills, Budgeting, Cooking, Safe Food Handling)

Capacity Building is "hard skill development." This stream incorporates education around specific skills identified as important by homeless youth. Certification programmes, ongoing training opportunities, and skills based workshops are designed to provide hands-on, practical experiences for youth to develop transferable life skills.

IV.   Youth Involvement (Youth Speakers Bureau, Youth Facilitators, Youth Leadership Council, Youth Research)

The fourth main stream provides opportunities for youth to assume leadership and advocacy roles. Through various projects, they are mobilised to communicate, organise, and advocate on behalf of other youth. Youth come to be recognised as community resources and have the opportunity to develop leadership, facilitation, public speaking, and advocacy skills.

These four innovative ways of engaging and sustaining youth in promoting a positive transition to adulthood have limitless potential. The following two examples highlight the transformative process youth experience as they come to make meaningful contributions to their communities and themselves.

Music Programme

Originally, the Music Programme was offered once, over an eight-week period led by a local musician/songwriter. It guided youth through the process of writing and editing songs, performing, and recording. The result was a compilation CD of their songs and a release "party" to showcase their talents and celebrate the achievement. This programme was so successful in promoting a higher level of self-perception and acquiring skills in creative expression and music recording that it has been offered on a yearly basis and now incorporates a youth facilitator.

A youth facilitator assists in harnessing the talents of the youth who participate by supporting and mentoring those new to the Music Programme. By having a peer facilitator, youth are shown how much they are valued as both participants and potential leaders. The incorporation of youth facilitators in this and other Special Initiatives allows young people the opportunity to gain better control over their own lives while positively influencing other youth.

Youth Speakers Bureau

The Youth Speakers Bureau is an important component of Phoenix's community education programming. It is made up of youth interested in having a "voice" in their community by providing education to youth and adults regarding issues affecting young people and homelessness. The Bureau has been developed as a place for "first voice experiences" to be brought forward and shared as a prevention mechanism with junior and senior high school students and other professionals working with young people. Their mission statement reads:

> *"Our goal is to create awareness among youth in our community of the issues related to homelessness. We hope to share our experiences and role model with other young people, so that they can make informed, healthy choices. We see ourselves as a resource and seek to understand and communicate our experiences for the benefit of other young people. By recognising the potential and resiliency of youth, we hope to empower others in improving their situations and brightening their futures."*

The participants (all of whom have been involved with other Phoenix programmes) cooperatively develop workshops and presentations for schools and community groups that address issues related to youth homelessness. Speakers share "real" experiences, both their own and those of other similar youth. The group receives training around group facilitation, public speaking, community development, ongoing support and guidance from staff. The Bureau illustrates the value of including youth in prevention efforts. Youth Speakers are role models, educators, mentors, and heroes to the young people and adults who have been privileged to share in their accomplishments.

Youth Development and Empowerment through Phoenix

The Special Initiatives project strives to integrate key components of youth development into programming and across the organisation in order to promote empowerment among participants. To accomplish this, programming includes, but is not limited to:

- acknowledging youth as resources and experts on their own lives;
- acknowledging youth as energetic, able citizens;

- providing youth with opportunities to meet and work with caring adults who provide support and guidance (staff, volunteers, and community members);
- providing creative forms of learning;
- providing holistic approaches to learning and programming;
- ensuring a continuum of care is provided through long-term services, supports, and follow-up; and,
- ensuring the quality implementation and evaluation of programming.

Special Initiatives has intentionally developed programmes and experiences for youth to develop social, personal, cognitive, civic, and moral competencies. Youth gain an awareness of their values, strengths, role, and the power of their contributions. Those who participate have been found to become more actively engaged and connect positively with other individuals and their communities. Special Initiatives has been important to sustaining an organisation-wide approach that emphasises developing assets and building resilience in youth across all Phoenix programmes. This has enhanced the association's ability to fully integrate innovative and complementary strategies into its work with youth deemed as at-risk.

HeartWood Centre for Community Youth Development

Since 1989, the HeartWood Centre for Community Youth Development's mission has been "to support the development of children and young people by linking them and their communities." HeartWood offers programming that helps connect communities meaningfully with their young people in ways that promote youth action as an integral part of building healthy communities. Programme activities include: leadership development, environmental education, community outreach, professional development in youth engagement, youth forums, research, and student engagement initiatives. HeartWood is considered a centre of excellence for youth engagement practices in the province of Nova Scotia and is recognised as one of the most innovative organisations in Canada working with youth and communities. The organisation works both locally and nationally, training adults and young adults in the skills and tools they require supporting youth action.

Young people represent the most consistently under-utilised resource in the leadership needs of youth-serving agencies and community development. In a time when communities and youth-serving agencies throughout North America are struggling with complex challenges and an absence of familiar guideposts to aid their decision-making — innovative ideas, fresh perspectives, and inspired actions are in short supply. Problem-solvers who are able to rise to the challenge unbridled by traditional thinking or established patterns of action are in high demand. Those who truly understand this challenge and seek solutions to the barriers facing community development are looking to youth for answers. HeartWood has discovered various ways to support community groups and individuals with their youth engagement efforts, currently supporting 35 communities and agency-based youth development initiatives.

HeartWood's approach encourages young people to connect with their community, and reciprocally the community to embrace its young people. Each community action team established is uniquely tailored to meet the needs of the participants and their communities. Here are some noteworthy examples:

1. A group of young people and adults are working to create a youth centre in their community. It is a long process, and as they struggle to maintain motivation, HeartWood is invited to present a workshop on the principles of youth inclusion.

2. Town leaders in another community want to hear what youth have to say regarding youth issues. A town meeting was organised and local youth were invited to participate. Over 100 young people let their voices be heard while HeartWood assists with facilitation.

3. A young woman works with her peers to change stereotypes

about youth by performing service projects in her community. HeartWood introduced her to a network of youth action teams with the same vision. Later, she is given an opportunity to tell her story of community youth action at a regional symposium for youth and youth-serving individuals and groups.

4. When several young people are charged with vandalism of a town cemetery, a local youth decides to challenge the growing stereotype of youth as troublemakers. With HeartWood's help, he organises a youth action team to rake leaves in the cemetery, giving the caretakers time to fix the damaged headstones.

5. A group of youth works toward personally changing their lives by moving away from high-risk, addictive behaviour. At their initiation, their adult supporters are asked to help them prevent younger children from becoming harmfully involved with drugs. HeartWood was invited to provide leadership training for the older youth and to network them with a family resource centre where they now help mentor children in need of positive role models.

A Framework for Action

Guiding this work, HeartWood has developed a Community Youth, Development Framework based on its research about variables that contribute to successful youth action teams. The Framework is intended for application when working with groups of young people, young adults, and adults within a given community or organisation. It blends both youth and community development and is designed as a blueprint to encourage, plan for, and support active engagement of youth within their communities and respective agencies. "Community" may be defined geographically, or by group, organisation, or by a network of shared interest. The Framework can be adapted to fit the specific needs that each community defines for itself.

Figure 7.2   HeartWood Centre for community youth development's framework

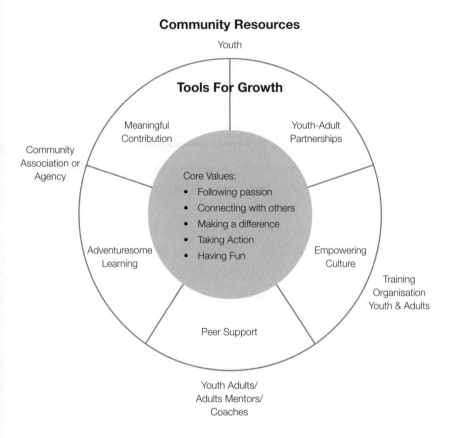

Community Resources

As one adult volunteer with HeartWood characterised his work: "It's an adventure, it's fun and exciting, and we're changing society — changing the world!" Community Youth Development (CYD) is the process of young people being engaged in meaningful participation through planning, decision-making, and programme delivery in government, organisational, institutional, and community settings. While encouraging the gifts and talents of individual young people, CYD places equal focus on the investment of these assets in the community. Individual youth and adults, organisations, and communities all benefit when youth are engaged as full and active participants (Hughes, 2000). The Framework identifies the core values, programme tools, and community resources essential to CYD.

The Framework is based on a research that applied an appreciative inquiry approach for data collection. Here, in-depth interviews were conducted with 54 participants from 12 youth action teams. An equal number of males and females, mainly from rural areas, were interviewed. Participants included 28 young people, 17 adult support people, and 9 community agency representatives who had supported or received service from a team.

There have been numerous benefits to this approach identified by participants. For individuals these include:

- living truer to one's values
- developing self-worth
- becoming a visionary
- seeking opportunities for learning
- taking the initiative for change
- making healthy lifestyle choices
- acting for the good of others

For communities and organisations the benefits include:

- youth supporting youth
- enriched community resources
- shared community vision
- youth making healthy choices
- youth-initiated activity
- genuine youth inclusion
- healthy youth-adult relationships

Youth engagement is the meaningful participation and sustained involvement of a young person in an activity that has a focus outside the individual (Pancer, Rose-Krasner, & Loiselle, 2002). When asked why they engaged as full and active participants, the young people interviewed articulated the core values of the Framework as:

- opportunity to follow their passions
- connections with peers and adults
- a sense that their work makes a difference to others
- the ability to take action
- having fun

The outer circle of the Framework (in Figure 7.2) specifies the community resources identified as facilitating the engagement of young people in community building and organisational development. Youth (and in particular, the recognition of the untapped potential of youth), supportive adults and young adults, community links and associations, and a youth training organisation are all fundamental to the implementation of a sustainable youth-engagement strategy. These community resources create the context within which an organisation or community can successfully implement the tools for growth that are also part of the Framework.

The Framework's Five Tools for Growth provides practical approaches to translate core values of youth engagement into practice. Each has been a component of the work HeartWood does.

Tool #1: Youth-Adult Partnerships

One adult member of a youth action team told researchers, "I think that it's key, that we do it together. It's not us and them. It's all of us participating together, all be our best." Such youth-adult partnerships engage both youth and adults in mutual growth and learning. As role models, adults provide youth with support and inspiration by sharing interests and experiences in an environment of equality and mutual respect. As mentors and coaches, supportive adults are also a resource for young people in connecting them with individuals or organisations. Reciprocally, adults who work with youth in healthy partnerships often find themselves inspired, energised, and increasingly committed to the organisations and communities they serve.

Tool #2: Peer Support

When supported by peers, individuals feel connected, encouraged, and appreciated. Peer support in the context of the Framework involves a balance of play and action, helping young people feel like part of a team or community while taking action that makes a meaningful contribution. As one youth member of a team said, "I think when it comes down to it, we're always going to be there for each other. We're connected and we're really, really close." Relationships rooted in mutual support and acceptance help group members nurture each other's strengths. In turn, their collective voice inspires them to take on challenges and face risks that they might avoid if acting alone.

Tool #3: Adventuresome Learning

Adventure is about exploration, excitement, challenge, mystery, and seeking for the unknown. Community Youth Action teams provide these opportunities. In the words of one youth, "It pushed my personal boundaries, so that was a thrill. It's given me the courage to take on things that I wouldn't have dared before." Young people are drawn to experiences that offer challenge, adventure, and new learning. Adventuresome learning acknowledges youth's needs for action by engaging participants in real-life experiences that challenge them to step outside their comfort zones.

Tool #4: Empowering Culture

"If we were serious about youth empowerment, then we had to make sure that we used meeting processes that said, right from the beginning, that this meeting was theirs." Such is the sentiment expressed by one adult on a Youth Action team. The teams meet the needs of young people for opportunities to demonstrate leadership and exercise real control and power through a group culture that incorporates trust, honesty, and open communication. This kind of empowering culture provides youth with a sense of responsibility for what happens, inspiring them to follow their passions and become co-authors of their vision of their community. .

Tool #5: Meaningful Contribution

Finally, for teams to function well, they must be both fun and encourage a youth's meaningful contribution, which is perceived as being part of something bigger than just the work at hand. Young people thrive when they feel needed, defining their self-worth in relation to their skills and capacities to make a difference. Research shows that the quality of their engagement is more important to their personal growth than the frequency or quantity of participation (Finn & Checkoway, 1998). As one youth team member explained regarding her work, "It's always fun and I always feel like I'm making a difference. That's very important to me." For another young person, participation made him feel a part of a collective of individuals striving to make his community better: "This is our community. We want to change it. We're not going to depend on someone else to change it. We're going to do it."

For practitioners working with young people, the Framework offers a field-tested tool for reflection on the day-to-day work of engaging youth meaningfully. The Five Tools for Growth suggest practical means for developing strategies and approaches to working with young people as partners in programme planning, development, and implementation. However, meaningful youth engagement requires a strong commitment from governing bodies both internal and external to the government structures. This requires providing the financial, human, and policy support to communities and organisations pursuing the work of youth engagement.

From Theory to Practice—And Back Again

As demonstrated in this chapter, efforts to enhance youth empowerment in Canada take a number of different paths. The two examples detailed above, the Phoenix Youth Programmes and HeartWood Centre for Community Youth Development each target very different populations. Phoenix seeks to give voice and resources for health to at risk youth (like Joanie) who may be homeless or at-risk of homelessness. HeartWood provides similar experiences for youth to have a voice and gain access to health resources, but mostly targets their interventions at youth in general, many who grow up seeking to find the power, purpose, and place that comes from being part of a community.

Both groups of youth, those at high and low risk, are generally misperceived by their communities. Contrary to what some might believe, Canadian youth are doing well, and even those most at risk are finding creative ways to sustain their health. Both high and low risk groups of youth say they are motivated to make a contribution to their communities, to participate in processes that affect their health and access to health resources which in turn, results in a sense of empowerment. In their search for this empowerment, youth exploit opportunities for relationships, access to social and health care services and resources, and experiences that bring them feelings of competence. Through praxis of action and reflection, youth find a powerful sense of themselves as contributors to their communities. This is best achieved when their communities make space for their youth. Both Phoenix and HeartWood foster healthy relationships, add resources to the lives of youth, and provide opportunities to build competencies through which a sense of personal control results. Both programmes are meant to foster youth empowerment, although each conducts their work in different ways.

While their approaches may vary, the examples above show that effective programming for youth in Canada challenges the mistaken perceived identities of children as vulnerable, clients, or adults-in-waiting. Instead, programmes like these, convey to youth their more positive roles in their communities, roles that cast them as resilient, participants, and community members in full standing. Each of these roles is synonymous with being empowered. Each relies on a web of services, relationships, and access to various other health resources at the level of the individual, family, and community.

Clearly, when it comes to empowerment, we know what youth need to succeed and feel powerful. Phoenix and HeartWood show us what is possible. However, despite their good work, the debilitating pervasive moral panic that grips communities in Canada makes the work of such organisations much more difficult. Ultimately, it will be up to Canadian youth themselves to challenge the stereotypes that disempower them. Effective programming provides a forum for both advantaged and disadvantaged youth to participate in a process of self and collective youth empowerment. With time, we can only hope that the way youth are perceived will change.

References

Bandura, A. (1998). Exercise of agency in personal and social change. In E. Sanavio (Ed.), *Behaviour and cognitive therapy today: Essays in honour of Hans J. Eysenck* (pp. 1–29). Oxford, UK: Pergamon.

Carrington, P. J. (2001). Changes in police charging of young offenders in Ontario and Saskatchewan after 1984. In T. Fleming, P. O'Reilly & B. Clark (Eds.), *Youth injustice: Canadian perspectives* (2nd ed.) (pp. 13–24). Toronto: Canadian Scholars' Press.

Cowen, E. L. (1991). In pursuit of wellness. *American Psychologist, 46*(4), 404–408.

Davidson, S., & Manion, I. G. (1996). Facing the challenge: mental health and illness in Canadian youth. *Pscyhology, Health & Medicine, 1*(1), 41–56.

Dumont, M., & Provost, M. A. (1999). Resilience in adolescents: Protective role of social support, coping strategies, self-esteem and social activities on experience of stress and depression. *Journal of Youth and Adolescence. 28*(3), 343–363.

Finn, J., & Checkoway, B. (1998). Young people as competent community builders: A challenge to social work. *Social Work,* *43*(4), 335–345.

Freire, P. (1970). *Pedagogy of the oppressed* (M. B. Ramos, Trans.). New York: The Seabury Press. (Original work published in 1968).

Garmezy, N. (1983). Stressors of childhood. In N. Garmezy & M. Rutter (Eds.), *Stress, coping, and development in children* (pp.43-84). New York: McGraw-Hill.

Hughes, D. M. (2000). Community youth development: A framework for action. *Community Youth Development Journal,* *1*(1). Available from www.cydjournal.org/ 2000Winter/Hughes.html.

Kieffer, C. H. (1984). Citizen empowerment: A developmental perspective. *Prevention in Human Services,* *3*(2/3), 9–36.

Lo, T. W. & Au, E. (2004). *Youth empowerment: International experiences.* Hong Kong: City University of Hong Kong.

National Youth Development Information Centre. (1998). *What is youth development?* Retrieved 9 May 2004, from www.nydic.org/ nydic/ programming/whatis/index.htm.

O'Reilly, P., & Fleming T. (2001). Squeegee wars: The state versus street youth. In T. Fleming, P. O'Reilly & B. Clark (Eds.), *Youth injustice: Canadian perspectives* (2nd ed.) (pp. 185–204). Toronto: Canadian Scholars' Press.

Offord, D. R., Boyle, M. H., Szatmari, P. Rae-Grant, N. I., Links, P. S., & Cadman, D., et al. (1987). Ontario child health study: Six-month prevalence of disorder and rates of service utilization. *Archives of General Psychiatry,* *44*(4), 832–836.

Pancer, M., Rose-Krasner, L., & Loiselle, L. D. (2002). Youth conferences as a context for engagement. *New Directions for Youth Development,* *96,* 47–64.

Prilleltensky, I., Peirson, L., & Nelson, G. (2001). Mapping the terrain: Framework for promoting family wellness and preventing child maltreatment. In I. Prilleltensky, G. Nelson, & L. Peirson (Eds.), *Promoting family wellness and preventing child maltreatment:* *Fundamentals for thinking and action* (pp. 3–40). Toronto, ON: University of Toronto Press.

Ryan, W. (1976). *Blaming the victim* (rev. ed.). New York: Vintage Books. (Original work published 1971).

Swift, C., & Levin, G. (1987). Empowerment: An emerging mental health technology. *Journal of Primary Prevention*, 8(1&2), 71–94.

Sykes, D., & Palmer, S. (2003). Treating adolescent girls with disrupted family bonds in residential care through a life stories programme. In K. Kufeldt & B. McKenzie (Eds.), *Child welfare: Connecting research, policy, and practice* (pp. 297–308). Waterloo, ON: Wilfrid Laurier Press.

Trocme, N., Phaneuf, G., Scarth, S., Fallon, B., & MacLaurin, B. (2003). The Canadian incidence study of reported child abuse and neglect: Methodology and major findings. In K. Kufeldt & B. McKenzie (Eds.), *Child welfare: Connecting research, policy, and practice* (pp. 13–26). Waterloo, ON: Wilfrid Laurier Press.

Ungar, M. (1995). *A naturalistic study of the relationship between the process of empowerment and mental health during adolescence.* Unpublished doctoral dissertation, Wilfrid Laurier University, Waterloo, Ontario, Canada.

Ungar, M. (2006). Strengths-based counseling with at-risk youth. *Thousand Oaks*. CA: Corwin Press.

Ungar, M., & Teram, E. (2000). Drifting towards mental health: High-risk adolescents and the process of empowerment. *Youth and Society*, 32(2), 228–252.

Vanier Institute of the Family. (2000). *Profiling Canada's Families II.* Ottawa, ON: The Vanier Institute of the Family.

Willms, D. (2002). A study of vulnerable children. In D. Willms (Ed.), *Vulnerable children* (pp. 3–22). Edmonton, AB: University of Alberta Press.

Zimmerman, M. A. (1990). Toward a theory of learned hopefulness: A structural model analysis of participation and empowerment. *Journal of Research in Personality*, 24, 71–86.

YOUTH EMPOWERMENT IN SINGAPORE: THEORY, EXPERIENCE, AND PRACTICE

8

Ngoh Tiong TAN

Introduction

Although the world's overall population is aging, youth of today are both a potential asset as well as a resource for the future. Youthful energy and idealism bring hope and provide the impetus for social change. Youth represent hope for tomorrow's better world.

The United Nations defined youth as individuals aged 15 to 24 years, whereas in the Asia-Pacific region, youth can range from 13 to 35 years (UNESCAP, 2004). Overall, the population has increased steadily, with over 60% of the world's youth currently living in the Asia-Pacific region.

The latest figure for the total population of Singapore is 4.2 million. The median age of Singaporeans has steadily increased over the years and is now 35.3 years. In 1970, the median age was only 20, in 1980 it was 24, 1990 it was 29, and at 2000 it was 34 years (Department of Statistics, 2000; see also www.singstat.gov.sg/keystats/c2000/topline11.pdf). Demographic data between the years 1990 and 2000 saw a percentage decrease (from 25% to 21%) in the population of those below 35 years and an increase (from about 10.5% to 14.5%) of those above 30 years old. In 2004, there were 983,000 youth, aged 15–34 years, living in Singapore (see www.singstat.gov.sg/keystats/c2000/topline9.pdf). This figure is 691,000, if youth are defined as individuals aged 15–29 years, as adopted by the Singapore's National Youth Council.

This chapter presents a rationale and theory of empowerment and focuses on Singapore's overall experience toward youth empowerment. Arising from empowerment theory is condition of meaningful participation such that youth are able to influence both local and national policies. Empowerment in this sense is about meeting real needs and aspirations. It involves the understanding of idealism and enormous potential energy of youth and harnessing it for constructive development and societal contribution (Lo & Au, 2004; Teen Empowerment, 2004). Youth also actively organise themselves as a power coalition for action and advocacy.

Table 8.1   Singapore's age demographics, 1990 and 2000

Age Groups	1990 (%)	2000 (%)
0–14	23.0	21.2
15–29	27.5	21.2
30–44	27.8	28.4
45–59	12.7	18.2
60 and above	9.0	10.7

Source: Department of Statistics (2000).

Development of collective power as such, is especially significant in the face of a progressively aging society like Singapore.

Youth and Juvenile Delinquency

A youth empowerment process is negatively correlated with criminalising behaviour. Developing countries all face rising crimes and delinquency rates. In Singapore in 2002, there was a 56% increase in the arrest of juveniles, aged 7 to 15 years, to 2,200 persons, with students forming more than two thirds (78%) of those arrested (Ho, 2003). Nearly half of these juveniles were arrested for theft and shoplifting.

To deal with teenage offenders in Singapore, the Inter-Ministry Committee on Youth Crime (IMYC) was formed in 1995. The IMYC consists of key stakeholders such as: the Ministry of Community Development and Sports, Ministry of Education, Ministry of Home Affairs, the Singapore Police Force, the Subordinate Courts, the Prisons Department, the National Council of Social Services, and the National Youth Council. They work collaboratively to prevent and educate local youth about committing crimes (Ho, 2003).

Since the formation of the IMYC in 1995, the numbers of youth aged 7–19, arrested in Singapore has steadily declined (Ho, 2002). The proportionate decrease from 1999 to 2001 has been a consistent trend (Ho, 2002). The number of youth arrested has decreased from 3,446 in 1999, to 2,986 in 2000, to 2,474 in 2001, calculated as a decline of 13% from 1999 to 2000, and a further decline of 17% from 2000 to 2001 (Ho, 2002).

Further analyses revealed that the number of youth arrested for offences related to public order decreased from years 2000 to 2001. Such offences included: unlawful assembly (down 40%), rioting (down 30%), serious hurt (down 55%), and possession of offensive weapons (down 37%) (Ho, 2002). These decreases bode well for our societal stability, and they have direct impact on youth development and empowerment.

Key areas of youth work focus on addressing the underlying causes of juvenile delinquency and transforming youth to function in mainstream society. Delinquency is often associated with a lack of parental supervision and discipline, negative media, peer influence, low self-esteem, and lack of self-discipline (Wong, 1996). It appears that youth from broken families, with absentee fathers, and family conflicts are more vulnerable to committing offences. Stress and tension at home may lead teenagers run away from their families to identify and affiliate with street corner gangs and other alienated youth (Choi & Lo, 2004).

Academic under achievement, low self-esteem, and a lack of self-discipline and social responsibility are characteristic profiles of delinquents (Wong, 1996). It is essential to deal with these factors when working with youth. Youth also need to develop skills in anger management, self-confidence, and a sense of purpose, so as to learn how to avoid negative peer influences and curtail negative behaviours such as gambling, drinking, and smoking (Ho, 2002). These are the lifelong and sustaining skills and attributes for successful negotiation of the adult world which youth in their "rites of passage" into functional society need to develop and assimilate. To be successful in the adult world, there are many societal demands and responsibilities that youth need to address.

Empowerment Theory

Empowerment is about the ability to harness resources to meet needs. It means providing for the youth's actual needs, not just an adult's understanding of their needs. Empowerment thus, necessitates being functional and competent in relation to fulfilling one's life tasks.

Empowerment is a dynamic concept and is the basis of social work practice. Social work is empowering as it seeks to release human and social power to promote personal, interpersonal, and structural competence in social functioning (DuBois & Miley, 1996). The ability to decide or control one's destiny is indeed empowering. Often, there are gaps between a youth's ideals and his/her environment (Chan, 2001; Ward, 1982). Thus, it is vital that youth programmes enhance the capacity for decision-making and autonomy over choices to influence those decisions. This can be accomplished through the provision of training, supervision, and guidance that promote self-efficacy. The development of opportunities and resources required for goal realisation and achievement of ideals are "part and parcel" of any successful empowerment strategy.

Empowerment involves five interrelated processes (Crawshaw, Mitchell, Bunton, & Green, 2000; Jessor, 1992; Karvonen, West, Sweeting, Rahkonen, & Young, 2001; Lee, 1991; Pandian & Tan, 2003; Tan, 1995):

1. Goal achievement based on the youth's own goals;

2. An agenda of action based on the needs of young people;

3. A long term commitment to work progressively on constructive programmes;

4. An equal partnership in participation between adults and youths; and,

5. A respect for diversity and non-judgmental valuing of the differences of youth.

To elaborate on these five processes of empowerment, first, the goals of services should be based on goals which the youth recognise and own as theirs. This means that achieving these goals must also be attainable. Young (1999) saw it as to "recognise, explore and challenge their senses of self and guide their actions . . . a closer correspondence between their goals and the sense of how to achieve them" (p. 88). Youth should be provided with opportunities to learn from their life experiences.

Second, the agenda for effective programmes should be based on the needs of young people rather than on adult interests (Jessor, 1992; Tan, 2003). Funding agencies often mandate the directions that such programmes should take. However, an empowerment approach should be based on growth in line with youth needs (Crawshaw et al., 2000).

Third, there must be a long term, rather than an episodic, commitment to work progressively on meaningful activities and constructive programmes. Communities will thus value these youth, and they are willing to invest in them in the long run—as they will be their future citizens (Pandian & Tan, 2003). Empowering activities as such, engage youth in developing skills and knowledge over their life span (Karvonen et al., 2001).

Fourth, the power relationship between adults and youth is one of the equals as in a true collaborative partnership. Adults should not control, and/or direct these interactions but empower youth to make their own decisions. This provides youth with avenues of greater involvement, participation, and thus greater commitment to any programme.

Finally here, there must be a healthy respect for diversity and non-judgmental valuing of the differences of youth. Youth, like all of us, wish to be treated with dignity, respect, and acceptance. Service delivery to youth should not have pre-judgemental programmes or stereotype them in any way (Pandian & Tan, 2003).

These five principles must be the basis of youth policies and programmes that promote youth empowerment. The various activities aimed at different levels of interventions may be collaboratively developed. The other side of empowerment and integration is the marginalisation of the youth and disempowerment.

The Singapore Model

There is generally a positive trend toward youth empowerment in Singapore, moving toward developmental and preventive interventions. Singapore's model focuses on an investment in people through the cornerstones of education, youth, and community development (Tan, 2003).

Singapore's approach is one of the "many helping hands." This is a collaborative model where government and non-government organisations (NGOs), as well as other sectors such as religious, community, and self-help groups are mobilised in working together to provide needed services. Formal as well as informal organisations work in complementary ways to meet a wide range of human, and specifically, youth's needs.

In Singapore, government leadership and initiatives are evident, especially in the provision of infrastructures for youth. Together with the NGOs and prevailing market forces, the state provides services at developmental, preventive, and remedial levels. High visibility of government projects including youth work, are promoted in Inter-Parliamentary committees (IMYC, 2004), the National Youth Council (NYC), and the People's Association. Although the state's initiatives and coordination are vital, the strategy for effective problem-solving and service delivery must incorporate in this process all of the various stakeholders.

The NYC (2004) views youth development as an active process by which young people are engaged, equipped, and empowered to become active and contributing citizens in society. It is a process which prepares youth to meet the challenges of the transition to adulthood through co-ordinated and progressive activities and experiences which help them become socially, morally, emotionally, physically, and cognitively competent (NYC, 2004; NYDIC, 1988). This model, instead of focusing on young people's deficits, works at building the creative capacities inherent in each young person. In the face of globalisation, we need to prepare youth to be "world-ready"—or those with the values, outlook, and skills to thrive and succeed in a global environment and yet maintain strong ties to their families, communities, and nation. These are youth who "dare to dream," have a "can do" and "never say die" attitude, and are able to "walk the talk," and "serve by doing" (NYC, 2004). The hope is for a new generation of resilient Singaporean youth with high aspirations, positive thinking, and values and principles that will enable them to make meaningful contributions to society, overall. They will be ready and prepared to compete in the knowledge-based, technological global economy. To achieve these goals, the NYC serves to increase the capability of youth organisations to provide services to them through funding and other forms of support. NYC also creates a supportive environment in which youth can participate in national education programmes, international exchanges, and projects which both develop youth and benefit the community as well (NYC, 2004).

There is an observed relationship between powerlessness and dysfunctional behaviour (Teen Empowerment, 2004). High-risk youth are often without opportunities for power in legitimate ways. In turn, some may resort to the use of weapons, involvement with gangs, drugs, risky sexual behaviours, and criminal and self-destructive acts to gain power. Youth need authentic and constructive opportunities to exercise their power (Teen Empowerment, 2004). Young (1999) suggested that young people also constantly challenge their perceived powerlessness and develop their sense of self and purpose through successfully negotiating these challenges.

Developmental Practice Framework

A social developmental framework is advocated for as the model for youth development and empowerment. This investment framework, as proposed by Midgley (1995), Midgley and Sherraden (1997), and Sherraden (1991), returns resources back into the economy. Investment in youth is thus perceived as a long term investment and developmental strategy. The focus of this model is to expand training and increase the formation of social capital. Mainstream developmental work includes partnerships with social and political systems and business corporations such as the Youth for Causes (2004) developed by YMCA of Singapore and sponsored by Citibank.

The Youth for Causes group, with the US$55,000 funding from the Citigroup Foundation, offers youth, aged 15–35 years, a platform to turn entrepreneurial ideas into reality, as well as raising money for charity. The list of welfare organisations, as beneficiaries of the project, include: children and youth, disabled, drug rehabilitation and after care, family, and other social service agencies. Each project is provided with $1,600 as seed money, to implement an idea that they came up with in order to help the particular group. The programme develops simultaneously leadership, project management, and entrepreneurial skills (Youth for Causes, 2004). Besides helping those in need (through this project), youth take initiative and also learn to mobilise and manage resources in their community, creatively working with the opportunities available and presented to them (Youth for Causes, 2004).

For the Citibank Youth for Causes 2003, a combined total net cash profit of more than $170,000 was raised through various project initiatives and was donated to 23 voluntary welfare organisations. For the project execution period, a remarkable total of 1,400 volunteers were also mobilised (Youth for Causes, 2004). These outcomes reflect the potential impact of youth participation. It was empowering to the extent that youth themselves exhibited creative talents, resolve, and resources for goal accomplishment. They were able to harness resources to make positive contributions to other less fortunate members of society. Mentors of Citibank, as adult resources, were the volunteers who served as advisors, teachers, and supports to these youth. The mentors were "to be enthusiastic and encouraging, helping the youth see a 'big picture' and resolve conflict constructively" (Youth for Causes, 2004). Mentors monitor participants' progress and are responsible for reminding them to adhere to the project proposal and budget. The mentors testified that it "was inspiring to experience the passion, energy and enthusiasm of the youth" and that they were "amazed by the determination of youth to go all out to make a difference . . . many people do not have such dedication or desire to give a little back to society" (Youth for Causes, 2004). Overall, the programme seeks to nurture youth to be concerned community leaders of tomorrow, and reportedly, it has accomplished its goals (Youth for Causes, 2004). The experiences afforded by this project provided for a positive value development, and a more caring and compassionate youth.

The project also provided evidence that volunteerism and caring for others is "alive and well" among Singaporean youth (Youth for Causes, 2004). Youth learn to handle adversity and problems encountered, and are able to be flexible and innovative in overcoming challenges as they arise. One of the winning teams, the "Care Bears", produced and sold an "inspirational journal" that raised $11,000 for the Children At-Risk Empowerment (CARE) Association. CARE provides for troubled students before and after-school care, as well as counselling services. One youth said, ". . . although I cannot save the world single-handedly, I believe that as long as I make an effort, in some small way, I can better the world for someone else" (Youth for Causes, 2004, p. 1). Other innovative Youth for Causes projects included: selling roses and Valentine day's balloons to raise money for Children's Cancer Foundation; using phone technology to raise money for Girls Brigade; and the production of photographic record of the elderly occupants of a Hospital.

In evaluating Youth for Causes, Eddie Khoo, Chairman of the Organising Committee for the project said, "What's key at the end of the day, is that the youth are able to gain the practical knowledge and experiences they need to do their parts for the local communities in which they live and work. This programme will enable youths to acquire further leadership skills and knowledge beyond the classroom" (Citigroup, 2004). The benefit of such a project is in its ability to facilitate networking among voluntary sector organisations and local best practices on resource mobilisation for strengthening the voluntary sector, overall (Citigroup, 2004).

A programme related to the Youth for Causes is the Service-Learning Project. Service-Learning is one of the tools for the Reach Youth Centre's programme (Ho, 2001). Service-Learning seeks to enhance the effectiveness of youth development programmes by "engaging them in a systematic and meaningful process to discover important values and lessons that enhance their life skills while performing needful service to the society" (Ho, 2001, p. 1). Altogether 160 youth from six schools were involved in Service-Learning which was supported by the National Youth Council and Central Singapore Community Development Council. Different welfare organisations, such as Club Rainbow, Bishan Home for the Intellectually Disabled, and the Singapore Association of the Visually Handicapped and World Vision were identified as beneficiaries. The youth "performed assigned tasks and sought out treasures with the beneficiaries" (Ho, 2001, p. 1). The aim was a realisation that the treasures are the beneficiaries themselves, and that the youth would learn something valuable about themselves and the community, respectively (Ho, 2001, p. 1).

Besides the above projects cited, school Community Involvement Projects, youth choirs, dramatic activities, other overseas humanitarian programmes, study trips, participation in cultural or sports festivals, as well as adventure programmes provide additional opportunities for the development of youth. A youth@venture homepage (website address: www.sg/nyc/adventure.htm) offers information and advice on the adventure programmes available to Singaporean youth (NYC, 2003).

All of these useful experiences provide opportunities for both doing as well as learning. Collaboration between adult mentors and youth along constructive experiences is empowering for both.

Finally, the needs of different parties involved, including the social service agencies, are met in various and respectful ways. Youth participation provides channels for integrating them directly into mainstream society.

Remedial and Preventive Youth Work

A National University of Singapore's study on Empowerment of Youth found that significant and growing numbers of young people in Singapore are still not getting their basic developmental needs met through current social, educational, or political structures (Community Matters, 2002; Pandian & Tan, 2003; Tan 2003). They are increasingly disconnected from their families, schools, and community institutions. Youth who have left the school system are at greater risk of experiencing low self-esteem that may lead them to seek out delinquent means of attaining these needs (Ho and Yip, 2003; Kaplan, 1984; Yip, 2001). Singapore is known to be a meritocratic and elitist society. School children and youth, in coping with societal demands, are experiencing increased stress and pressure on a daily basis. Thus, youth who are unable to cope with the existing academic and mainstream system may be disadvantaged and ill equipped for their future.

The laws affecting Singaporean children below the age of 14 and young persons who are aged 14 and above, but below 16 years of age, are contained in the Children and Young Persons Act (CAP. 38). The definition of a juvenile is one who is 7 years or above and below the age of 16. The purpose of the Act is to protect children and young persons and make provisions for the handling of juvenile offenders in juvenile courts and approved homes. There are some offences that apply to juveniles only, not to adults. Regulations that affect youth include the minimum age of 18 years for purchasing alcohol and cigarettes, or to smoke in a public place, obtaining a driver's license as well as entry into nightclubs.

A Special Marriage License is also required for people below the age of 18 wanting to get married. For Muslim marriages, the minimum age is 16 and the parents must be present if the male is below 21 years of age. The legal minimum age for movies categorised as Restricted Artistic R(A) is 21 years of age (Health Promotion Board, 2004; Youth Research Network, 2004). Delinquency, as in smoking and drinking, is thus an infringement of the legal statues when the young people have not attained the required age permitted for such acts.

Preventive programmes should receive greater emphasis (Tan, 1995; 2002). These programmes include those that deal with pre-delinquency issues, such programmes which strengthen families, and those served by community-based agencies that provide youth and other community services. Youth need outreach activities and alternative platforms to have their needs met in healthy outlets or through socially acceptable means. Youth programmes delivered by social service agencies thus far, are preventive or rehabilitative in nature (Ho, 2002).

Remedial intervention is also recommended to deal with youth who are in trouble with the law and who navigate outside the mainstream of the formal education and employment systems. Youth work also often incorporates with such preventive elements. The key focus of preventive interventions is in the strengthening of individuals and their families through a range of youth and family services.

Streetwise Programme

An example of youth empowerment in Singapore is the Streetwise Programme (SWP), initiated in 1997 by the Inter Ministry Youth Crime Committee (IMYC, 2004), and coordinated by the National Youth Council. The primary aim of SWP is to reduce juvenile delinquency by targeting a specific group of wayward youth who have drifted into street corner gangs. SWP is conceptualised as a non-residential community-based treatment programme for juvenile offenders who are arrested for gang related activities.

The programme objectives are to change the behaviour of

youth gang members by enhancing their self-esteem, personal responsibility, conflict-resolution skills, and their abilities to manage through the provision of opportunities of creative expressions. SWP is a multi-faceted approach in partnership with the police, prisons, and juvenile courts and is administered by the youth or family service organisations (IMYC, 2004).

In seeking to prevent youth from drifting into gangs, the juvenile court may refer certain young offenders to the SWP, as a condition of their probation. The aim is to provide an opportunity for youth to change and dissociate from other gang members in such instances. Police referrals and placement into SWP are through the Secret Societies Branch of the Criminal Investigation Department. Under the police referral system, a youth would be eligible for the programme if s/he has not committed any offence; is age 13 to 18; is a Singapore Citizen or Singapore Permanent Resident; and will reside in Singapore for the next 12 months from the date of enrolment into the programme (IMYC, 2004).

A youth may be associated with a secret society but have the desire to "turn over a new leaf". S/he has to agree to the conditions of the SWP and sign a contractual letter of undertaking (IMYC, 2004). His/her parents must also agree to co-operate with social workers and attend all guidance sessions and activities organised by the agency as required. They must carry out other instructions offered by the social worker. Voluntary self-referrals for the SWP are also accepted, where youth have realised their mistakes and wish to leave the influence and pressure of gangs. Since the SWP is a voluntary diversionary programme, it does not have control over clients and families. Hence, a downward trend in attendance has been observed in some of the SWP projects.

The four respective social service agencies administering SWP help youth make a fresh start in their life with a series of counselling, life skills, recreational, and social programmes like art, music, sports, and career guidance. SWP also includes a visit to a prison. For some youth, court conditions and prescribed activities are attached to their programme participation. One such activity involves the opportunity for youth to see for themselves, the desolate conditions in the prison, as well as the tough regime prisoners must go through. This is intended to serve as a warning to youth so as to encourage them to avoid further trouble with the law (NYC, 2004).

Overall, the SWP develops a structured and disciplined lifestyle among youth. Youth attend activities and sessions held in the Social Service Centres' either before or after their school sessions keeping them (ideally) favourably pre-disposed. There is time allocated there for both homework and recreation. This community approach provides a constructive alternative in terms of healthy pursuits for delinquent youth. In an evaluation, SWP is viewed as a comprehensive programme, consisting of a range of activities such as sports activities, group work, and constructive hobbies that balance the restrictions of the juvenile probation supervision (Pandian & Tan, 2003). The developmental portions of the programme also aid in the prevention of future youth problems.

Teen Development Programme

In evaluating the Teen Development Programme (TDP), funded under the Streetwise Programme, Yeo (1998) observed that it had undergone various changes. The heavy educational stance from the inception of the programme consists of self-development, e.g. enhanced self-identity, relationship-building such as male-female, peer and parental relationships, and a heightened sense of societal responsibilities. There is also an emphasis on education and career as well as skill development, e.g. problem-solving and conflict management skills. Parent meetings have also positively evolved into parent education and supporting group (Yeo, 1998). Counsellors also assess youth in the SWP who have potential for positive change, overall.

Yeo (1998) found that the evaluation part of TDP was not consistently applied and as a result, he instituted his own outcome measures. As to whether youth found the programme to be useful, the average score obtained was a 3.5 on a 5-point Likert-scale. Although youth did not disclose their personal problems to staff, the mean was only 2.3; they apparently enjoyed their time at the TDP, scoring it at a relatively high mean of 4.1 out of the maximum of 5 on the scale (Yeo, 1998). These figures provided tentative empirical detachment indication of the effectiveness of the SWP and specifically, the TDP.

Generally, in terms of social and youth agency programmes, emphasis is often placed on remedial activities rather than on vague developmental needs of youth. The SWP and other related programmes (besides the remedial orientation) also have a preventive focus in changing the behaviour of youth gang members by enhancing their self-esteem, personal responsibility, conflict resolution skills, and ability to manage anger. This is achieved through the provision of positive creative outlets, such as art, sports, and musical activities.

Cirque du Monde

Cirque du Monde, another similar project, closely follows this creativity notion. Here, circus and acrobatic techniques are offered as an alternative means of empowering youth (Pandian & Tan, 2003). The teen circus also provides the means for legitimate income generation and the development of discipline and employable skills. Project Kemistry, a spin-off from Cirque du Monde, uses the circus programme to reach out these troubled or delinquent youth. This is also developmental in nature, utilising arts as an alternative learning approach to re-build the character of such youth. It provides constructive, enriching opportunities for growth through a series of creative activities. Perhaps involving students, families, and the school, and being comprehensive and integrative, would enhance this project's overall effectiveness. Working with families to foster support and enhance positive communication also adds value to the programme (Pandian & Tan, 2003). As this programme is based on the principle of voluntary participation, it is assumed not only a higher client self-motivation, but also a possibility of dropping out and discontinuation of youth participation. These are challenges that social work programmes face in reality. It is, however, integral to the cornerstone principles of self-determination and empowerment.

Project Bridge

Project Bridge which reaches out to youth at-risk is another initiative of the Inter Ministry Committee on Youth Crime (IMYC), launched in June 2000, by the Community Development Council, YMCA and the NYC. Project Bridge, based in youth centres, reaches out to those who had left school prematurely. It works closely with schools in the community with programmes including counselling, referrals for job attachments or training, and encouraging social skills, leadership, and personal development in youth (Ho, 2002). Project Bridge also provides tuition, personal coaching to develop learning skills, and effective study methods to enhance the academic link of the youth.

Guidance Programme

The Ministry of Community Development and Sports and the National Youth Council have implemented yet another programme for youth apprehended for random petty offences, such as shoplifting and theft, and street-corner gang activities. It is called the Guidance Programme. This programme provides guidance and counsel to youth through informal, as well as organised activities.

Other Prevention Programmes

The Ministry of Education, with the support of the National Council of Social Services, provides teacher-counsellors and school-based social work as a further prevention strategy. The teacher-counsellors counsel and work with students to impart life skills. Training includes instilling conflict resolution and management skills in the youth. Police, through this project, provide prevention and educational talks in schools (Ho, 2002). This affords resources to youth increasing their utilisation of, as well as accessibility to other societal systems. IMYC, together with the National Crime Prevention Council (NCPC), has produced a set of exhibition panels to discourage students from committing crimes. This is an ongoing educational campaign involving the Police, NCPC, and the schools. The collaborative approach by the IMYC has generally been productive, overall (Ho, 2003).

Another joint project of the Subordinate Courts and the Ministry of Education, trains secondary school student leaders to mediate peer disputes. Prevention programmes including school assembly talks, Community Network Forums, Police-School Liaison System, Out-of-School Youths Working Group, and the National Drug Abuse Awareness Campaign target the prevention of delinquency. In the courts, Family Conferences, Juvenile Offender Behaviour Criteria, Guidance Programme, "boot-camp," school-probation-courts link-up, and the Youth Family Care Programme are primarily rehabilitative in nature (Tan, 2003).

Another youth intervention project, tried in the juvenile court, is family conferencing between the offender and his family, with the victim of the offence and his family. The intention here is to allow the offender to understand the consequences of his/her actions and bring about heartfelt remorse and change. This project has both preventive and remedial elements and ultimately, it seeks to prevent recidivism.

These programmes, with varying results, are the initial efforts of youth work in Singapore. Using such methods of proactive outreach and enhancing and developing the potential of at-risk youth has great potential, as we have noted to date. They provide an alternative avenue for youth identity and affiliation. Moreover, new avenues for youth expression are also available through the various youth programmes noted previously. They need however, to be developed and driven more by the youth themselves, rather than adults. Youth initiative and leadership are essential benchmarks for strategic empowerment, also a trust and respect are vital to move the empowerment process forward.

Overall, efforts to reach and engage high-risk teens must provide youth with ways of achieving viable positions of legitimate power, i.e. the ability to make decisions and take action with the potential to substantially impact their schools, workplaces, and communities (Teen Empowerment, 2004). The long term strategy in empowering youth is not only to provide remedial and preventive programmes, but also to strengthen education, employment, and health of the youth (Tan, 2003). The importance of positive values rooted to the family, community, and nation is also vital (Ho & Yip, 2003; Tan, 2003). The centre of empowerment is the development of the youth's inner spiritual core for purposeful and meaningful human direction.

Conclusion

As a meritocratic society, Singapore places high achievers, be they educational or economic, on a pedestal. As a result of the preoccupation with academic excellence, students who have different aptitudes and inclinations other than in the academic arena, are not given due recognition and credit (Pandian & Tan, 2003; Singapore 21 Committee, 1999). Instead of social and political exclusion, all youth need to be included in the core operating systems of our society. Youth differences in abilities and talents need to be accepted, valued, and celebrated.

Working with both mainstream and disadvantaged youth is a key strategy to preserve and foster human and social capital. Thus, youth are empowered in both having their needs met and further to contribute to society. Youth also need to organise themselves as a power base for further action. Youth participation and action are the keys to a vibrant and progressive society.

Youth empowerment involves the facilitation of youth advocacy and voice within the system so that it can be heard and heeded. It is about meaningful participation by youth to influence policy and bring about real change (NACC, 2004). This involves an awareness-raising of issues which impacts on young people as well as the promotion of the participation of young people, especially in decision-making processes, overall (UNESCAP, 2004). Youth are the future of the world and empowering youth is actually a human empowerment toward a better world of great hope, not only in Singapore but in any nation which hopes to thrive and develop.

References

Chan, W. L. (2001). *Empowering delinquents: A guidance programme groupwork.* Honours Thesis, Department of Social Work and Psychology, National University of Singapore.

Choi, A., & Lo, T.W. (2004). *Fighting youth crime: A comparative study of two little dragons in Asia* (2nd Ed.). Singapore: Eastern University Press.

Citigroup. (2004). *Philanthropy—Corporate Citizenship.* Retrieved 11 May 2004, from www.citigroup.com/citigroup/citizen/philanthropy/021022a.htm.

Community Matters (2002). *Engaging the least engaged youth.* Retrieved 5 September 2002, from http://commatters.org/youth/engage.htm.

Crawshaw, P., Mitchell, W., Bunton, R., & Green, E. (2000). Youth empowerment and youth research: Expertise, subjection and control. *Youth and Policy, 60,* 1–17.

Department of Statistics. (2000). Singapore census of population 2000, *Advanced Data Release No 4.* Singapore Department of Statistics, December 2000.

DuBois, B., & Miley, K. K. (1996). *Social work: An empowering profession* (2nd ed.). Boston: Allyn Bacon.

Health Promotion Board. (2004). Retrieved 11 May 2004, from www.teencentral.gov.sg.

Ho, K. C., & Yip, J. (2003). *Youth.sg.* Singapore: National Youth Council.

Ho, P. K. (2001). Speech by Associate Professor Ho Peng Kee, Minister of State for Law and Home Affairs and Chairman of the Inter-Ministry Committee on Youth Crime at the official launch of Reach Youth Centre, 16 June 2001, Singapore.

Ho, P. K. (2002). Keynote address by Associate Professor Ho Peng Kee,

Senior Minister of State (Law and Home Affairs) at the ASEAN Seminar on Urban Youth Work II, 19 March 2002, Singapore.

Ho, P. K. (2003). Speech by Associate Professor Ho Peng Kee, Senior Minister of State (Law and Home Affairs) at the official launch of "Stop Stop Theft" Programme, 16 July 2003, Singapore.

Inter Ministry Committee on Youth Crime (IMYC). (2004). *Streetwise Programme*. Retrieved 11 May 2004, from www.imyc.org.sg/prog_rehab_02.html.

Jessor, R. (1992). Risk behaviour in adolescence: A psychosocial framework for understanding and action. *Journal of Adolescent Health Care, 12,* 597–605.

Kaplan, H. B. (1984). *Patterns of juvenile delinquency.* Beverly Hills: Sage Publications.

Karvonen, S., West, P., Sweeting, H., Rahkonen, O., & Young, R. (2001). Lifestyle, social class and health-related behaviour: A cross-cultural comparison of 15 year olds in Glasgow and Helsinki. *Journal of Youth Studies, 4(4),* 393–413.

Lee, F. F. L. (1991). Empowerment model in youth work. *Asia Pacific Journal of Social Work, 9(2),* 36–103.

Lo, T. W. & Au, E. (2004). *Youth empowerment: International experiences.* Hong Kong: City University of Hong Kong.

Midgley, J. (1995). *Social development: The developmental perspective in social welfare.* Thousand Oaks, CA: Sage.

Midgley, J., & Sherraden, M. (1997). *Alternatives to social security: An international inquiry.* Westport, CT: Auburn House.

National Association of Counsel for Children (NACC). (2004). *Youth Empowerment.* Retrieved 11 May 2004, from www.naccchildlaw.org/training/youth.html.

NYC. (2003). *Adventure.* www.sg/nyc/adventure.htm.

NYC. (2004). *National Youth Council.* www.sg/nyc.

NYDIC. (1988). *National Youth Development Information Centre, 1988.* Singapore: National Youth Council.

Pandian, S., & Tan, M. F. (2003). *A youth empowerment model.* Working Paper, Department of Social Work and Psychology, National University of Singapore.

Sherraden, M. W. (1991). *Assets and the poor: A new American welfare policy.* Armonk, NY: M. E. Sharpe.

Singapore 21 Committee. (1999). *Summary of the deliberations of the subject committees to the Singapore 21 Committee.* Unpublished paper. Singapore.

Tan, N. T. (1995). The challenge to preventive youth work. *Asia Pacific Journal of Social Work,* 5(2), 68–74.

Tan, N. T. (2002, March). *Issues and challenges of Asian youth.* Plenary paper presented at ASEAN Seminar on Urban Youth Work II, Orchard Hotel, National Youth Council, Singapore.

Tan N. T. (2003, November). *Strategies for the development of human and social capital for youths in a changing world.* Plenary Paper presented at International Conference on Working with Youth in a Rapidly Changing World, Department of Social Work, Hong Kong Baptist University, Hong Kong.

Teen Empowerment. (2004). *Teen Empowerment Model.* Retrieved 11 May 2004, from www.teenempowerment.com/model.html.

UNESCAP. (2004). *Having Asia-Pacific UN Focal Point for Youth,* Retrieved 11 May 2004, from www.unescap-healthdev.org/youth/index.htm.

Ward, D. (1982). *Give them a break: Social action by young people at risk and in trouble.* Leicester: National Youth Bureau.

Wong K. S. (1996). Speech by Mr Wong Kan Seng, Minister for Home Affairs at the 1996 Seminar on Reducing Juvenile Delinquency, Organised by the Inter-Ministry Committee on Juvenile Delinquency, 30 November 1996, Singapore.

Yeo, W. T. (1998). *Evaluation of the Talent Development Programme.* Academic Exercise, Department of Social Work & Psychology, National University of Singapore.

Yip, K. L. (2001). *Deviant pathways? A journey into the lives of early school leavers.* Academic Exercise, Department of Sociology, National University of Singapore.

Young, K. (1999). The youth worker as guide, philosopher and friend – the realities of participation and empowerment. In S. Banks (Ed.), *Ethical issues in youth work* (pp. 77–92). London: Routledge.

Youth for Causes (2004). Retrieved 11 May 2004 from www.youthforcauses.com/about.htm.

Youth Research Network. (2004). Retrieved 11 May 2004, from www.nyc.gov.sg/yrn/statures.asp.

PROJECT PASSPORT: EMPOWERING YOUNG MINORITY WOMEN THROUGH A VOLUNTEER PROGRAMME IN THE UNITED STATES

9

Monit CHEUNG

Acknowledgements

This study is based on a research grant funded by Small Grants Programme Application, University of Houston, co-researched with Dr. Maxine Weinman Epstein of the University of Houston, and Dr. Peggy Smith and Dr. Ruth Buzi of the Teen Health Clinic at the Baylor College of Medicine.

Introduction

The area of immigrant urban children and youth is a critical one. Cultural adaptation, combined with care and concern, is a required component for practice and research on urban immigrant children and youth. Feldman (1998) indicated that immigrant and second-generation families, who reside in large urban cities, will be an increasing population of interest in future society. These families are of interest because their numbers have increased to more than three times that of the growth of children in non-immigrant families.

In Houston Texas, our research team at the Teen Health Clinic conducted research about adolescent mental health issues. In one study, we reported that female teens, especially ethnic minorities who attended family planning clinics, tended to demonstrate more mental health problems and symptoms, as well as high-risk behaviours (Buzi, Weinman, & Smith, 2000). Many do not understand the concept of "willingness to help needy strangers" (Cheung, 2006) because they themselves need help.

In order to help these teens better understand the concept of self-help and volunteerism, we developed a programme called "Project Passport." It is based upon a framework which integrates attachment and resiliency in teens' asset development. "Project Passport" is promoted as a certified volunteer programme which aims to attract and recruit minority teens to learn adaptive life long skills. It stresses the use of a structured curriculum design (i.e. learning to re-attach) and "hands-on" activities (i.e. learning to keep one's commitment) in order to encompass the 40 developmental assets recommended by our Search Institute data (1997). The programme also uses resiliency theory to emphasise the various components by providing: a) a caring, supportive adult, b) meaningful activities, and c) high expectations for the behaviour of young people (Gabriel, Hopson, Haskins, & Powell, 1996). The purpose of this chapter is to describe how to use this field tested curriculum with incentives to promote the idea of volunteerism while helping the female teens to build their assets.

The Need

"Project Passport" was initiated because the need for mental health services for children, youth, and adolescents in the greater Houston area was substantial. The 2003 Report of the Children and Adolescents Committee of the Mental Health Needs Council, Inc., found that approximately 108,478 (11%) of children and adolescents who resided in Harris County were likely to have met the criteria for severe emotional disturbance, and 19,723 (2%) were likely to need public mental health services. In the city of Houston, it is estimated that 19,130 children under 18 years of age need publicly funded mental health services for a diagnosable mental illness.

Since Houston is an ethnically diverse city with a population of 2,000,000 composed of 5% Asian/Pacific Islander, 25% Black/African American, 31% White/European, and 37% Hispanic/Latino (U.S. Census Bureau, 2001), any intervention for inner city youth must include culturally relevant services for high-risk migrant, immigrant, and mobile adolescent populations.

Data on mental health needs among N=281 female family planning patients at the Baylor College of Medicine Teen Health Clinic showed a high frequency of family and relationship problems as well as symptoms of nervousness, depression, and anger (Buzi et al., 2000). A recent study, among N=110 adolescents at the Houston Teen Health Clinic, showed that resiliency in combination with family support affected depression symptoms among indigent adolescents (Weinman, Buzi, Smith, & Mumford, 2003). These findings suggested that several of the resiliency domains, as measured by the Individual Protective Factors Index (IPFI), as well as family support measured by the Family Support Scale (FSS), were associated with depressive symptoms. Their findings also suggested that 16.4% of the teens in the clinic could be classified as clinically depressed and as needing further evaluation.

These results supported the contention that adolescents are indeed resilient and possess unique characteristics, values, beliefs and support systems. Resilience factors enable them to cope with life stressors and to avoid depressive symptoms more effectively than those who have not established resilience. Given this reality, "Project Passport" was developed as an intervention that fostered attachment, enhanced individual protective factors, and attempted to ameliorate the effects of high-risk environments.

Theoretical Framework

Research has shown that teens who had concrete educational plans and goals tended to be motivated to volunteer to help others (Johnson, Beebe, Mortimer, & Snyder, 1998). Further, those who participated in recreational volunteer activities tended to see increases in skill development, self-esteem, social networking, sense of community, and empowerment (Stroud, Miller, Stuart, & Adams, 2006). Volunteerism is a self-help concept that builds on the resiliency theoretical framework suggested by Rutter (1985; 1987; 1999). Figure 9.1 shows how these theoretical principles underpin "Project Passport."

Resiliency, as noted in Figure 9.1, is conceptualised as a dynamic process involving an interaction between risk and protective factors which modify the effects of adverse life events. Before a young woman can reduce her risk, she has to build resiliency through a process that also involves the reduction of negative chain reactions and the establishment of self-esteem, self-efficacy, and positive opportunities.

Numerous studies over the past two decades have found that individuals who progressed to healthier lives despite adversity possessed protective factors that buffered them from the negative forces or stresses to which they were exposed (Mueller, 2005; Nicholson, Collins, & Holmer, 2004). The framework of using youth development as a way to provide positive building blocks that young people need for success is based on the theories of resiliency and attachment.

Research conducted at the Search Institute (1997) studied more than 500,000 6th–12th graders and identified 40 developmental assets necessary to help youth experience positive outcomes e.g.

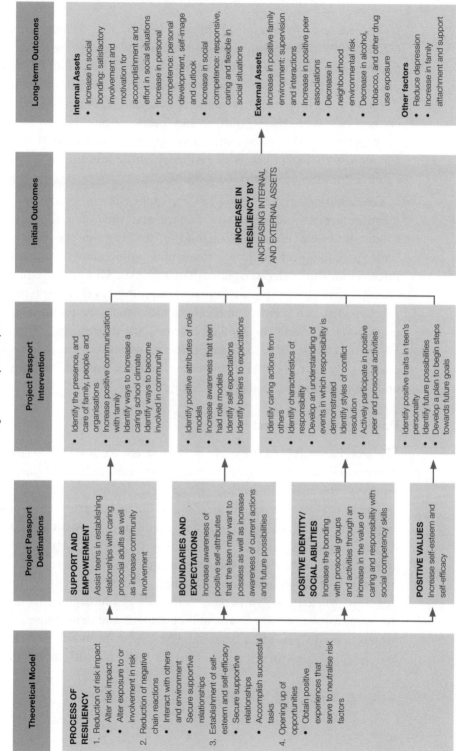

Figure 9.1 Project Passport

school success, maintaining physical health, and helping others (Scales, 1999). Their findings suggested that adolescents with higher numbers of assets are less likely to have high-risk behaviours such as unplanned pregnancies, sexual acting out, drug abuse, and school dropout. Attachment theory suggests that young people can rebuild connections with their families and peers despite initial deficits or problems, and subsequently develop skills to enable them to function with higher levels of resiliency and commitment in their communities (Solomon & George, 1999).

In addition, there is a growing emphasis on psychiatry to identifying risk and protective factors and their causal linkages to disease. One promising method is to examine the effect of both psychological and environmental vulnerability and their interrelationship (Merikangas & Risch, 2003). Our interest in the effects of resiliency on depressive symptoms takes into account psychological and environmental factors, such as mobility and migration, as well as familial factors in depression. "Project Passport" consists of various supportive activities to help adolescents design their own definition of success, practice conflict resolution, and eventually exercise adult leadership.

Purpose of this Project

"Project Passport" recruits female volunteers to attend a certified programme in order to help them learn life skills that aim at reducing the risk of teenage pregnancy. Volunteer participants enhance resiliency through five main domains: a) support and empowerment, b) boundaries and expectations, c) positive values, d) social abilities, and e) positive identity. Participants learn to analyse their protective factors, called internal and external assets, by participating in innovative learning activities based on these domains. Most teens who come to the Clinic are deemed to be at high-risk for pregnancy, STDs, and/or alcohol and drug abuse. This project aims to provide a personal assessment inventory, exercises, and learning activities for the teens as well as tools to help the counsellor provide support and awareness. The more vulnerable teens are, the more they can benefit from the protective aspects of the 40 assets (Scales, 1999). For all groups, cultures, disciplines, and philosophies, the more the assets are increased, the fewer risks and the more positive behaviours youth generally experience.

According to the Search Institute (1997), teens who have 31 or more of the assets (only 8%) are considered as "high asset youth". Conversely, one in five young people are deemed "asset poor" with 0–10 assets. The average teen has less than one-half of the ascribed 40 assets. In addition, the number of assets decreases as the teen gets older. High asset youth, even those with developmental deficiencies such as experiencing violence, spending too much time alone, or being physically abused, are more resilient to risk factors than those in the low asset group.

This project addresses positive youth development constructs rather than focusing on typical problem behaviours (Catalano, Berglund, Ryan, Lonczak, & Hawkins, 1998). Themes common to success in these types of programmes include methods which: strengthen social, emotional, behavioural, cognitive, and moral competencies; build self-efficacy; shape messages from family and the community about clear norms for youth behaviour; increase healthy bonding with adults, peers, and children; expand opportunities and recognition for youth; provide structure and consistency in programme delivery; and intervene for at least nine months or more.

Although single site interventions can be effective, combining the resources of the family, the school, and the community are significant factors that ensure success. Therefore, implementing the 40 developmental assets in as many other areas of the teen's life as possible provides additional likelihood for positive outcomes (Catalano et al., 1998). A study by Gager and Elias (1997) determined that resiliency paradigm prevention programmes are successful even in high risk school districts, but only when the programme aligns itself with the school's mission and programmes are well planned and carried out. This mission oriented alignment ensures that the programme becomes part of the school's culture and is able to be implemented by trained personnel.

Positive involvement in pro-social institutions is linked to less truancy, drug use, and general delinquency than for teens that do not have an attachment to these groups. Social alienation is a signature personality characteristic among teens who use drugs (Liddle & Hogue, 2000). Unstable school environments, frequent transitions, and limited or no involvement in the community also places adolescents at-risk for substance abuse. The single most influential precursor of drug use and other behavioural problems is an adolescent's association with anti-social peers. Strong connections to pro-social institutions are critical factors in positive adjustment, overall. Academic success and investment in school, involvement in recreational activities, and association with pro-social peers help insulate adolescents from behavioural problems.

"Project Passport's" Approach

Traditionally, adolescent sexual risk and substance abuse prevention programmes have focused on risk factors, rather than the enhancement of resiliency (Kaplan & Turner, 1996). This project takes a unique strengths-based approach derived from a theoretical framework of resiliency as conceptualised by Rutter (1985; 1987; 1999). Rutter defined resiliency as "the relative resistance to psychosocial risk experiences". Therefore, resilient individuals will tend to experience relatively positive outcomes despite their experiences with various risk situations. Rutter described the developmental and situational mechanisms which facilitate the process of resiliency as: reduction of risk impact, reduction of negative chain reactions, establishment of self-esteem and self-efficacy, and the opening up of positive opportunities. Thus, the enhancement of resiliency was selected as the prevention modality in order to reduce risk behaviours of those in this programme. Rutter's

(1985; 1987; 1999) theoretical framework of resiliency integrates concepts of Bandura's (1977) social learning theory and Bowlby's (1969; 1973; 1980) attachment theory.

An important aspect of social learning theory is vicarious learning, which suggests that behavioural acquisition occurs by observing others. Another key aspect is self-efficacy, or the belief that one can achieve desired goals through one's own actions (Catalano et al., 1998). It has been found that teens who are self-efficacious are more successful in dealing with adverse circumstances (Robbins, Chatterjee, & Canda, 1998). For example, a recent study found that self-efficacy and the ability to articulate coping responses were important characteristics among resilient adolescent participants who were facing adversity (Hamill, 2002).

Bowlby's attachment theory stresses the importance of connections with caregivers during childhood, and the importance of attachments with peers and significant others during adolescence (West, Rose, Spreng, Sheldon-Keller, & Adam, 1998). The quality of a child's bonds with caregivers is an essential aspect of positive development in becoming a healthy adult (Catalano et al., 1998). Thus, the degree to which the developing individual becomes resistant to stressful life events is determined by patterns of attachment early in life (Svanberg, 1998). However, Bowlby (1969; 1973; 1980) suggested that individuals are still capable of re-attachment during other stages of life, such as adolescence, through relationship building and mastering behaviours. Strategies to promote positive bonding, combined with the development of skills, have proven to be an effective intervention for at-risk adolescents (Catalano et al., 1998). Thus, a key component of the proposed programme is to help teens reorganise and build new attachment relationships with other pro-social peers and healthy families.

"Project Passport" is a 12-hour, 6-session programme that focuses on enhancing resiliency through the development of the teens' 40 internal and external developmental assets (see Table 9.1) which serve to buffer and reduce risky sexual, and/or substance

Table 9.1   The 40 external and internal developmental assets (Seales, 1999)

External Assets	Internal Assets
Support	**Commitment to Learning**
1. Family support	21. Achievement motivation
2. Positive family communication	22. School engagement
3. Other adult relationships	23. Homework
4. Caring neighbourhood	24. Bonding to school
5. Caring school climate	25. Reading for pleasure
6. Parental involvement in schooling	
	Positive Values
Empowerment	26. Caring
7. Community values youth	27. Equality and social justice
8. Youth as resources	28. Integrity
9. Service to others	29. Honesty
10. Safety	30. Responsibility
	31. Restraint
Boundaries and Expectations	
11. Family boundaries	**Social Competencies**
12. School boundaries	32. Planning and decision making
13. Neighbourhood boundaries	33. Interpersonal competence
14. Adult role models	34. Cultural competence
15. Positive peer influence	35. Resistance skills
16. High expectations	36. Peaceful conflict resolution
Constructive Use of Time	**Positive Identity**
17. Creative activities	37. Personal power
18. Youth programmes	38. Self-esteem
19. Religious community	39. Sense of purpose
20. Time at home	40. Positive view of the future

abuse behaviours. The programme is tailored to teens based on their life stories, in order to empower them. Such empowerment allows teens to identify and expand upon their unique set of existing internal and external assets in addition to acquiring new ones.

"Project Passport" is designed to facilitate the process of resiliency through a series of exercises (see Table 9.2 for an exercise example that helps one assess their 40 assets). The constructs of resiliency are integrated into these exercises within the five "Destinations". The exercises in these destinations facilitate the reduction of risk and negative chain reactions; the establishment of self-esteem and self-efficacy; and the opening up of opportunities by: a) assisting teens in establishing relationships with caring adults; b) increasing teens' involvement within their communities and environment; c) increasing teens' awareness of positive self-attributes; d) increasing teens' awareness of the importance of current actions on future possibilities; and e) increasing teens' social competency skills and bonding with pro-social groups and activities.

It is important to respect a teen client's own personal experiences in order for this intervention to be effective. Participants participate in the activities in each of the five Destinations, either individually or in small groups, and discuss the learning process with their counsellors. The exercises are simple, positive, and aim to assist the adolescent in discovering that positive changes are possible for them. At the end, a university-awarded Certificate is conferred to emphasise that this programme is a learning process, rather than a treatment programme per se. The aim here is to strengthen the adolescents' confidence in the overall learning process, enhance their commitment to continuous and ongoing asset development, and apply learned skills to their daily lives.

Two manuals have been developed to administer "Project Passport". The Therapists' Manual is divided into the five Destinations, and is used by licensed therapists. The Teens' Manual is taken home by participants. Taking into consideration that high-risk clients do not return to the Clinic on a regular basis, it is important to adapt the curriculum to their lives and appointment schedules. Utilising the health-focused Clinic, this programme encourages adolescents to use the Clinic as a point of service for their overall well-being.

Table 9.2   Assessing your 40 assets

Check each statement that is true for you (√).

☐ 1. I feel loved and supported in my family.

☐ 2. I can go to my parents for advice and support. We talk with each other often about many different things, including serious issues.

☐ 3. I know at least three adults (besides my parents) I can go to for advice and support.

☐ 4. My neighbours give me support and encouragement. They care about me.

☐ 5. My school is a caring, encouraging place to be.

☐ 6. My parents are actively involved in helping me succeed in school.

☐ 7. I feel valued and appreciated by adults in my community.

☐ 8. I'm given useful roles and meaningful things to do in my community.

☐ 9. I do an hour or more of community service each week.

☐ 10. I feel safe at home, at school, and in my neighbourhood.

☐ 11. My family has both clear rules and consequences for my behavior. They also monitor my whereabouts.

☐ 12. My school has clear rules and consequences for my behavior.

☐ 13. My neighbours take responsibility for monitoring my behavior.

☐ 14. My parents and other adults in my life model positive, responsible behavior.

☐ 15. My best friends model responsible behavior. They're a good influence on me.

☐ 16. My parents and teachers encourage me to do well.

☐ 17. I spend three or more hours each week in lessons or practice in music, theatre, or other arts.

☐ 18. I spend three or more hours each week in school or community sports, clubs or organisations.

☐ 19. I spend one or more hours each week in religious services or spiritual activities.

☐ 20. I go out with friends with nothing special to do two or fewer nights each week.

☐ 21. I want to do well in school.

☐ 22. I like to learn new things.

☐ 23. I do an hour or more of homework each school day.

☐ 24. I care about my school.

☐ 25. I spend three or more hours each week reading for pleasure.

☐ 26. I believe that it's really important to help other people.

☐ 27. I want to help promote equality and reduce world poverty and hunger.

☐ 28. I act on my convictions and stand up for my beliefs.

☐ 29. I tell the truth—even when it's not easy.

☐ 30. I take responsibility for my actions and decisions.

☐ 31. I believe that it's important for me not to be sexually active or to use alcohol or other drugs.

☐ 32. I'm good at planning ahead and making decisions.

☐ 33. I'm good at making and keeping friends.

☐ 34. I know and feel comfortable around people of different cultural, racial, and/ or ethnic backgrounds.

☐ 35. I resist negative peer pressure and avoid dangerous situations.

☐ 36. I try to resolve conflicts non-violently.

☐ 37. I feel that I have control over many things that happen to me.

☐ 38. I feel good about myself.

☐ 39. I believe that my life has a purpose.

☐ 40. I feel positive about my future.

Add up the total number of checks. How many do you have? _____

The curriculum is flexible and can be adapted to individual needs, and participants are encouraged to complete asset activities at home. The therapist works to create a therapeutic bond with participants so that the teens will be more likely to return to the Clinic to discuss the activities with the therapist. These discussions may take place in small groups or individually, on weekly or bi-weekly basis for the six sessions. In addition, a case manager follows up with each participant prior to the next scheduled visit, usually within a month. In our experience, all adolescents who seek services from various Teen Health Clinic locations speak English, but bilingual staff are available when needed.

Curricular Areas

Resilience has been described as the ability to cope positively with adversity. Synonymous terms used to describe resilience are hardiness and invulnerability. By focusing on resiliency, we gain an understanding of how people deal with and overcome life challenges and adversities. With this context, we are able to build on these traits and factors in order to protect high-risk teens. Some of the characteristics and traits of a resilient teen include the following (Edari & McManus, 1990):

- Competence-capacity represents an event internally and the ability to organise
- incoming information into meaningful categories which become clues for behaviour (i.e. reflectiveness, impulse control, realistic assessment of options, and social problem skills)
- Well-developed sense of self
- Activism
- Higher self-esteem
- Sense of power
- Ability to exercise a degree of control over situations and events

- Superior social skills
- Cooperativeness
- Sensitivity
- Participatory propensity
- Well-developed sense of curiosity about people, things, and ideas
- Adaptability and flexibility
- Empathy
- Easygoing disposition and a good sense of humour
- Having a warm and positive relationship with an adult
- Having an ability to distance oneself in thinking and acting independently in relation to troubled families and caregivers
- Responses to danger: an awareness and ability to respond quickly to threatening events
- Maturity: to respond to situations beyond the developmental norm for that age
- Dissociation of affect: ability to disengage oneself from emotional involvement
- Information seeking: ability to build a repertoire of knowledge regarding potential hazards
- Positive anticipation: the capacity to fantasise positively about the future
- Risk taking: the ability to assume responsibility over taking a calculated risk
- Loved: feeling of being loved and cared for
- Idealisation of an aggressor's competence: identifying with an aggressor's positive traits in order to maintain self-esteem
- Relationships for survival: an ability to cultivate relationships that are conducive to survival
- Reinterpreting experiences: an ability to reconcile painful past events with current status

- Altruism: deriving pleasure and satisfaction from helping others

- Optimism and hope: maintaining positive expectations about the future

These factors (described above) can be collapsed into three main areas with the following sub-headings:

1. Risk Factors and Resiliency and How They Interact
2. Role of the Family in Enhancing Resiliency
   a. Care and Support
   b. Resiliency and Family Structure
   c. High Expectations
   d. Encouraging Participation
3. Role of the Individual in Developing Resiliency
   a. Imaginers of Their Own Destiny
   b. Developing a "Tough Cookie" Attitude
   c. Playing the "School Game" Properly
   d. Engagement in Regular Renewal
   e. Developing Caring Relationships

As the curriculum is offered, participants work at asset development in these main and sub-areas in ways that allow them to accrue assets which are individualised to their needs.

The Five Destinations

With the emphasis on resiliency, family relationships, and individual characteristics, "Project Passport" is designed with five destinations, each aiming to achieve some aspects of the 40 assets.

Destination 1: Support and Empowerment

Teens need to experience the presence, care, help, and love of their family members as well as other people, organisations, and institutions. The purpose of this module is to help teens identify supportive adults in their life. Exercises in this destination assist the teens in understanding the importance of their actions and how they affect those around them. In situations where a supportive parent seems to be non-existent, the hope is that the teen will identify other adults who would support and encourage her to form and strengthen healthy relationships.

Ideally, teens grow up in a positive, nurturing environment. Parenting styles that monitor and control teen behaviour in a caring and consistent manner provide support and encouragement, support psychological and emotional independence, and allow for the most positive transition from teenager to adult. Positive growth for teens occurs in environments which offer guidance, structure, a variety of experiences, and encouragement. It may be the absence of support from families, societal institutions, communities, and friends that explain the failure of some adolescents to achieve successful adulthood.

In this destination, obstacles to family support are discussed. Issues, such as poverty, prejudice, and discrimination based on race, ethnicity, and social class, may produce feelings of anger, frustration, confusion, distrust, lack of connectedness with the larger society, and feelings of helplessness and hopelessness. However, these negative effects may be moderated somewhat by positive experiences in the family and community. Schools can also function as a protective factor for teens who experience prejudice and discrimination. As long as administrators and teachers maintain high expectations for youth regardless of their race, ethnicity, or socioeconomic status, students can develop positive attitudes.

Research on resiliency has been consistent in determining qualities that are associated with competence and good psychosocial functioning during or following adverse experiences. Two of the most widely reported predictors of resilience appear to be relationships with caring, pro-social adults and teens' possession of good intellectual functioning (Masten & Coatsworth, 1998). Thus, a close bond with an effective parent or other adult is related to better outcomes overall, among children with ordinary lives, as well as among children who face the threats of marital discord, child maltreatment, homelessness, or multi-faceted risks.

Destination 2: Boundaries and Expectations

In order to develop a sense of identity, teens are encouraged to look at their surrounding environments including their families, school, friends and themselves. They may experiment and test the values of those around them and develop a sense of who they are, what they want out of life, and what kinds of people they hope to be in the future. One of the activities in this destination is to identify role models in their lives and list positive attributes of those people. By naming these people and exploring positive qualities, teens may move toward a better understanding of their own identity. By thinking realistically about expectations of their parents and other significant people, teens will also likely assess whether they agree with these expectations, and why. Such assessment helps them arrive at answers to questions such as who they are becoming, and explore the choices that they are making now that may interfere with who they plan to be in the future. In forming an identity, it is important for the teens to understand that what they want out of the future, is more important than chasing after the past (Zastrow & Kirst-Ashman, 2001).

Destinations 3 and 4: Positive Values and Social Competencies

Research indicates that teens who are disengaged from school, parents, family, and other pro-social institutions are at increased risk for behavioural problems (McNamera, 2000). School programmes that both allow and encourage high-risk students to participate in shared decision-making, cooperative learning, and positive changes result in an enhanced sense of school attachment and belonging, as well as reduced dropout rates and improved retention and graduation rates. When circumstances exclude teens from participation in pro-social activities, they tend to associate with peers who display problematic behaviours, or withdraw altogether.

Destinations 3 and 4 include exercises to increase the values of caring and responsibility with social competency skills such as empathy, sensitivity, friendship, and peaceful conflict resolution. These areas of self-development are critical to bonding with pro-social groups and activities, thus decreasing the possibility of engaging in other high-risk behaviours.

Destination 5: Developing a Positive Identity

Resilient teens possess two prominent characteristics: positive self-esteem and self-efficacy (Turner, Norman, & Zung, 1995). Self-esteem is defined as a belief that one's ideal self-image and actual self-image are the same. Self-efficacy is a self-perception that one has the ability to successfully perform specific tasks. People who have a high level of self-efficacy believe that they can master difficult tasks and will put forth the effort to deal with stressful situations. Teens who possess both high self-esteem and self-efficacy have positive feelings about themselves and their ability to control what happens to them.

One goal of "Passport Project" is to use small groups in a safe environment where ideas and feelings can be shared openly and honestly with others. However, it may be more effective for some teens to meet individually with a counsellor in order to discuss personal issues related to self-esteem and self-efficacy. Research has shown that a girl's level of self-esteem decreases during her teen years (Turner et al., 1995). However, there is also evidence that a girl's self-esteem, self-efficacy, and problem-solving skills can be enhanced in gender-specific prevention programmes (Turner et al., 1995).

Practice Implications

After research with more than 500,000 6th- to 12th-grade students, the Search Institute recognised that there are 40 assets that provide some protection for teens against unhealthy behaviours (Scales, 1999). "Project Passport" integrates the use of these 40 developmental assets to help teen girls establish a healthier self-identity. It is assumed that the more assets a young person has, the less likely that the teen is to engage in risky behaviour. These assets appear to provide one with protective factors that enable a teen to experience positive outcomes such as school success, physical health, voluntary participation in self-care, and helping others. Assets are the positive building blocks that can be increased with the assistance of the family, caring adults, and the community at large.

These assets are sub-categorised into eight topics. Support, empowerment, boundaries, expectations, and constructive use of time are external assets that the young person receives from the adults in her life and in her environment. The internal assets are commitment to learning, positive values, social competencies, and positive identity. These last four assets are the values, skills, and experiences that the teen develops in order to guide herself in her decision-making processes (see Table 9.1 on p. 236).

Young people do not grow up in social isolation. Because of gender inequity, more adolescent girls are affected differently by their family and societal culture, in terms of perception, decision-making, behaviour, and view of the future, than boys. As they mature, teenagers develop the cognitive ability to begin analysing their feelings and developing their own sense of self-worth (Lo & Au, 2004). They then begin to understand what is in their best interest, not only for today but also for the future. By asking them "Where do you think you are going to be in 5 or 10 years", adults can begin to implant in youth the idea that they do have a future. Youth can learn that engaging in risky behaviours may delay their personal development and limit their opportunities to build a positive future (Johnson, Bassin, & Shaw Inc., 1998).

Rather than addressing social problems, unintended pregnancy, drug abuse, suicide, and violence, as separate concerns needing separate solutions, we have found that more effective results can be obtained by integrating the youth into a prevention programme that addresses overall life passage, education, and preparation. By developing life skills that focus on future goals and the risks that would interfere with that process, youth are able to examine the roles that will limit their future by engaging in unsafe behaviours.

More than ever, young people all over the world are growing up in circumstances that put them at-risk for involvement in potentially harmful behaviours, that offer them few opportunities, and that make some feel truly hopeless about their future. These teens need the support of caring adults who can equip them with the knowledge, skill, and attitudes they need not just to survive but to thrive (Johnson, Bassin, & Shaw Inc., 1998). Literature on resiliency suggests that interpersonal relationships are important, and volunteerism provides opportunities for building relationship skills. In "Project Passport", all five destinations aim to stimulate ideas about attaining strong and supportive connections with caring adults (Debold, Brown, Weseen, & Brookins, 1999). Studies have shown the importance of bonding to the family and bonding to pro-social resources as being pivotal in protecting teens from anti-social outcomes. Strong parent-adolescent attachments provide a safe place for adolescents to grow and graduate to emotional independence that respects the autonomy and the connectiveness of these teens (Liddle & Hogue, 2000). If these parental attachments are threatened or non-existent, it is hoped that their social participation in self-care and volunteer programmes will help them establish healthy relationships with other adults, such as teachers, neighbours, and extended family members. The concept of volunteerism in this project highlights the importance of achieving mentorship attachment from a unique curriculum-based intervention programme.

References

Bandura, A. (1977). *A social learning theory.* Englewood Cliffs, NJ: Prentice-Hall.

Bowlby, J. (1969). *Attachment and loss: Attachment.* London: Hogarth Press.

Bowlby, J. (1973). *Attachment and loss: Separation, anxiety and loss.* London: Hogarth Press.

Bowlby, J. (1980). *Attachment and loss: Loss, sadness and depression.* London: Hogarth Press.

Buzi, R., Weinman, M. L., & Smith, P. B. (2000). Mental health problems and symptoms among adolescents attending a family planning clinic. *North American Journal of Psychology, 2*(2), 337–346.

Catalano, R. F., Berglund, M. L., Ryan, J. A. M., Lonczak, H. S., & Hawkins, J. D. (1998). *Positive youth development in the United States: Research findings on evaluations of positive youth development programmes.* Retrieved 25 May 2006, from www.aspe.hhs.gov/hsp/positiveyouthdev99.

Cheung, C. (2006). Experiential learning strategies for promoting adolescents' voluntarism in Hong Kong. *Child and Youth Care Forum, 35*(1), 57–78.

Debold, E., Brown, L. M., Weseen, S., & Brookins, G. K. (1999). Cultivating hardiness zones for adolescent girls. A reconceptualization of resilience in relationships with caring adult. In N. G. Johnson, M. C. Roberts, & J. Worell (Eds.), *Beyond appearance: A new look at adolescent girls* (pp. 181–204). Washington, DC: American Psychological Association.

Edari, R., & McManus, P. (1990). Risk and resiliency factors for violence. *Violence among Children and Adolescents, 45*(2), 293–305.

Feldman, R. A. (1998). From the point/counterpoint editor: Catch the wave. *Journal of Social Work Education, 34,* 162–164.

Gabriel, R. M., Hopson, T., Haskins, M., & Powell, K. E. (1996). Building relationships and resilience in the prevention of youth violence. *American Journal of Preventive Medicine, 12*(Suppl. 2), 48–55.

Gager, P. J., & Elias, M. (1997). Implementing prevention programmes in high risk environments: Application of the resiliency paradigm. *American Journal of Orthopsychiatry, 67*(3), 363–373.

Hamill, S. K. (2002). Resilience and self-efficacy: The importance of efficacy beliefs and coping mechanisms in resilient adolescents. *Colgate University Journal of the Sciences in Psychology, 35*, 115–146.

Johnson, Bassin, & Shaw, Inc. (1998). *Preventing adolescent pregnancy: A youth development approach.* Developed for the Family and Youth Services under Contract No. 105–92–1709 from the Administration on Children, Youth and Families. Washington, DC: U.S. Department of Health and Human Services.

Johnson, M. K., Beebe, T., Mortimer, J. T., & Snyder, M. (1998). Volunteerism in adolescence: A process perspective. *Journal of Research on Adolescence, 8*(3), 309–332.

Kaplan, C. P., & Turner, S. (1996). Promoting resilience strategies: A modified consultation model. *Social Work in Education, 18*(3), 158–169.

Liddle, H. A., & Hogue, A. (2000). A family based developmental-ecological preventive intervention for high-risk adolescents. *Journal of Marital and Family Therapy, 26*(3), 265–279.

Lo, T. W. & Au, E. (2004). *Youth empowerment: International experiences.* Hong Kong: City University of Hong Kong.

Masten, A. S., & Coatsworth, J. D. (1998). The development of competence in favourable and unfavourable environments. *American Psychologist, 53*(2), 205–220.

McNamera, K. (2000). Outcomes associated with service involvement among disengaged youth. *Journal of Drug Education, 30*(2), 229–245.

Merikangas, K. R., & Risch, N. (2003). Will the genomics revolution revolutionise psychiatry? *American Journal of Psychiatry, 160*(4), 625–635.

Mueller, A. (2005). Antidote to learned helplessness: Empowering youth through service. *Reclaiming Children and Youth, 14*(1), 16–19.

Nicholson, H. J., Collins, C., & Holmer, H. (2004). Youth as people: The protective aspects of youth development in after-school settings. *Annals of the American Academy of Political and Social Science, 591*, 55–71.

Robbins, S. P., Chatterjee, P., & Canda, E. R. (1998). *Contemporary human behaviour theory: A critical perspective for social work.* Boston: Allyn & Bacon.

Rutter, M. (1985). Family and school influences on cognitive development. *Journal of Child Psychology and Psychiatry, 26,* 638–704.

Rutter, M. (1987). Psychosocial resilience and protective mechanisms. *American Journal of Orthopsychiatry, 57*(3), 316–331.

Rutter, M. (1999). Resilience concepts and findings: Implications for family therapy. *Journal of Family Therapy, 21,* 159–160.

Scales, P. C. (1999). Reducing risks and building developmental assets: Essential actions for promoting adolescent health. *Journal of School Health, 69*(3), 113–119.

Search Institute. (1997). *Forty developmental assets.* Minneapolis, MN: Author.

Solomon, J., & George, C. (1999). The place of disorganisation in attachment theory: Linking classic observations with contemporary findings. In J. Solomon & C. George (Eds.), *Attachment disorganisation* (pp. 3–32). New York: Guilford Press.

Stroud, S., Miller, K. D., Stuart, J. S., & Adams, B. (2006). *A winning recipe for volunteerism.* Parks & Recreations, 00312215, 41(1).

Svanberg, P. O. G. (1998). Attachment, resilience and prevention. *Journal of Mental Health, 7*(6), 543–579.

Turner, S., Norman, E., & Zunz, S. (1995). Enhancing resiliency in girls and boys: A case for gender specific adolescent prevention programmeming, *The Journal of Primary Prevention, 16*(1), 25–38.

U.S. Census Bureau. (2001). *Census 2000 Briefs.* Retrieved 25 May 2006, from www.census.gov/population/www/cen2000/briefs.html.

Weinman, M., Buzi, R., Smith, P. B., & Mumford, D. M. (2003). Associations of family support, resiliency and depression symptoms among indigent teens attending a family planning clinic. *Psychological Reports, 93,* 719–731.

West, M., Rose, M. S., Spreng, S., Sheldon-Keller, A., & Adam, K. (1998). Adolescent attachment questionnaire: A brief assessment of attachment in adolescence. *Journal of Youth and Adolescence, 27*(5), 661–673.

Zastrow, C., & Kirst-Ashman, K. (2001). *Understanding human behavior and the social environment* (5th ed.). Belmont, CA: Brooks/Cole.

YOUTH EMPOWERMENT AND SELF-ACTUALISATION: EXPERIENCES IN SHANGHAI, CHINA

10

T. Wing LO, Songxing SU, and Guoping JIANG

Introduction

Empowerment is defined by scholars in accordance with their own values, belief systems, cultural and political backgrounds; in general, most agree that empowerment is a process of giving power and authority to the powerless, or enabling someone to gain mastery over their affairs and achieve their personal goals. Pernell (1986) contends that empowerment is the capacity to influence the forces affecting one's life space for one's own and others' benefit. To be empowered is regarded as being able to connect with others in a mutually productive way (Shrewsbury, 1987). Empowerment emphasises multiple dimensions of competence, and can be achieved through different levels of intervention, including individuals, families, organisations, and communities (Saleebey, 1996; Wolff, 1987). Empowerment is a process of increasing personal, interpersonal or political power (Gutiérrez, 1994), achieving control over one's destiny, and acquiring the competence to make change at the individual and systems levels (Pinderhughes, 1995). Rappaport (1987) has summarised two main levels of empowerment, including "both individual determination over one's own life and democratic participation in the life of one's community. . . . Empowerment conveys both a psychological sense of personal control or influence and a concern with actual social influence, political power, and legal rights" (p. 121). These two levels of empowerment are of special value to the following discussion of youth volunteerism in China.

Individual Level

On the individual level, empowerment has been related to personal development. It is an act of strengthening an individual's beliefs in his or her sense of effectiveness (Conger, 1989). Empowerment is a personal and social process which liberates one's own strengths, competence, creativity, and freedom of action. To be empowered is to feel the power to act and grow (Morley, 1995). Power is obtained as an individual move from a condition of relative powerlessness to one of relative power (Staples, 1990). Moreover, empowerment can be regarded as spiritual enlightenment. Certain religions and philosophies tend to promote empowerment through spiritual rather than material fulfilment (Servian, 1996).

Community Level

At the community level, empowerment has been regarded as freedom from government. It has been used to describe the freedom felt in the 1960s by people in rebelling against authority (Neville, 1995). Solomon (1976), as an advocator of empowerment in the 1970s, asserted that as long as African Americans occupy a powerless position in American society, empowering the oppressed is key to the achievement of autonomy, equality, and self-affirmation. Empowerment could be an access to democratic processes, including the rights to vote, and to take part through various means in political decisions and policies. According to the World Bank, "empowerment is the expansion of assets and capabilities of poor people to participate in, negotiate with, influence, control, and hold accountable institutions that affect their lives" (Narayan, 2002, p. 14). Thus, empowerment implies access to power. Issues of power, ownership of power, inequalities of power, and the acquisition and redistribution of power centre around empowerment.

Other than empowering people, it has been suggested that empowerment could be a manipulative strategy. Morley (1995) suggests that the term "empowerment" is designed to disguise the harsh consumer-oriented market values of New Right policies. It is also part of the "manipulative, victim-blaming ideology suggesting that oppressed groups have the power to change their material circumstances through psychological restructuring" (Morley, 1995, p. 8).

This chapter will examine the development of youth volunteerism in China with reference to these two levels of empowerment. Before such examination, a brief discussion of the socio-political development of China in the past three decades will be provided for the analysis.

The Development of Youth Volunteerism in China

Pre-Reform Period

In Mao's China, class struggle was the first imperative. Due to the excessive capitalist and imperialist exploitation in the Guomintong regime, the ever-growing misery of labour and peasants brought about a new revolutionary break under the dictatorship of the proletariat, represented by the Communist Party (CCP). The CCP played a central role in the ideological reproduction of social and economic relations in which there was neither private property nor wage-labour, and neither poverty nor riches under communism. Class struggle was characterised by the "mass line" in political leadership, "popular justice" in judicial policy, "continuing revolution" in social development and the "Red and expert" ideal as an educational goal (Brady, 1982). For continuing revolution to emerge, there would be no consensual, but a coercive form of domination by the proletariat. The mass line signified that the CCP would dictate, colonise and destroy the class and political enemies, and would never abandon its monopoly of power under the People's Democratic Dictatorship. To achieve this goal, the CCP had to sustain the "mass line" leadership, in which the masses were led by the CCP, not vice versa.

The CCP tried to develop a new paradisiacal state in which private property and all forms of coercion would be abolished and the lives of masses protected. It adopted the strategy of high employment, low wage and high welfare, attempting to provide employment and protection for all, with a guarantee of standard wages and a full range of subsidies and welfare in cash and in kind. Basic food items were also subsidised to help keep people's lives simple. All people could then "eat from the big rice bowl". Thus, the state provided comprehensive welfare programmes to achieve its socialist ideals: "The morals advocated in the old society—parents should be kind to their children, children should be filial to their parents, brothers should love and respect each other—can be transformed into socialist ethics of mutual understanding, mutual love and mutual help" (*Beijing Review*, 42, p. 29, quoted in Ogden,

1992, p. 330). Many of these ideals were implemented by work units and mass organisations, as outlined below:

Removal of Bourgeois Elements

After the communist takeover of China in 1949, enterprises run by "bureaucratic bourgeoisie" in cities were confiscated. The landlords and businessmen, including even the benevolent, who were formerly the main sources of donation for relief, were purged because they were regarded as the exploiting class (Gardner, 1969; Brady, 1982; Ladany, 1988; Lo, 1993). In addition, a campaign to re-examine the nature of charitable organisations was conducted to assure that only those serving genuine welfare purposes could continue to exist (Chen, 1994). Needless to say, the examination of political background was one of the criteria. Welfare institutions run by the Guomintang, religious bodies and international charitable organisations were taken over by the CCP as they were regarded as the agents of the imperialists and capitalists who exploited China. Immediately after the takeover, in view of various natural disasters and the chaos caused by the civil war and the change of government, the CCP established the Production and Save-the-Disaster Committees in various parts of China. The committees mobilised the general public to prevent flooding so as to protect agricultural production. Different remedial measures, such as relief, health care and settlement of refugees, were carried out to help the victims. To pursue such cause, a large number of volunteers were mobilised to help in the relief activities.

Welfare Protection

In the 1950's, labour insurance was introduced to employees of state and collective enterprises (Chow, 1988). Workers and their family members could turn to their work units or production teams for help in times of need. Work units provided workers with a full range of occupational welfare, such as housing, medical care, nursery, transportation allowance, holiday houses, recreational activities and retirement pension. Some individuals did not fall under this welfare support network, such as the elderly, the destitute, the handicapped, and the "three-nos"—no family, no means of living, and no-one to rely on. Services were provided for these individuals by the civil affairs bureaux, which relied heavily on volunteers to support their works.

Mass Organisations

Simultaneously, mass organisations were formed. The Women's Federation, Labour Union, Communist Youth League, Street Offices, and Residents' Committees organised social services, promoted mutual help, and provided a variety of functions, including conflict mediation, environment improvement, mutual help, neighbourhood support, political education, grassroots feedback, and assistance to families in need (Chan & Chow, 1992). Essentially, these mass organisations were run by volunteers who would support the Party line.

In the pre-reform era, China had committed itself to certain welfare state functions, such as state subsidised education, child care, housing, medical care, food, and social security for the old and disabled. However, the low economic development could not support the huge capital needed to achieve the ideals of a welfare state. Welfare expenditure was so inadequate that it failed even to ensure for everyone a living above the subsistence level. Increasing welfare demand has created pressing financial burden on the state whose socialist ideals guarantee universal and comprehensive coverage of social and welfare services. Without adequate financial resources, the CCP had to rely on volunteers from the mass organisations. Thus, the welfare philosophy increasingly adopted by the CCP gradually moved from state social welfare to community care, informal care, and mutual help. In this respect, the mass organisations had vital roles to play. The fact that most welfare establishments were still run by such mass organisations as the rural collectives and residents' committees clearly indicates that in a socialist country like China, welfare and volunteerism did not depart from state control. The organisations served vital political control functions for the CCP to advance its continuing revolution.

The Great Volunteer—Leifeng

Another critical event in the history of volunteerism in China is the legend of Leifeng, titled "Chairman Mao's good solider". Being born to a poor family in 1940, he was an orphan at the age of 7, and was brought up by village-mates. He joined the People's Liberation Army in 1960 and later the CCP. He died in an accident while on duty in 1962. Leifeng was well known for his ardent love for communism, the collectives, battle companions, the masses, and doing public good. For example, he donated his savings by stinting himself to the people in need; he also influenced and encouraged young people's development with exemplary behaviour, such as acting as a counsellor in after-school activities. Because of his altruism and "red" background, he was hand-picked by the CCP as a model of the great volunteer. A campaign entitled "Learning from Leifeng" was then launched across the country. In primary and secondary schools in particular, young people were asked to follow the good example of Leifeng, to be volunteers and successors of communism.

The reason why Leifeng was raised to the national level is related to the internal and external constraints faced by China at that particular historical juncture. Leifeng was a typical role model who devoted his whole life unselfishly to the nation in line with Mao Zedong's thought and socialist ideals. Setting him up as a model volunteer helped the CCP educate the entire nation, especially young people, purify bourgeois elements, and strengthen the socialist values of "serving the people", thus laying down a solid foundation for communism. In addition, China had completed the Land Reform, Cooperation Campaign, the Three Great Remold, and People Commune Campaign. However, these campaigns did not bring people out of poverty. At the same time, China encountered three years of natural disasters, diplomatic upheavals with the Soviet Union and counterattacks from Taiwan. Leifeng, as a combination of political and moral symbolism, fitted well into a role model who called on and inspired Chinese people, the essence of communism at such a critical time. The "Learning from Leifeng" slogan was repeatedly used during the national leader's term-shift so as to strengthen social morale and maintain the leaders' authority. Thus, empowering youth through volunteerism under the leadership of mass organisations was in turn empowering the CCP.

In the Cultural Revolution and its aftermath, the "Learning from Leifeng" spirit was promoted to guide Chinese youth to contribute to their society. Youths were mobilised by mass organisations to "learn from Leifeng" through volunteering for the nation and CCP. Following the unselfish model of Leifeng, this played a positive role in cultivating youths' world view, life perspective, and socialist values in the period of planned economy. Empowerment holds the perspective that the less influence from the authority, the more autonomous space youth have to potentially grow and develop. The rise and development of volunteerism in China in the early days does not exactly embody such a principle of empowerment. Because of longstanding political reasons, empowerment continues to be an unfamiliar and unpopular concept in mainland China.

Even today, mainland Chinese often use the term self-actualisation to describe the empowerment of an individual. However, in the pre-reform period, the word "self-actualisation" left many with an impression of selfishness—as it was not part of the state but an individually centred value and practice. Needless to say, self-actualisation was dismissed as it was regarded as a rather bourgeoisie concept. Consequently, coercive practices of volunteering through mass movement and campaigns that denied individual choices were adopted. Self-actualisation in China during this period was regarded as deviant, and thus prohibited in public forums (Su & Hu, 2000). As such, the purpose and forms of youth empowerment, in the sense of self-actualisation, counted for little because to maintain the interests of the CCP was always of overriding importance.

Post-Reform Period

Deng returned to power in 1978 after ten years of political turmoil and economic austerity during the Cultural Revolution which had made the Chinese masses apathetic towards class struggle and plain life. Young people wanted self-actualisation rather than to follow the Party line (Yip & Lo, 1996). Following the decrease of revolutionary enthusiasm and mass participation, centralised planning also resulted in economic difficulties and failures. In an attempt to solve these problems and to win the consent and acquiescence of the masses, the rulers turned to capitalist techniques. Thus the real power over the means of production has gradually gravitated into the hands of the managerial elite. The separation of Party control from enterprise management began to emerge. Under these circumstances, managers run their enterprises from a profit-oriented perspective, rely for their guidance and control more and more on the impersonal pressures of the market. The number of private and collective-owned enterprises, alongside state-owned enterprises, has been on the rise. This also results in the increase of casual, temporary, and contract workers due to the introduction of responsibility, leasing, and contract system. Welfare benefits to workers are undermined or kept to a minimum in order to maximise profits.

Today, when private enterprises become a vital economic force under the new socialist market economy, the rigid structure of state-owned enterprises cannot compete with their flexible non-state-owned counterparts and become economically vulnerable. To adjust to the competitive nature of the socialist market economy, some enterprises have to discard the past "eating from the big rice bowl" principle and to upgrade their workforce by eliminating incompetent and redundant workers. Coupled with the close-down of those mismanaged private enterprises, this leads to a high employment rate among workers in cities. Thus, the increasing number of laid-off workers or workers on contract terms and not covered by labour insurance, the increase of industrial injury and occupational hazard due to low standard of industrial safety, and the increase of the elderly population require stronger state commitment in labour protection, social security, retirement pension and other welfare services. Moreover, changes in household structure and family life, the increase in the number of one-child families, the drifting population and migrant workers in cities have also created high demands for social welfare (Au, 1996; Gao, 1996).

The "open door" policy "ignores the social and moral aspect of socialist transformation and measures development only in steel tonnage and transport mileage" (Brady, 1982, p. 245), and the get-rich-quick atmosphere has "systematically widened social inequalities in wages, power and prestige and [has] reversed the egalitarian spirit of the Cultural Revolution" (Brady, 1982, p. 223). Once profit and loss have been raised to sacred importance, the interest and well-being of the powerless is undermined. Moreover, when individualism and materialism abound, the mass organisations began to lose popularity. For instance, the Street Offices and Residents' Committees, which rely on the retired people and volunteers to take care of the needy, find difficulty in recruiting younger volunteers because they are often engaged in longer working hours or are too busy in preparing for public examinations. Without volunteers, many services offered by these organisations would fail to operate (Cheung, 2006).

In the 1990s, volunteerism was actualised through a series of activities in various cities such as: the Youth Volunteer Work Federation launched in Shenzhen in 1990, the Loving Heart Association established in Peking University in 1993, and the Youth Volunteer Action promoted by the Communist Youth League in 1994. Since then, the Communist Youth League has provided a social stage for youth to develop their social roles and display their abilities. Through such participation, youth volunteers learn new knowledge and skills and foster their leadership and adaptable abilities for self-development through the process of serving others and dedicating themselves to their communities. They adapt their activities to fit the "Learning from Leifeng" project with new transformational approaches and content. Doing for others what is altruistic, showing compassion, taking pleasure in helping others and dedication to society, are the steps toward self-empowerment (Cheung & Ngai, 2000; Penner, 2002). Volunteer activities are now based on individuals' choice without restraining their freedom. This differs significantly from the mass movement of the past (Xu, 2003).

While youth value to society has changed dramatically since the implementation of the expanded market economy, the "Learning from Leifeng" approach has been transformed in accordance with the acceptance of, and current requirements of, the volunteer movement in our modern times. For example, what youth want are self-learning and actualising opportunities. Therefore, what the CCP needs to determine is how to change from "asking youth to learn from Leifeng" to "youth wanting to learn from Leifeng". How to offset the effects of the traditional modes of mass mobilisation and planned intervention deserves youth workers' timely interventions.

Since the economic reform and "open door" policies, many longstanding ideological conflicts have been amended (Cheng, 1996). Today, self-consciousness and self-awareness are more positively recognised, and youth are deemed as individuals with their own psychological, emotional, social needs and leisure activities (Yip & Lo, 1996), instead of passive objects living under controlling policies embedded in political ideology. It is acknowledged that self-actualisation is to realise one's potentiality to achieve one's maximum capacity. Thus, attention is paid to the individual characteristics or developmental needs of youth to help them achieve life objectives at different junctures of their growth and transition. Throughout this process, youth may be provided with opportunities to self-discover, self-analyse, self-evaluate, and self-educate. Society not only cares about youth self-development and self-actualisation, but also encourages them to integrate more fully into society. It is posited that promoting or practicing empowerment should be an important part of youth policy with more overall social acceptance and community involvement. As such, "autonomy", "responsibility", and "confidence" emphasised in empowerment theory are the basic elements of self-actualisation (see Chapters 4–5). However, only the individual level of empowerment, not community level of empowerment, is recognised because in Chinese culture and politics, power always belongs to the ruling party. Putting youth empowerment in its historical and political context in China, it is largely related to self-actualisation rather than Solomon's (1976) perspective of delegation of power from authority to the powerless.

Youth Volunteerism: The Case of Shanghai

In Shanghai, volunteerism has a long history. In February of 1980, the first youth volunteer team, an outgrowth of the "Learning from Leifeng" project, was born in the Shanghai Third Bicycle Factory. Between 1993 and 1994, more than 1,000 youth participated in various volunteer activities, such as the "Carrying Orphan" and "International Volunteer Day." Subsequently, the Shanghai Volunteer Association was founded in 1995. Later, branches at district levels were established, liaison stations were also set up on the street or town level, and volunteer teams were formed in local work units. The Shanghai Volunteer Association has grown considerably since 1997 with nearly a million youth volunteers regularly involved in local social activities and services. Through recruitment and allocation, systematic training, regular assessment, and positive reinforcement through various awards, a service framework for youth volunteers has been established in Shanghai. Consequently, Shanghai founded the Adult Volunteer Reserve with 5,000 branches across the city, and 100,000 volunteer reserve members. A few of these various and prominent volunteer initiatives will now be presented as testimonies to this community organisation.

Caring for Disadvantaged Groups

As one would assume, there are some unavoidable social problems in the rapidly developing urbanisation of Shanghai. The emergence of various disadvantaged groups is inevitable with such economic and population growth. Shanghai volunteers often help deprived individuals on a one-to-one intervention basis. That is, one volunteer or one volunteer team provides regular services to a person in need of care, or a deprived family. Such services and activities may involve health care, daily living care, psychological or emotional support, education, and skills training. Shanghai youth volunteers provide these services for service recipients after school, after work, and/or during holiday times. Some of the groups served include: children from single parent families, the disabled, the floating population, employees who are laid-off, retired workers, and elderly living alone.

Supporting Large-Scale National and Community Activities

Since the birth of the volunteer movement in Shanghai, youth volunteers have provided support to numerous national and international initiatives. Some examples are the Third Peasant Athletic Meeting, the First Special Olympics in the Asia-Pacific Region, the Eighth National Athletic Meeting, and the Asia-Pacific Economic Cooperation (APEC) meeting. Volunteers have also joined to assist rescue work in Hunan Province, maintained traffic order for the local government, and assisted in building a clean and beautiful environment through large-scale community programmes, such as the "Seven-Undos" educational programme, the "Building National Clean City" programme, and the "Tree Planting" programme.

Providing Professional Services

Volunteers with higher educational backgrounds make use of their knowledge to help needy individuals in the local community. In many universities, student volunteers initiate and organise programmes such as: "helping the poor to use technology," "supporting education and wiping out illiteracy," and "delivering medical care in rural areas." Volunteers also help workers alleviate difficulties and anxieties associated with work stress. Youth volunteers from rural areas help people living below the poverty line fight against poverty. All in all, such volunteer support services have spread to many fields of urban and rural lives, and their altruism has been recognised by society. People have indeed noted that "Leifeng is back," and they see how a harmonious society can be enhanced through various youth organised volunteer services.

Empowering School Students through Volunteer Services

Helping students succeed is both an empowerment process and objective. Success is defined by students who have reached the basic requirements of compulsory education and who have acquired self-confidence, self-actualisation, and social responsibility. A successful education in school intends to help adolescents improve both their self-image and self-concept. Thus, they may form an intrinsic mechanism of self-learning or continued education, and finally, become a successful person in either school or society (Lei & Qu, 1998).

However, some youth are committing "failure education" in China. Judging students solely by using examination tests or scores have put tremendous pressure on many students. Too many failures cause students to lose their self-confidence and for many may lead to inferiority complexes. Further, to increase the proportion of students entering college, many schools offer extra home assignments to students, which can suppress their potential and optimal learning.

The goal and essence of education is to help students learn, grow, and actualise. One problem is that some students are disempowered, instead of becoming empowered, in their educational institutions. Such negative consequences should be challenged openly. The educational system should guarantee the success for the majority of students, which means that every student should have an opportunity for self-actualisation. One method to help students build their self-confidence is by participation in meaningful volunteer services.

The slogan of "make the first move, to be a youth volunteer" has inspired many high school students in Shanghai. Increasingly, more high schools have encouraged and directed students to participate in volunteer activities. For instance, students aged 16 to 18 were expected to achieve a target of 60 class hours of credit for volunteer services. Based on student interest as well as physical and psychological characteristics, schools have carried out specific volunteer programmes, such as public good work (e.g. cleaning), love heart action (e.g. concerning the underprivileged groups), and civic education (e.g. no smoking and obeying traffic regulations). The volunteer group at the Shanghai Kongjiang Middle School is an outstanding example. They have many passionate examples reflecting students' self-actualisation and self-development in this regard. Here are three of their recent success stories.

Story One

Minjie, a grade 9 student, recovered from leukaemia after seven years of a difficult personal struggle. She had been the youngest cancer patient on record (at the time) in Shanghai. Minjie's story made students aware of the existence of "another world"—one of pain, suffering, hope, and resilience. That is, there were many children suffering from leukaemia in a hospital close to their school who were in need of care and help. Students posted an announcement in their school recruiting volunteers to care for these patients. A volunteer team named "The Journey of Love Heart" was founded. Through their participation, the volunteer team became more aware of the needs of such deprived groups in their community. They learned that older neighbours may need emotional comfort; that some children from poorer families faced the prospect of dropping out of school; and, that some children had difficulties handling situations in their families due to unexpected crises. Such lessons through volunteering impacted many students.

Story Two

In a hospital ward on International Children's Day, volunteers' comic playacting, dance, and performance resulted in patients' happiness through laughter. Volunteers noted that one boy with a bandaged head riveted his eyes joyfully on their performance. His expression showed his zest for life. However, one week later, the hospital volunteers could not find him anymore, as he had died. Nurses told the volunteers that he wanted to hear "the big brothers and sisters singing again." Knowing this, the volunteers added a new programme termed "ward education." In this way, they taught patients under the age of 8 to read picture stories, patients from 9 to 10 years old to write Chinese characters, and all children to sing. Such teaching activities inspired the volunteers to study harder at school and to be good role models for the children.

Story Three

The "Flying Swallow Volunteer Group" in Class 1 of Grade 8 helped a 70-year-old childless woman who had difficulty moving around at home. Ten members of the group visited her each week bringing her needed goods, doing the housework for her, and having heart-to-heart talks with her. The woman was so moved that she asked the School Principal to thank the Flying Swallow on her behalf. In fact, there were many class-based volunteer groups like the Flying Swallow. Students took initiative to form groups and provide volunteer services in the community. Tasks conducted by the students here included drafting the group's constitution, formulating and implementing plans, and evaluating the services they provided. A branch of the Communist Youth League helped them achieve their goals.

Such examples of volunteer activities taught these students the true meaning of love, dedication, social responsibility, social commitment and the spirit of empowerment and self-actualisation

(Cheung & Ngai, 2000). There was an obvious integration of achieving individual life objectives and meeting social and community needs in these examples of volunteering in Shanghai high schools.

Conclusion: The Journey to Empowerment through Volunteerism

There are billions of youth in China. They are both capable and eager to make a better life for themselves and their families. Empowerment of youth in China and the rise and development of volunteer services in Shanghai show real promise of a better society for the future (Dai & Jin, 1998; Xu, 2003).

Development of Individual Consciousness

It is well known that China has a long feudal history. Historically, feudal culture has influenced the development of Chinese society deeply. Chinese society moved from the focus on individuals and families or clans in feudal times, to individuals in a collective nation in a communist regime. Somewhere lost in this journey was the development of the individual self. Therefore, Chinese people are not historically "individually-conscious."

Although the feudal dynasty was overthrown by the "1911 Revolution," and the "Enlightening Movement" erupted in 1919, individual consciousness was still not formed in China. After the breakdown of the Cultural Revolution, Chinese individual consciousness began to emerge. A youth named "Pan Xiao" wrote to the *Journal of China Youth*, and ignited a nationwide debate about the meaning of life. Dissatisfaction with the cultural collectivism as expressed in various mass movements in China, young people began to question, "What are we living for?" This philosophical question showed that youths were thinking of individual rights and responsibility alongside social and national development. After the debate, confusion among youth seemed less certain.

A national survey in 1996 revealed that 73% of youth interviewed considered that realising individual self-value needed to be more recognised by society. Thus, Chinese youth began to examine relationships between individuals and society and between self-actualisation and meeting community and social needs. Today, youth volunteers join hands to serve society as independent individuals, rather than as part of a political ideology. There is no question that the self-consciousness of Chinese youth has increased considerably through their participation in volunteer activities (Zhang, 1986; Ha & Lo, 2006).

For volunteers, having freedom of choice is an important premise. As mentioned earlier, there was no concept of "the individual" *per se* in the thousands of years of Chinese history. Everything belonged to the clan or collective, including one's time after school or work. It was not until 1979, that China began to introduce the idea of leisure time into one's individual life. This marked the first time that an individual's personal time (after school or work) belonged to themselves alone. In fact, what youth can control now is not only their leisure time, but also other aspects of their life (Yip & Lo, 1996; Su & Hu, 2000).

For example, youth employment opportunities were previously assigned by the state in the past, whereas now youths can choose their jobs via the market economy. Today, generally speaking, Chinese citizens have much more freedom in choosing jobs, acquiring wealth, travelling freely, and participating in their respective communities. They now have the option of "doing something, or not doing anything." The Shanghai volunteer activities noted above, demonstrate this reality. Today, volunteer activities are very different from the "Learning from Leifeng" programme, which was promoted by the CCP leaders and actualised through a "top-down" approach. The former is conducted through open recruitment and more freedom of choice; the latter was done through organisational coerciveness and collective participation.

Practising Altruist Values and Self-Actualisation

Youth volunteerism in China today is clearly driven by a greater sense of altruism. There is no apparent conflict in such altruism based on self-determination, which aims to achieve self-actualisation through responding to societal needs (Cheung & Ngai, 2000). However, since the value orientations of self-actualisation are diverse, volunteers' altruistic orientations are also diverse. This is an inevitable result of developing youth empowerment at the current stage of economic and socio-political development in China.

When one considers altruism, the word first reminds us of unselfishness. Volunteerism demonstrates young people's precious unselfish spirit, which is at the core of volunteer activities. However, such "dedication" is not totally "unselfish", as it includes various motives and value orientations. For example, some youth help people feel good about themselves, others serve society to gain unique life experiences; some youth see helping others as an opportunity to improve their own self-image and self-confidence, while others volunteer to gain a sense of belonging to their communities. All of these motives are positive, and they are no different from the motives of volunteers in the West (Okun & Michel, 2006; Omoto & Snyder, 1995; Penner, 2002). In sum, youth volunteerism is important to obtain opportunities to gain new knowledge and new life skills, broaden their worldview, improve organisational and leadership abilities in the process of doing public good, re-instilling community pride, and genuinely helping others live and grow. Such altruistic behaviour can make young people more spiritually satisfied and enhance their feeling of social responsibility and commitment (Ha & Lo, 2006). Volunteerism can be described by the following metaphor: "giving another a rose, while the aroma lingers on." This signifies that young people are more intrinsically and spiritually happy when they receive no rewards for their volunteer work. In other words, young people are clearly empowered through this process of self-actualisation by volunteering (Dai & Jin, 1998).

The experiences in Shanghai, China, noted in this chapter, clearly exemplify that volunteerism is here to stay in Chinese culture, and youth hold the key to it becoming a part of our exciting future. They are actually empowered if they have or can create choices in life, are aware of the implications of those choices, make an informed decision freely, take action based on that decision, and accept responsibility for the consequences of that action (Commonwealth Secretariat, 1998). Participation in voluntary programmes will reduce the sense of powerlessness of youth. The empowered youth will be able to manage their emotions, skills, knowledge, and resources toward bettering their performances in what are required of them in their social roles. They will increase their participation in positive roles, understand their social identities, and reduce the negative effect of rolelessness. As such, they will gain satisfaction and enhance their self-esteem. The empowered youth will become aware of their rights and abilities in gaining control over themselves and influencing others, if they are given room to contribute to making decision, and if their opinions are considered and incorporated in the shaping of policies that affect them.

References

Au, E. (1996). Divorcing and single parenting in contemporary China: Challenges to family restructuring. In T. Wing Lo & Joseph Cheng (Eds.), *Social welfare development in China: Constraints and challenges*. Chicago: Imprint Publications, 121–134.

Brady, J. P. (1982). *Justice and politics in People's China: Legal order or continuing revolution?* New York: Academic Press.

Chan, C., & Chow, N. (1992). *More welfare after economic reform?* Hong Kong: University of Hong Kong.

Chen, Liangjin (1994). *Encyclopedia of Chinese social work*. Beijing: Chinese Society Press.

Cheng, J. (1996). Socialism with Chinese characteristics: Development models and value changes since 1949. In T. Wing Lo & Joseph

Cheng (Eds.), *Social welfare development in China: Constraints and challenges.* Chicago: Imprint Publications, 1–28.

Cheung, C. K., & Ngai, N. P. (2000) Service role commitment among participants of centres for children and youth. *Childhood, 7,* 27–42.

Cheung, J. (2006) Determinants of sustained volunteerism. In IAVE (2006) *10ᵗʰ IAVE Asia-Pacific Regional Volunteer Conference: Conference proceedings.* Hong Kong: Agency for Volunteer Service.

Chow, N. (1988). *The administration and financing of social security in China.* Hong Kong: University of Hong Kong.

Commonwealth Secretariat. (1998). *Plan of action on youth empowerment to the year 2005.* London: Commonwealth Foundation.

Conger, J. (1989). Leadership: The art of empowering others. *The Academy of Management Executive, 3*(1), 17–24.

Dai, W., & Jin, D. (1998). *Dedication and honours: A research on Shanghai volunteers.* Shanghai: Shanghai University Press.

Gao, M. (1996). Welfare needs and problems of migrant workers in South China. In T. Wing Lo & Joseph Cheng (Eds.), *Social welfare development in China: Constraints and challenges.* Chicago: Imprint Publications, 101–120.

Gardner, J. (1969). The Wu-fan Campaign in Shanghai: A study in the consolidation of urban control. In A. D. Barnett (Ed.), *Chinese communist politics in action.* Seattle: University of Washington Press, 477–539.

Gutiérrez, L. M. (1994). Beyond coping: An empowerment perspective on stressful life events. *Journal of Sociology and Social Welfare, 21*(3), 201–219.

Ha, Y. H., & Lo, S. C. (2006) Elderly volunteering as empowerment. In IAVE (2006) *10ᵗʰ IAVE Asia-Pacific Regional Volunteer Conference: Conference proceedings.* Hong Kong: Agency for Volunteer Service.

Ladany, L. (1988). *The Communist Party of China and Marxism 1921–1985.* London: C. Hurst.

Lei, S., & Qu, T. (1998). *Education experiment and education thoughts.* Chengdu: Sichuan Education Press.

Lo, T. W. (1993). *Corruption and politics in Hong Kong and China.* Buckingham: Open University Press.

Morley, L. (1995). Empowerment and the New Right. *Youth and Policy, 51,* 1–10.

Narayan, D. (Ed.). (2002). *Empowerment and poverty reduction: A sourcebook.* The World Bank.

Neville, R. (1995). *Hippie, hippie shake.* London: Bloomsbury.

Ogden, S. (1992). *China's unresolved issues.* New Jersey: Prentice-Hall.

Okun, M. A., & Michel, J. (2006) Sense of community and being a volunteer among the young-old. *The Journal of Applied Gerontology, 25*(2), 173–88.

Omoto, A. M., & Snyder, M. (1995). Sustained helping without obligation: Motivation, longevity of service, and perceived attitude change among AIDS volunteers. *Journal of Personality and Social Psychology, 68,* 671–686.

Penner, L. A. (200) The causes of sustained volunteerism: An interactionist perspective. *Journal of Social Issues, 58,* 447–467.

Pernell, R. (1986). Empowerment and social group. In M. Parnes (Ed.), *Innovations in social group work: Feedback from practice to theory.* Selected proceedings of the 5th Symposium of Social Work with Groups. New York: The Haworth Press, 107–118.

Pinderhughes, E. (1995). Empowering diverse populations: Family practice in the 21st century. *Families in Society, 76*(3), 131–146.

Rappaport, J. (1987). Terms of empowerment/exemplars of prevention: Toward a theory for community psychology. *American Journal of Community Psychology, 15*(2), 121–144.

Saleebey, D. (1996). The strengths perspective in social work practice: Extensions and cautions. *Social Work, 41*(3), 296–305.

Servian, R. (1996). *Theorising empowerment: Individual power and community care.* Bristol: Policy Press.

Shrewsbury, C. (1987). What is feminist pedagogy? *Women's Studies Quarterly, XV* (3 & 6), 6–14.

Solomon, B. (1976). *Black empowerment: Social work in oppressed communities.* New York: Columbia University Press.

Staples, L. (1990). Powerful ideas about empowerment. *Administration in Social Work, 14*(1), 29–42.

Su, S., & Hu, Z. (2000). *Separation and integration: Values of contemporary youth*. Shanghai: Shanghai Social Science Academy Press.

Wolff, T. (1987). Community psychology and empowerment: An activist's insight. *American Journal of Community Psychology, 15*, 151–166.

Xu, J. (2003). *Changing fate by personality*. Beijing: Huawen Press.

Yip, C. Y., & Lo, T. W. (1996). Popular Culture: Its Impact on Young People in Guangdong. In T. Wing Lo, & Joseph Cheng (Eds.), *Social welfare development in China: Constraints and challenges*. Chicago: Imprint Publications, 145–162.

Zhang, Z. (1986). *On university students' psychology*. Chongqing: Southwestern Normal University Press.

YOUTH EMPOWERMENT IN FRANCE: ACTION AND REACTION

11

Dan FERRAND-BECHMANN

Introduction

In France, the Reseau National de Jeunes Associations—National Network of Junior Associations (RNJA) works in cooperation with local authorities and other volunteer associations to support community youth activities such as sports, leisure, cultural, humanitarian, and "solidarity" actions.[1]

Experiences gained from developing and managing such projects are intended to help them master various knowledge, skills, and abilities they will need to become active, participating adult citizens. These experiences are seen as stepping stones to continued participation in society in the future (Lo & Au, 2004).

Empowerment

Empowerment as we define it, addresses issues about the control of one's life and the capacity to have one's actions valued to gain status and power in society, despite one's age or gender. However, it also addresses broader questions such as knowledge in action (Schön, 1983), a one's ability to be "the actor of self", as well as different sociological analyses of the participation and "autonomisation" of young citizens for the acquisition of self-directedness and purpose.

French Canadians define "empowerment" as a consequence of collective community action. Surprisingly, there is no French term for empowerment. Despite the reluctance of French Canadians to use English,[2] they nonetheless use the English expression "empowerment" (Ferrand-Bechmann, 1998). "To be able to act" (pouvoir d'agir) might be one possible translation of this concept, but in France as in other French-speaking countries, we have not yet come to consensus on an accepted expression. To empower a person means enabling the obtaining of power by someone; power to do but also power to define one's self, purposes and needs on one's own terms. But even the translation "to be able to act" does not reflect the exact meaning of the concept of empowerment.

Empowerment has been related to personal and social

development as "the act of strengthening an individual's beliefs in his or her sense of effectiveness" (Conger, 1989, p. 18). Power in action, to be able to act, or empowerment allows empowered people to feel more confident, to have a better self-image, and to develop a better identity. In helping relationships, people trust those who empower them and those who empower, trust empowerment's beneficiaries. In "Rules for Radicals," Saul Alinsky (1976) described how deprived people in poor areas had been helped to react collectively to their landlords. This social reformer explained empowerment within the context of grassroots organisations.

The use of empowerment has not become widespread at the academic, political, and professional levels of social work, social psychology, and social administration in France. French voluntary organisations and institutions prefer other overarching concepts because they are mainly managed by leaders and professionals and the volunteers who assist others.

Volunteerism

Some authors criticise voluntary action in social work on the grounds that it is often envisaged as the consequence of, or the solution to, a reduction of public expenditures. Thus, the according of status to volunteers is seen as a symbolic reward to those who could not be paid. Indeed, this is the reason why systems of voluntary action have developed in countries without welfare and where paid staff in social work is limited.

In countries and societies where family and primary supports, neighbourhood and community connections have declined, voluntary action is a possible solution to the decline in the "ability to act" or empowerment. Young adults could help their peers or older persons on an unpaid basis in a complementary role to welfare, and/or for paid services. It really is impossible to offer any explanation why this altruism is not more studied and supported by public agencies. European policies focus only on European voluntary programmes that are complementary, and often subsidiary, to public welfare, in general.

One outcome of volunteerism in non-profit organisations is the reinforcement of the social fabric. The way many organisations are rooted in their community and in neighbourhoods, meaning the geographical proximity, is a precious social capital for the society. Many needs could be answered at this level. Even in societies where the welfare state is prominent, the production and benefits of community action are important in the long term, as a source of conviviality. Community action binds individuals and furthers partnership and collaboration between citizens and their organisations.

To volunteer, to advocate, to donate money to needy people, or to sustain a political or social cause, all are the same types of responses of active citizenship and provide positive contributions to the society. Yet, to give time or money or to be an activist also has different assumptions, dimensions, and characteristics. Young adults who give their time are also giving their energy and their life, i.e. they commit themselves. Often, they would be called activists. Not all citizens volunteer and many are not willing to give their time to help organisations or their communities. Altruism and social involvement are contradictory to other main utilitarist norms and values (Caillé, 2003). Although it satisfies a human and social need to help, young persons especially may look for relationships on an egalitarian and not hierarchical basis, outside of processes such as competition, performance, or other market systems with a desire for personal autonomy.

Does this mean that if young adults do not look or search either for altruism, generosity or involvement, they could not be empowered? In our conceptual framework, they could become powerful in terms of money, power, etc. but we would use the term empowerment to describe their actions. This concept implies involvement in moral and ethical values in the society in which they live and are being educated.

Indeed, young adults are often quite generous. They give their time and money to other young people either in their communities, friends, or to humanitarian actions and non-governmental organisations. Even young people who do not have a lot of money show a generosity of spirit. Many young adults share cigarettes, drinks, and lodgings with other peers. They may also give money or help people begging on the streets. In a recent study of an older generation (university students), we observed that they would not accept money offered by the non-profit organisation where they were volunteering (Ferrand-Bechmann, 2000). They volunteered and therefore, would not accept any financial compensation for their time (Houzel, 2003). Their action was a "total altruistic act," or a humanitarian one. In a form of utopian idealism they willingly offered both time and human capital. This type of action is highly valued in our society.

Eventually, as some of this generation comes into care by the welfare state and local authorities at cost for society,[3] the status and admiration for those who take care of themselves and who "serve" society is reinforced. One can point to the contrast between, on the one hand, public programmes that provide leisure, sports activities, cultural activities, education and training, etc. and on the other hand, other sorts of self-help groups or autonomous organisations where users are actors and have responsibilities. The latter acts more on a horizontal basis with mutual and non-hierarchical relationships. In the former, young adults are consumers; in the latter they are actors. In the former, there would likely be paid social workers; and, in the latter the paid staffs either is few (or none).

Motivation

Young adults volunteer and act with various motives. These are typically both altruistic as well as pragmatic. Data are lacking in France about the relationship between altruism and volunteering. Motivation, considering that it pushes one to act or not to act, constitutes the driving element of any individual commitment in the dynamics of action.

Youth may take action to be allowed access to public facilities such as stadiums, skate parks, etc. Or they may proactively engage themselves to socialise and meet friends. They might also act out of ethnic or religious motives, or out of guilt or coercion. Some youth are oppositional and extremist, and/or endorse violence or criminal behaviour. Others preach love, peace, and harmony. Some are racists and others are willing to fight against racism and other forms of discrimination. Some become actively involved in their local communities; others go overseas. Some are looking to begin a career within voluntary organisations, others are just looking to have fun and spend some time with friends and other groups. Some are searching to become independent from their families and to become responsible adults. Others are very much tied to family links and bonds and, even within the context of a voluntary organisation, would only be involved with their immediate and extended family members. Understanding the motivational triggers for youth within this context seems not only important but essential in outreaching and supporting them to volunteer.

As indicated previously, young people get involved for various pragmatic and practical reasons; however, they typically develop a sense of civic responsibility once they have spent some time working together positively within a group. And if they take root in the local community or neighbourhood, they have the possibility of entering the greater community, and even into life itself, like part of an initiation ritual, as stated in the first part of the title of a book by Lapassade "L'entrée dans la vie. . ." (Lapassade, 1963). We can, therefore, say that they have learned to act and thus, we find ourselves back at the central theme of this book—empowerment, or more simply—"mastering something which is important" (le Bossé, 1994).

Examples from the Junior Associations in France

"Children have the rights to freedom of expression" is indicated in the International Convention for Children's Rights. However, French law does not necessarily always allow for children to do this.

In general, "associations" in France do not open their boardroom doors to young people due to their general mistrust of youth. Even though "associations" are structures that usually provide services to youth, they are typically managed by adults, who are volunteers and salaried workers. Often, young people are neither allowed to have a say nor allowed to take on responsibilities within these structures and thus, cannot take action. Unfortunately, this is part of a general trend as the expertise and "know-how" of those concerned is often undervalued (Cheyssial, 2002).

Further, young people are rarely allowed to voice their opinions and take part in decision-making, especially as they are considered as young or inexperienced about life. Few say anything about this, since it involves the "protection of minors," and because administrators are more concerned about the social-cultural activity aspect of the various programmes they offer.[4] Yet, under the impetus of the Ministry of Education, Youth and Research, a new programme called "Envie d'Agir" (The Desire to Act) was launched a few years ago in France; this was deemed a novel idea.

And yet, young people have the potential to become involved in very legitimate and constructive projects. It should be noted here that young people are more inclined to set up associative networks and get involved in "community action" types of initiatives which result in forms of local social development. Successful youth initiatives are not noticed or recognised as they are often "out of the norm" and considered as "not standard." Young people are often the object of, and are subject to, policies that are set up by social and inclusion programmes, as they are supervised, yet they are rarely praised. Little is known or said about their knowledge and learning, the extra-curricular training, and experiences acquired within the framework of these "associations," which should be validated. For example, in our study of this national network of junior associations (RNJA),[5] it was found that parents and teachers often ignored and did not promote the experiences young people obtained from these associations.

Youth is a fragile age cohort which is both protected and

misunderstood. Realistically, our society does not know how to include them meaningfully in its ranks, which creates a mismatch of age and social expectation. There are very young soldiers. There are very old students. . . . There are very young mothers. . . and there are "Tanguys."[6] Youth are recognised when society needs young people, however most of the time they are denied opportunities to develop their own specific identity as an autonomous age group.

To be young is to be part of a cohort which adopts the same issues, conflicts, challenges, happiness, problems, and concerns. Young people experience the same collective situations and try hard to build situations together so as to form a "group" to identify and coalesce with. It is difficult to group all young people together for research purposes. Some studies therefore, are categorised by age groups, gender, educational levels, religious groups, and communities. However, they are universal when it comes to their life styles, and/or the way in which they assert themselves, as noted in a popular song in the 1960s:

> *"All the boys and girls around my age, they hold each other by the hand in pairs . . ."* [7].

Youth is a social category that transcends many identities and affiliates actors with multiple profiles and potentially offers them the power of those who are together and who can act together. The young president of an association said that he was happy to have grouped young people together to prove that young people are "not just good for nothings and scum that hang around the streets." Youth want to re-adjust the power of those less-fortunate, and so they are empowering themselves (le Bossé, 1994). This allows them to defend such values as equality and fraternity.

Young people often lack social capital and suffer from various paradoxical tensions namely: between desire and reality; and between globalisation and local identity; and between a call for citizenship and political role models. Many social institutions and authorities no longer have any sign posts which they can follow.

Yet views on receding altruism and on an environment of future uncertainty do not really depict the youth who we saw and who we would qualify as being inventive, strategic and creative, and who are struggling to gain new rights. We met and observed several groups; here are a few noteworthy examples:

- Nine young women collected money to go to Senegal. They were preparing a medical-social baccalaureate. Many of them want to become nurses. "We didn't go on a tourist trip over there. We lived like they do. We want to connect with their issues and concerns. We think we were there to discover and learn and not to tell them: this is how you should do it."

- Another group wanted a place where they could set up cultural activities for the young people in their neighbourhood. These were recreational activities of course, but some had a charitable goal.

- One group wanted "public walls" and free spray-paint. "Ever since we painted a mural in the neighbourhood, the old people and other young people changed their minds about us. They see us in a different light. Before that, they thought we were little hoodlums." The youth have an image that society has of them, and changing this image is important if they wish to be perceived differently.

- There were female dance groups that contributed to expanding and promoting the hip-hop culture and participated in fashion shows.

- Some young women created a group to pay tribute to a friend who died at the age of 15. They dreamed of founding an association to help children in Haiti, where their friend was originally from. They appeared mature and seemed to have a vision and experience. However, they were concerned about creating the type of association that the French 1901 Association Act allowed.

- One group of youngsters wanted to make robots so that they could participate in the TV science show "E=M6." This is made up of young people who refuse to hold "honorary" positions and who make decisions as a group for various activities.

- Another group project by 30 young people provided Internet initiation sessions to a large number of their friends. The president was 16 years old and had a volunteer outlook and a sense of social responsibility.

- Another group requested funds to build a skate park in the neighbourhood. Before this project, they skated in the streets. Their aim was to better themselves, to improve their skateboarding skills, to play music, and to meet others. They would provide skating classes to help justify this investment.

- At a local radio station, two young men demonstrated exceptional organisational skills and professionalism. One wants to be a journalist, the other an actor, and they established this radio station. Both of them hoped to learn to be more confident about their futures. A sure outcome of the impact of this initiative was the fact that their teachers acknowledged their activity by listening to their radio station.

For many, an "association" is a tool to obtain help, a place to meet and gain positive recognition, which is important in their eyes because they need to be recognised. An association provides them further with managerial and organisational skills and with a sense of stability and social responsibility.

Effective coordinators are adults who support them while at the same time, allow them to be self-sufficient. Many young people want to transfer something to and teach the "little ones," and they said that they did not learn a lot from the so-called trainers.[8]

They are also not really perplexed by the bureaucratic paperwork and administrative procedures. According to our study, only half of them seemed to be discouraged by the administrative paperwork and the slowness of bureaucracy and only a fourth of them by the responsibility entailed, and by the fact that they had to open a bank account.

Innovative, Strategic and Creative Practices

Their first meeting at town hall, which represented an establishment and transitioning to another world—the adult world, makes youth aware of the need to be organised, and of the necessity to formalise their ideas into an "official" organisation. Becoming part of an organisational network provides them with recognition and self-esteem, and groups often mentioned that they became more at ease in their relationships with adults through this process. Table 11.1 lists the types of learning experiences (from the associations project) that youth reported in the two main skill areas of decision-making and organisational aspects.

Becoming a "1901 association" may be discouraging for some young people. Yet, we were struck by their sense of responsibility, their maturity, the energy, and activity that they put into their projects as well as their seriousness, including the accounting aspects. Even though many groups were frustrated about the slowness of bureaucracy, and the tediousness of certain tasks, they

Table 11.1   Youth learning experiences and skills from junior associations

Decision-making Skills	%
Unanimous	24.2
With a member majority	24.2
With a board majority	6.6
The president decides	8.2
No answer	21.7

Organisational skills	Answers N=244
Internal regulations	118
A notebook	126
A contribution	131
Statutes	131
A Charter	14

were proud of what they had done, overall. The association gave them the satisfaction that they may not always get from public education, as sometimes motivation, energy and creativity are stifled in the school system.

For the good (academic) students, the association takes away their free time, but not their classtime.[9] There is a type of self-reliance that comes from the appropriation of knowledge, as we have already seen in organisations where adults are involved.[10] Some say—"We don't learn that at school!" For example, the dancers and skateboarders learned from cassettes, and "they don't think they can learn a lot from their teachers."

As in the study on European volunteer services,[11] we realised that young people invent their own forms of learning, and the results are often unexpected, since the knowledge obtained is sound and significant. In our study of the RNJA, almost of all the groups were pretty much at the start of the learning curve process, when they will be able to create, as they are in a "realisation" stage, of involvement and commitment.

The Birth of a Project and Motivations

Luck and necessity and the will to do something and to act at last, a project emerges from a meeting, from the need for equipment or a place to grow. Somewhere between a creation that is more or less programmed and nurtured by coordinators and a fortuitous birth, the "associations" of these young adults do not always evolve in the ways that they were created. Some of them take off again when they enter the "associative" ranks. Others die out, like choked out plants or perhaps because the young people could not deal with the constraints and conflicts they encountered. Several associations we called could be categorised as "absent subscribers," for they are on the official list supplied by the RNJA, yet there was no one available to answer our questions.

The need to express themselves, to carry out a temporary or durable project, to search for partners, the need to be seen, to be recognised, to affirm their identity, and the need for socialisation and empowerment are reasons for the birth of these "associations." The youth would like to make a certain practice official; they want to perfect their skills for work purposes or for a project based on solidarity. There are a multitude of reasons between what they say and why they actually do it, and here were some things said:

1. *To do what you want with your friends.*

2. *This avoids hanging out and getting into trouble.*

3. *To invest in the neighbourhood.*

4. *To advance together.*

5. *Many people speak poorly of youth; we want to change the "ghetto" image of our neighbourhood and show them that we are capable of doing something else, and that there is more to it than just money.*

6. *Renounce rather than do business.*

7. *To prove to yourself that you can do something.*

8. *Music, we are born with it, but at school we only learn history.*

9. *This is better than what we do at school.*

Figure 11.1 (see p. 288) shows the various areas of support that youth said they received from to conduct JA projects.

The corresponding Figure 11.2 (see p. 289) shows the perceived accomplishment and gains the youth said they achieved from participants in JA projects.

Learning Experiences

On the whole, the experience was a positive one for 91.4% of the youth surveyed, as it constituted a sort of initiation to working in an association. Further, more than half wanted to continue to participate in associative activities after the age of 18. On the whole, the young people learn numerous association experiences and rules (see Figure 11.2 and Table 11.1).

Figure 11.1   From whom you received support in order to carry out JA projects

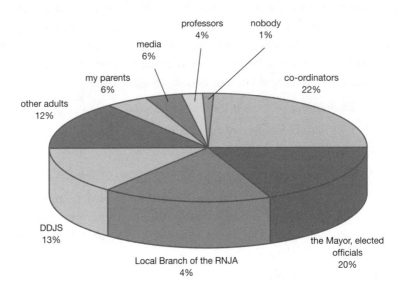

Parents had various attitudes concerning the commitment of their children to JAs. Not all parents supported this practice, fearing that associative or volunteer work would hinder their school studies. We noted that the women elected at the "Ligue"[12] sometimes complained that their children were not involved.

Teachers were often unaware of their JA work, and some youngsters did not feel that they were being supported by them.[13] The image of these associations is not really well known or advertised, even in the educational field, given their recent development.

Finally, some of the youth from one of the groups, "the restless ones," no longer attended school. Since they did hip-hop, they were advised to sign up at an expensive classical dance school. And yet, these same youngsters had the "know-how," knowledge and skills; the only problem was that it was neither recognised nor validated in their school courses.

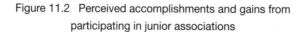

Figure 11.2   Perceived accomplishments and gains from participating in junior associations

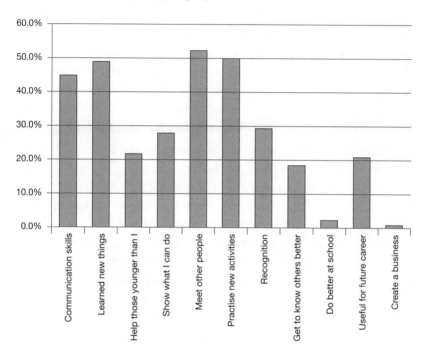

Conclusion[14]

We saw clearly in our work the emergence of new and innovative practices from young minors and their will for self-sufficiency and their desire to act. For certain groups, a "junior association" was simply a way to obtain equipment, a place to meet, support, or something else, but once they were "caught in the net," they established and implicated themselves in some of the most open-minded and interdependent projects. The network that organised junior associations is located at the crossroads of the adult and youth worlds, and is caught between the desire to "laissez-faire" and at the same time, the desire to be available, to listen, and to simply be "side-by-side" with youth.

Certain practices should be considered in terms of acquired knowledge. We found that it would be interesting and beneficial if the public education sector were to better regard the "know-how" of its youth. For instance, we need to take a look not only at the curriculum learned in school, but also at the competencies and skills that certain young people acquire through their extracurricular activities. We feel that elementary and middle schools should better consider the fact that these youngsters bear civic and civil knowledge and competencies, and the sooner they are learned, the better.

Training for associative and volunteer work, civic involvement and citizenship is necessary for France's future. Through funding, junior associations can serve as a stepping stone for future youth. Since this study, the number of junior associations has strongly increased, which only proves the dynamism and viability of this network and of the youth themselves. Young people coalesce around common practices and sectors of involvement that belong to their age groups; the simple fact of living in a socially uniform neighbourhood does not really lead to a great social mix. The followings are some final observations in our study:

- Traditional structures, sports groups that are the most attended and the "associations" from the "Education Populaire" movement certainly play an important role, since we noted that junior associations developed themselves even more in innovative fields.

- Phenomena linked to power developed in these groups and young people took on strong leadership roles.

- We noted youth solidarity which demonstrated their rejection of certain forms of social inequality in these initiatives.

- Youth are discovering new ways of living, of getting involved, and of tapping into new networks, yet at the same time they are inclined to be associated with their families.

- Project groups are indeed a means of social integration; however they were limited in time, resources, physical space, and neighbourhood.

End Notes

1. In France, practically all non-profit organisations fall under the umbrella term "Association loi 1901", which refers to the 1901 Act that enables and governs volunteer organisations. These associations may range from recreational centres which provide activities to the local community, to sports clubs, and even to organisations with a humanitarian aim.

2. They speak of a "parking lot" as a "stationnement", or of "shopping" as "magasiner".

3. In France the "missions locales" are public agencies giving jobs, counselling and training to young people between 16 and 25 years old.

4. In France there are numerous public structures that help the youth and "associations" that organise activities for them.

5. In a recent study of this national network of junior associations, we studied the activities and projects undertaken in it, as well as the aims, motivations, representations, self-image and problems the youth face, including how they may be restricted and how they gain power. The question of empowerment is at the core of this study. Nevertheless, we have also taken a look at how young participants are valorised or stigmatised by adults. What do these young people learn and what do they teach their younger friends? To whom are they transmitting their projects? What are the effects of their activities on their neighbourhood and on local development? How do teachers and parents react? Is the action of these junior associations seen as part of the public or private sphere? What may be the lessons of these experiments especially in terms of empowerment?

6. Allusion to the recent film titled *Tanguy* concerning a young adult who still lives with his parents and who won't or can't leave.

7. A song by Françoise Hardy which was popular in the 1960s:

    Tous les Garçons et les Filles
    Françoise Hardy
    Tous les garçons et les filles de mon âge
    Se promènent dans la rue deux par deux
    Tous les garçons et les filles de mon âge
    Savent bien ce que c'est qu'être heureux

Et les yeux dans les yeux
Et la main dans la main
Ils s'en vont amoureux
Sans peur du lendemain

In a free translation :

all boys and girls of my age
are walking in the street together
they know what is to be happy
and eyes in the eyes
hands in hands
they are in love
They are not afraid of the day after!
all boys and girls of my age
are walking in the street together.

8. We consulted the thesis by Renaud Camilleri "Hip, Hop and the Transmission of Knowledge" University Paris 8, UFR 8 2003

9. It should be noted that some of these young people are good students. They are very active in Junior Associations (JA) and on top of this they work (but this doesn't appear in the statistics).

10. Please refer to the CESOL report and study on "the paths of knowledge in associations" under the direction of Dan Ferrand Bechmann.

11. Evaluation for the French part of the structure realised in 1998.

12. Under the direction of Dan Ferrand-Bechmann, Pratiques Associatives au Féminin, CESOL for the Ligue de l'Enseignement. 2003.

13. The Ministry of Education is here too being innovative by launching an educational commitment programme.

14. Since this conference, in 2007, I have published a book *L'Engagement Bénévole des Etudiants, Le Pouvoir d'Agir*, that focuses on students voluntary action in universities. Readers may also like to read another new book of mine *Tribulations D'Une Sociologue* published by L'Harmattan.

References

Alinsky, S. (1976). *Manuel de l'Educateur Social*. Paris le Seuil.

Ferrand-Bechmann, D. (1998). *Travail social en cette faim de siècle*. Conférence à Hull, Université Ciriec, Quebec.

Ferrand-Bechmann, D. (2000). Motivations et engagement des étudiants bénévoles à l'afev. CESOL published in chapter XI in Becquet, V. et de Linares, C. (2005), *Quand les Jeunes s'engagent, entre expérimentations et constructions identitaires*. Paris: L'Harmattan.

Ferrand-Bechmann, D. (sous la dir) (2007). Préface de Bernard Kouchner, *L'Engagement Bénévole des Etudiants le Pouvoir d'Agir*. Paris: L'Harmattan.

Caillé, A. (2003). *Critique de la raison utilitaire: Manifeste du MAUSS*. Paris: La Découverte.

Cheyssial, A. (2002). *La quantité négligeable*. Thèse de 3e cycle Université de Paris 8.

Conger, J. (1989). Leadership: The art of empowering others. *The Academy of Management Executive, 3*(1), 17–24.

Houzel, G. (2003). *Les engagements bénévoles des étudiants*. Paris: La Documentation Française.

Lapassade, G. (1963). *L'entrée dans la vie. Essai sur l'inachèvement de l'homme*. Bourgeois C., & D. de Roux (Eds.). Paris.

le Bossé, Y. (1994). Empowerment et pratiques sociales: Illustration d'une utopie prise au sérieux. *Nouvelles Pratiques Sociales, 9*(1), 127–145.

Lo, T. W. & Au, E. (2004). *Youth empowerment: International experiences*. Hong Kong: City University of Hong Kong.

Schön, D. A. (1983). *The reflective practitioner: How professionals think in action*. New York: Basic Books.

part three

Conclusion

This part presents one concluding chapter to the book by Liu and Holosko. It discusses how youth empowerment as a theoretical concept and youth volunteerism as an example can offer us a direction and a vision to move onward and upward in youth work. A synthesised youth empowerment model is also concluded.

ONWARD AND UPWARD: YOUTH ARE THE FUTURE!

12

Elaine S. C. LIU and Michael J. HOLOSKO

Introduction

As we look retrospectively at the eleven chapters in this book about youth, empowerment and volunteerism from countries all over the world, we were stuck by some recurring thoughts. The first is that "Marshall McLuhans" (1962) insightful forecast tabled some 45 years ago which rings loud and true—is that we really do now live in a global village! And this village is hot-wired by warp-speed technologies which not only link or connect us together, but allow us to share, to dialogue, to inform, to teach and to learn openly from one another (Dunlop & Holosko, 2006). The edited chapters in this text clearly serve as testimony to this "globalisation information sharing" phenomena.

The content mix of chapters in the book move from theoretical to practical, and all are laden with rich and illustrative examples of how youth, when given the opportunity, can have an impact in the communities in which they reside. As we noted, some countries have been slower than others to respond to this reality. However, all demonstrated that they are keenly aware of the power of youth— that is, when they become truly empowered. In turn, such awareness presents as a groundswell of overall public awareness embedded in the socio-political fabric of the social institutions of the many nations in our global village.

Extending this notion a bit further, we offer a new twist on the old African saying, *"It takes a village to raise a child"*. Our take on this now is—"It takes a child or (youth) to raise a village". Because as youth become empowered, not only do they become more self-actualised as they "put back something to their communities", but the "village" in turn, becomes a better place in which to live, for all of its citizens.

When we became involved in these youth conferences, initiatives, international outreach, curriculum offerings, etc., the concept of empowerment was a rather elusive one. Indeed, it seemed rather idiosyncratic, culturally specific, multi-faceted and defined more by developmental notions oriented to "how one becomes empowered"—rather than "how one can become disempowered" (Holosko, Leslie, & Cassano, 2001). It was also more leaning toward how individuals became empowered, not organisations or communities (Holosko et al., 2001; Lo & Au, 2004).

For us, this text has addressed many of these concerns. That is, understanding that empowerment is a process foremost and that it unfolds differently for different individuals, is an important first step in this conceptual unraveling. Second, is to truly listen and learn from the numerous rich examples presented herein, "the real word" and those communities in which youth and community empowerment have occurred.

Synthesising a Model of Youth Empowerment

Based on the above, we present an aspirational conceptualisation of the process of youth empowerment in Figure 12.1.

As indicated in Figure 12.1, the actualising process of empowerment is presented in a developmental four step-wise progression. It occurs from a first step of self-awareness → to a decision to act → to a cognitive self-appraisal → to self-actualisation. Although this chapter shows how volunteerism can be used to drive this process, many other factors can similarly trigger the empowerment process e.g. achievement in a skill, athletic

Figure 12.1 The actualising process of youth empowerment

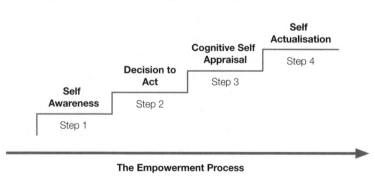

development, academic achievement, job skills and occupational achievement, acquiring friends, working with a team toward a positive goal, developing good relationship skills, finding one's path in life, and a spiritual awakening, etc.

Step 1, self-awareness in Figure 12.1, was deemed by youth (in this text) and stated as "I am" and therefore, "I can!" A belief in self then, was pre-requisite for triggering this initial self-awareness. Next, was a decision to act on some project, programme, or volunteer initiative. In Step 2, youth incorporated and expressed their awareness into sayings such as "I like this", "I can do this", or "This is fun". Here, they explored what they honestly liked or disliked, and seemed to gravitate to those volunteer experiences which they thought were both fun and worthwhile.

The next Step 3 called cognitive self-appraisal was where youth began to find out just how worthwhile their volunteer experiences were, not only to themselves but to others, including their friends, parents, teachers, individuals they helped, various organisations and communities. This involved a deeper self-reflection and issues such as "I really like this", "I can make an impact", "I enjoy doing this with others, who like doing this", or "This is worthwhile", came to the fore and were often articulated. The final Step 4 self-actualisation was an awaking of self-respect, compassion for others and caring for their community—all at the same time. Here, youth championed issues such as "I am important", "I can make a difference", or "People like me for who I am—not just what I am doing".

As such, the empowerment process is one that can be delineated in four sequential steps as illustrated in Figure 12.1. Further, it should be noted that different youth became empowered at different steps in this process. Additionally, not all youth achieved the same actualisation levels in all four steps in this process. However, such is the nature of any process and since empowerment is worthwhile and needed for one's self-growth and self-development, any form of empowerment or actualisation was deemed a good thing, overall. What is more important and germane however was that all of the youth involved in these volunteer programmes/projects/initatives were somewhere on this developmental four step continuum of empowering themselves.

Figure 12.2 builds further on understanding this process and presents a synergistic and conceptual framework showing how youth who volunteered in various projects/programmes/initiatives became actualised. It shows how the process of empowerment through volunteerism was facilitated by four key factors: i) a belief in youth, ii) social/human resources, iii) volunteer projects/programmes/initiatives, and iv) individual and community outcomes. This framework is dynamic and shows how each element in it infuses and influences the next one in a circuitous pattern. Energy, synergy and the continual interaction of these elements in turn, accrues and fuels the process of youth empowerment accordingly.

At the top of Figure 12.2, a belief in youth is a foremost requisite to triggering this conceptualisation. We were reminded (in many of the chapters) that such a belief doesn't typically emanate

Figure 12.2   Conceptual framework: Empowering youth through volunteerism

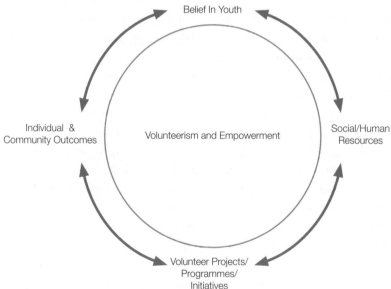

from larger social/cultural contexts or institutions, but from smaller organisations such as youth groups, associations, schools, universities, etc. When these organisations committed themselves to a sincere belief in youth, it had the consequent result of instilling that same belief in the youth themselves. As such, "since you believed in me—I too believed in myself", was echoed in various examples cited in the text.

Then came the issue of social/human resources required to do the volunteer work. In this sense, many youth were keenly aware of the time commitments, social and economic capital involved, and their willingness to become involved in volunteering. These for many, were carefully factored into the issue of social/human resources accordingly. In many countries like China, Korea, Japan, Singapore for examples, the pressures of their school work, extant family responsibilities caused such youth to be creative and prudent time managers, when their time demands were taxed. We were duly impressed however, in each of these instances how they "found the time", when they had to, to commit to volunteerism in their respective communities. And for many, the volunteerism ↔ empowerment process was a symbiotic one which energised itself, as the more they volunteered, the more they wanted to volunteer.

In regard to the various projects/programmes and volunteer initiatives, there is an old Chinese proverb that seems appropriate to mention here; "If you take care of the work . . . everything else will take care of itself". Indeed, this text is rife with numerous creative examples of both small scale one-to-one volunteer acts, to large scale international projects/programmes. In all of these, we were reminded that when individuals were committed to something they truly cared about and valued, it was done with passion, enthusiasm and compassion. Further, when these youth could see for themselves that they were making a difference in the lives of individuals, and/or bettering their communities, they were positively reinforced by the symbiotic and energising volunteering ↔ empowerment process.

The final component of the conceptual framework, individual and community outcomes was the actual tangible results of these volunteering experiences. These included both those small, humane, delicate and very touching interpersonal outcomes such as: a smile on an elderly person's face, a clean apartment, the joy of a person happy to see their volunteer come to the hospital or elderly care facility; and also included things such as: seeing a community park being cleaned up, rivers and streams being ecologically revived, or being involved with a team of rescue workers providing large scale international disaster relief to individuals who became homeless overnight. Indeed, for these youth seeing was believing. We consciously tried to include many of these examples throughout the book, as these were the real stories behind the volunteerism ↔ empowerment process.

Onward and Upward!

The above two models show how empowerment is a process that can advance youth development through volunteerism. Moving onward and upward, and extending this thought a bit, if youth empowerment is the ultimate goal of all kinds of youth work, and using youth volunteerism as an example (as illustrated in this text), what then will be the future direction of youth volunteerism?

In the Copenhagen World Summit on Social Development held in 1995, 117 countries pledged to implement ten commitments to alleviate poverty, promote full-time employment, and secure social integration. To advance these goals, members of this conference made reference to the important role played globally, by voluntary and community organisations. The Government of Japan further suggested a special session be held in June 2000, to address the importance of volunteerism for social development. Subsequently, an Expert Working Group from different regions of the world met in November 2000 in New York, and they re-confirmed the notion that volunteers indeed play a significant role in social development and integration, both in industrialised and developing countries (United Nations Volunteers, 2002).

Of the volunteer activities noted, most were delivered, and/

or co-ordinated by non-governmental organisations, professional associations, trade unions, and de-centralised government services. In all of these previous discussions at international levels—youth, elderly persons, disabled persons, and families among other social groups were specially mentioned of being the basic vehicles in volunteer service delivery. It is estimated that volunteers in some countries contribute between 8% and 14% of the overall Gross Domestic Product (GDP) to their nations. In another research study done in the 1990s the volunteer sector accounted for around 4.6% of the GDP of 22 countries surveyed (United Nations Volunteers, 1999).

Besides counting the contribution of volunteerism economically, the experiences of volunteering confirm youth engagement with society and contribute to a nation's social integration, cohesiveness and stability. By the very nature of the work itself, many volunteer projects pay special attention to the welfare and needs of marginalised and excluded groups, and they play important roles in building citizenship and harmony. If we look at the levels of participation cited in this chapter, youth volunteers were involved from community to organisational levels, from private to public sectors, from individuals to communities, and from national to international projects. Further, these happened across different cultural and political systems and across developing, transitional and developed countries.

However, there have been some critics to the volunteer movement overall, and how it relates to youth, in particular. Despite the previously mentioned economic benefits to primarily health and human service agencies, for some youth, these experiences served the needs of the organisation more so than the youth volunteers themselves. For instance, if one examines the tasks performed by youth volunteers, some could argue that they are rather menial, tangential, limited, simplistic, conservative, and technical.

Further, they serve as adjuncts to agency service delivery, technical assistance, labour force supply, and social welfare delivery. Thus, these youth volunteers become "organisational enablers," filling the gaps of paid professionals to undertake essential tasks needed by the agency. In turn, they have rather delimited opportunities for personal growth during their volunteer experiences, and in this regard they simply sustain the organisations' mandate.

The theory of "sustained volunteerism" shows how organisational attributes and practices and volunteers' relationship with the organisation are important factors in contributing to this phenomena (Penner, 2002). What is needed is to move beyond this theory, to assist youth in becoming more meaningfully actualised through various volunteer experiences. This text clearly exemplifies numerous instances of volunteers who are deemed as "contributors to social capacity development."

These volunteers are characterised by freely choosing a target group or social issue and are guided by their interests, passions, or moral imperatives as chosen by them. They work to attend to social problems that are largely ignored by the conventional service delivery system and wish to alter the direction of the agency and its development. Volunteers who are involved at this level of participation usually demonstrate the values of commitment and solidarity, have a belief in collective action, value public good, and are committed to human rights and gender equality. These qualities ensure greater likelihood of empowerment, if young volunteers could achieve them through volunteerism.

Finally, putting this discussion into the context of a theory of youth empowerment and youth volunteerism, governments as policy-makers and agencies as service providers should be aware that an (apparently) good idea such as youth volunteerism could still be underused or even misused, if we do not examine it critically with an ultimate sense of how it is an actualising and a meaningful experience for youth. As such, youth volunteer experiences should all be oriented to empowering not disempowering youth. We hope that after reading this text, you too, will take this correct positive message forward.

References

Dunlop, J., & Holosko. M. J. (Eds.). (2006). *Information technology and evidence-based social work practice.* Binghampton, New York: The Haworth Press Inc.

Holosko, M., Leslie, D., & Cassano, D. R. (2001). How service users become empowered in human service organisations: The Empowerment Model. *International Journal of Health Care Quality Assurance, 14*(2), 126–132.

Lo, T. W. & Au, E. (2004). *Youth empowerment: International experiences.* Hong Kong: City University of Hong Kong.

McLuhan, M. (1962). *The Gutenberg Galaxy: The making of Typographic Man.* Toronto, Ont: University of Toronto Press.

Penner, L. A. (2002). Dispositional & organisational influence on sustained volunteerism: An interactionist perspective. *Journal of Social Issues, 58*(3), 447–467.

United Nations Volunteers (1999). *Expert working group meeting on volunteering and social development.* New York: November 29–30, 1999.

United Nations Development Programme. (2002). *Capacity for development: New solutions to old problems.* Fukuda-Parr, S., Lopes, C., & Malik, K. (Eds.). New York: Earthscan Publications.

Index

關心青少年系列

本系列已出版的書籍

做個A+青少年——
積極心理學必修的8堂課
岳曉東 著
ISBN: 978-962-937-149-4
154 x 229毫米，320頁

違規路段——
高危青少年服務理論與實踐
香港遊樂場協會 編
ISBN: 978-962-937-151-7
154 x 229毫米，240頁

盜與罪——
青少年犯罪預防理論與對策
李紫媚 著
ISBN: 978-962-937-150-0
154 x 229毫米，248頁

追星與粉絲——
青少年偶像崇拜探析
岳曉東 著
ISBN: 978-962-937-134-0
154 x 229毫米，288頁

解構青少年犯罪及對策——
香港、新加坡和上海的經驗
盧鐵榮、蔡紹基、蘇頌興 著
ISBN: 978-962-937-121-0
154 x 229毫米，296頁